Lemuel Hopkins

American Poems

Vol. 1

Lemuel Hopkins

American Poems
Vol. 1

ISBN/EAN: 9783337477028

Printed in Europe, USA, Canada, Australia, Japan

Cover: Foto ©Thomas Meinert / pixelio.de

More available books at **www.hansebooks.com**

AMERICAN POEMS,

P R E F A C E.

IN the following pages, the Public, according to the promise of the Publishers, is presented with a Volume of American Poems; partly Selected, and partly Original. In undertaking this Work, they have been actuated by a variety of motives, and drawn onward by a number of objects. When looking round them, they saw many Poems, written by the most eminent American Authors, from the loose manner of their publishment, known only to a few of their particular acquaintance, and unheard of by the generality of their Countrymen. The value of the performances, and the regard which authors generally feel for their literary offspring, left them no room to doubt, but that, at some future period, each person would think it not unworth the while to collect what he had scattered. But this period was uncertain; and the publishers tho't that it would not be rendering an unacceptable service to the Public, if they undertook the business of collecting, and arranging each Author's productions in a volume, which from its size should claim a more universal attention.—Beside the smaller Poems of Gentlemen, distinguish'd for their poetical talents, many others, of very great merit, have appeared in the different Periodical publications of the United States. Performances of this kind, falling from the pens of persons not intent on literary fame; or intent on reputation different from poetical reputation; or whose names have not yet been dignified by national applause; especial-

c

ly as many of them are adapted to particular and local oc-
cafions; notwithftanding their defert, are conftantly lia-
ble to be forgotten and loft.   And the publifhers have ob-
ferved it to be a matter of much regret, among perfons of
reading and tafte, that the frail fecurity of an obfcure news-
paper, was the only one they had for fome of the hanfom-
eft fpecimens of American Poetry.   To afford a ftronger,
and more durable fecurity, is one of the objects of this
Publication.—Among other things, it did not appear to be
a matter altogether deftitute of ufefulnefs, to bring together, in one view, the feveral poetical productions of the different States.   By this means a more certain eftimation
can be made of the comparative merit of their various wri-
ters; a more thorough acquaintance may be obtained of the
ftate of the belles-lettres in the individual parts of the Union; and hereby will be promoted a more intimate combi-
nation of literary interefts.—It efpecially feemed a matter
of importance, to draw forth, for the amufement of the
lovers of poetry, thofe Poems which, for want of a Repof-
itory of this kind, alone, were withheld from the Public.
It was eafy to forefee, that many perfons, acting with a
proper regard to the worth of their own writings, would
readily give up that advantage, which news-papers beftow,
of having them known to every body; if they could by
means of a Work like the prefent one, fecure them a certain
conveyance to the attention of the fcientific and refined.
It was likewife the wifh of the Publifhers, to excite the
attention of thofe poffeffed of talents and leifure, to fimi-
lar purfuits; by holding out to them a Work where, united with the like performances of the moft celebrated
among their Countrymen, their Poems may be equally fe-

cure of prefervation and notice.—Thefe have been the in-
tentions of the Publifhers.   How far their defign is accom-
plifhed, is not for them to determine.   That it fhould be
completely fo, was not to be expected.   This is but the beginning of an Undertaking; and they hope, not an un-
promifing one.   The Public alone, have the power to coun-
tenance and fupport them in its accomplifhment.—Should
the Volume, now publifhed, meet with that fuccefs which
the value of the Poems it contains feems to warrant, it is
the intention of the Publifhers to add another; and to con-
tinue the Collection as long as the *prefent fupply* of Materials, and *that* for which, in future, they may be indebt-
ed to the generofity of the literarty, will enable them.

They have, now, only to return, to their fubfcribers,
their moft unfeignedly grateful acknowledgments for the
generous fupport which they have afforded them; and to
exprefs a hope, that tho' the publication owing to fome
unfortunate circumftances, has been delayed longer than
their firft purpofe, no other expectation, which they have
held forth, may be difappointed on a careful examination of
the Work.

Litchfield (Connecticut) June 1793.

POSTSCRIPT.

IT is the intention of the Editors, as mentioned in the Preface, to purfue their defign ; and, fhould fufficient encouragement appear, to publifh a Second Volume, in the courfe of the next two years. —Many difappointments, the ill health of one of the Editors, and other circumftances, too complicated and painful to mention, have contributed to render their part of this Work lefs perfect than their expectations, and promifes. They intend to finifh the fucceeding Volume, or Volumes, in a more elegant manner ; and, if a fecond edition of the prefent volume fhould be called for, it is their further intention to make it equal, in beauty, to the others ; to all of which fuitable, and well-executed decorations fhall be added.

CONTENTS.

SELECTED POETRY.

ORIGINAL POETRY.

ELEGY on the TIMES.

First printed at BOSTON, *Sept.* 20*th*, 1774.

By JOHN TRUMBULL, *Esq.*

OH BOSTON! late with ev'ry pleasure crown'd,
    Where Commerce triumph'd on the favoring gales,
And each pleas'd eye, that rov'd in prospect round,
    Hail'd thy bright spires and bless'd thy op'ning sails!

Thy plenteous marts with rich profusion smil'd;
    The gay throng crouded in thy spacious streets;
From either IND thy chearful stores were fill'd;
    Thy ports were gladden'd with unnumber'd fleets.

For there more fair than in their native vales,
    Tall groves of masts arose in beauteous pride;
The waves were whiten'd by the swelling sails,
    And plenty wafted on the neighb'ring tide.

Alas, how chang'd! the swelling sails no more
    Catch the fair winds and wanton in the sky;
But hostile beaks affright the guarded shore,
    And pointed thunders all access deny.

C

Where the bold Cape its warning forehead rears,
  Where tyrant Vengeance waved her magic wand,
Far from the fight each friendly veſſel veers,
  Calls the kind gales and flies the fatal ſtrand.

The ruin'd Merchant turns his mournful eyes
  From the drear ſhore and deſolated way;
Thy ſilent marts unuſual glooms ſurprize,
  And through thy ſtreets the ſons of rapine ſtray.

Such the dread ſtillneſs of the deſert night,
  When brooding horror ſettles on the groves;
While powers of darkneſs claim their hateful right,
  And fierce for prey the ſavage tyger roves.

Along thy fields, which late in beauty ſhone
  With lowing herds and graſſy veſture fair,
The inſulting tents of barbarous troops are ſtrown,
  And bloody ſtandards ſtain the peaceful air.

Are theſe thy deeds, oh Britain? this the praiſe,
  That points the growing luſtre of thy name?
Theſe glorious works that in thy latter days,
  Gild the bright period of thine early fame?

Shall thy ſtrong fleets, with awful ſails unfurl'd,
  On Freedom's ſhrines the unhallow'd vengeance bend?
And leave forlorn the deſolated world,
  Cruſh'd—every foe, and ruin'd—every friend!

And damp'd alas! thy ſoul-inſpiring ray,
  Where Virtue prompted and where Genius ſoar'd,
Or quench'd in darkneſs, and the gloomy ſway
  Of Senates venal and the liveried Lord!

There fhame fits blazon'd on the unmeaning brow,
　　And o'er the fcene thy factious Nobles wait,
Prompt the mixt tumult of the noify fhow,
　　Guide the blind vote and rule the mock debate.

To thefe how vain, in weary woes forlorn,
　　With fearful hands the fond complaint to raife,
Lift fruitlefs offerings to the ear of Scorn—
　　Of fervile vows and well-diffembled praife!

Will the grim favage of the nightly fold
　　Learn from their cries the blamelefs flock to fpare?
Will the deaf gods, that frown in molten gold,
　　Blefs the dup'd hand, that fpreads the proftrate prayer

With what pleas'd hope before the face of Pride,
　　We rear'd our fuppliant eyes with filial awe;
While loud Difdain with ruffian voice reply'd,
　　And Injury triumph'd in the garb of Law!

While Peers enraptur'd hail the unmanly wrong,
　　See Ribaldry, vile proftitute of fhame,
Stretch the brib'd hand and prompt the venal tongue,
　　To blaft the laurels of a FRANKLIN's fame!

But will the Sage, whofe philofophic foul,
　　Controul'd the lightning in its fierce career,
Hear'd unappal'd the aerial thunders roll,
　　And taught the bolts of vengeance where to fteer;—

Will he, while echoing to his juft renown
　　The voice of kingdoms fwells the loud applaufe;
Heed the weak malice of a Courtier's frown,
　　Or dread the coward infolence of laws?

See envying Britain rends the facred bays;
　　Illuded Juftice pens the mock decree;
While Infamy her darling fcroll difplays,
　　And points well pleas'd, oh, WEDDERBURNE, to thee!

For nought avails the virtues of the heart,
　　The vengeful bolt no Mufe's laurels ward;
From Britain's rage, and death's relentlefs dart,
　　No worth can fave us, and no fame can guard.

O'er hallow'd bounds fee dire Oppreffion roll;
　　Fair Freedom buried in the whelming flood;
Nor charter'd rights the tyrant courfe controul,
　　Though feal'd by Kings and witnefs'd in our blood.

No more fhall Juftice with unbiafs'd hand,
　　From lawlefs Rapine fnatch her trembling prey,
While in her balance by *fupreme* command
　　Hang the dead weights of minifterial fway.

(For taught by pain, our injur'd bofoms feel
　　The potent claims whence all our woes began,
And own *fupreme* the power, that could repeal,
　　Thofe laws of heaven, that guard the rights of man.)

In vain we hope from Britain's haughty pride
　　An hand to fave us, or an heart to blefs;
'Tis ftrength, our own, muft ftem the rufhing tide,
　　And our own virtue yield the wifh'd fuccefs.

But, oh, my friends, the arm of blood* reftrain!
　　(No rage intemperate aids the public weal)
Nor bafely blend (too daring, but in vain)
　　The affaffin's madnefs with the patriot's zeal.

[For *the Note, fee next page.*]

Shall the fields blush, with vital crimſon ſtain'd,
   When blind reſentment marks the victim'd breaſt ?
Will reeking life, by vengeful hands prophan'd,
   Our wrongs relieve, or charm our woes to reſt ?

Ours be the manly firmneſs of the ſage,
   From ſhameleſs foes the ungrateful wounds to bear ;
Alike remov'd from baſeneſs and from rage,
   The flames of faction, and the chills of fear.

Check the vaſt torrent of commercial gain,
   That buys our ruin at a price ſo rare ;
And while we ſcorn Britannia's ſervile chain,
   Diſdain the livery of her marts to wear.

For ſhall the luſt of faſhions and of ſhow,
   The curſt idolatry of ſilks and lace,
Bid our proud robes inſult our Country's woe,
   And welcome Slav'ry in the glare of dreſs?

Will the blind dupe, in liveried tinſel gay,
   Boaſt the ſhamed trappings, that adorn the ſlave ?
Will the fond mourner change his ſad array,
   To attend in gorgeous pomp a parent's grave ?

---

* *This is not meant as a caution againſt defending our rights with our blood, if we ſhould be driven to that extremity ; but only againſt the impolitic zeal of thoſe, who ſeem deſirous to let looſe the rage of popular reſentment, and bring matters immediately to a criſis in this Province.*

No! the rich produce of our fertile foil,
  Shall cloath the neatnefs of our chearful train,
While heaven-born virtues blefs the pious toil,
  And gild the humble veftures of the plain.

No foreign labour in the Afian field
  Shall weave her filks to deck the wanton age,
But, as in Rome, the furrow'd vale fhall yield
  The unvanquifh'd Chieftain and paternal Sage.

And ye, whofe heaven in ermin'd pomp to fhine,
  To run with joy the vain, luxurious round,
Blefs the full banquet with the charms of wine,
  And roll the thundering chariot o'er the ground!

For this, while guis'd in fycophantic fmile,
  With hearts all mindlefs of your country's pain,
Your flattering falfhoods feed the ears of Guile,
  And barter freedom for the dreams of gain! .

Are thefe the joys, on vaffal'd climes that wait—
  In downs of eafe luxuriant to repofe,
Quaff ftreams nectareous in the domes of ftate,
  And blaze in fplendor of imperial fhows?

No—the hard hand, the tortur'd brow of Care,
  The thatch-roof'd hamlet and defencelefs fhed,
The tatter'd garb, that meets the inclement air,
  The famifh'd table, and the matted bed.—

Thefe are their fate—In vain the arm of toil
  With gifts autumnal crowns the bearded plain;
In vain glad Summer prompts the genial foil,   .
  And Spring diffolves in foftening fhowers in vain;

There favage Power extends his difmal fhade,
    And chill Oppreffion, with her frofts fevere,
Sheds her dire blaftings o'er the fpringing blade,
    And robs the expecting labours of the year.

So muft we fink?—and at the ftern command
    That bears the terrors of a tyrant's word,
Bend the crouch'd knee and raife the fuppliant hand,
    The fcorn'd, dependant, vaffals of a Lord?

The wintry ravage of the ftorm to meet,
    Brave the fcorch'd vapours of the autumnal air,
Then pour the hard-earn'd harveft at his feet,
    And beg fome pittance from our pains to fhare?

But not for this, by heaven and virtue led,
    From the mad rule of hierarchal pride,
From flavifh chains our injur'd fathers fled,
    And follow'd freedom on the advent'rous tide;

Dar'd the wild horrors of thefe climes unknown,
    The infidious favage, and the crimfon'd plain,
To us bequeath'd the prize, their woes had won,
    Nor deem'd they fuffer'd, or they bled in vain.

And think'ft thou, NORTH, the fons of fuch a race,
    Where beams of glory bleft their purpled morn,
Will fhrink unnerv'd before a tyrant's face,
    Nor meet thy louring infolence with fcorn?

Look thro' the circuit of the extended fhore,
    That checks the furges of the Atlantic deep!
What weak eye trembles at the frowns of pow'r?
    What leaden foul invites the bands of fleep?

How Goodnefs warms each heaven-illumin'd heart!
  What generous gifts the woes of want affuage,
And fympathetic tears of pity ftart,
  To aid the deftin'd victims of thy rage!

No clamourous faction with unhallow'd zeal
  To wayward madnefs wakes the impaffion'd throng;
No thoughtlefs furies fheath their breafts with fteel,
  Or call the fword to avenge the oppreffive wrong.

Fraternal bands with vows accordant join;
  One guardian Genius, one enrapturing Soul
Nerves the bold arm, inflames the juft defign,
  Combines, infpirits, and illumes, the whole.

Now meet the Fathers of this weftern clime;
  Nor names more noble graced the rolls of fame,
When Spartan firmnefs brav'd the wrecks of time,
  Or Rome's bold virtues fann'd the heroic flame.

Not deeper thought th' immortal Sage infpir'd,
  On Solon's lips when Grecian fenates hung;
Nor manlier eloquence the bofom fir'd,
  When genius thunder'd from the Athenian tongue.

And hopes thy pride to match the patriot ftrain
  By the brib'd flave in penfion'd lifts enroll'd;
Or awe their councils by the voice prophane,
  That wakes to utterance at the calls of gold?

Can frowns of terror daunt the warrior's deeds,
  Where guilt is ftranger to the ingenuous heart?
Or Craft illude, where godlike Science fheds
  The beams of knowledge and the gifts of art?

Go, raife thy hand, and with its magic pow'r
   Pencil with night the fun's afcending ray,
Bid the broad veil eclipfe the noon-tide hour,
   And damps of ftygian darknefs fhroud the day.—

(Such night as lours o'er Britain's fated land,
   Where raylefs fhades the darken'd throne furround ;
Nor deeper glooms at Mofes' waving wand,
   Pour'd their thick horrors o'er the Memphian ground.)

Bid heav'ns dread thunders at thy voice expire,
   Or chain the angry vengeance of the waves ;
Then hope thy breath can chill th' eternal fire,
   And free fouls pinion with the bonds of flaves.

Thou canft not hope—Attend the flight of days,
   View the bold deeds, that wait the dawning age,
Where Time's ftrong arm, that rules the mighty maze,
   Shifts the proud actors on this earthly ftage !

Then tell us, NORTH,—for thou art fure to know ;
   For have not Kings and fortune made thee great ?
Or lurks not genius in th' ennobled brow,
   And dwells not wifdom in the robes of ftate ?

Tell how the pow'rs of luxury and pride,
   Taint thy pure zephyrs with their poifon'd breath ;
How dark Corruption fpreads th' envenom'd tide,
   And Britain trembles on the verge of death.

And tell how, rapt by Freedom's deathlefs flame,
   And foft'ring influence of the fav'ring fkies,
This Weftern World, the laft recefs of fame,
   Sees in her wilds a new-born empire rife :

D

A new-born Empire, whose afcendant hour
　　Defies the foes, that would its life deftroy,
And like Alcides, with its infant power
　　Shall crufh thofe ferpents, who its reft annoy.

Then look thro' time, and with extended eye,
　　Pierce the deep veil of fate's obfcure domain!
The morning dawns, th' effulgent ftar is nigh,
　　And crimfon'd glories deck her rifing reign!

Behold afar beneath the cloud of days,
　　Where reft the wonders of afcending fame;
What Heroes rife, immortal heirs of praife!
　　What fields of death with conq'ring ftandards flame!

See her throng'd cities' warlike gates unfold!
　　What tow'ring armies ftretch their banners wide,
Where cold Ontario's icy waves are roll'd,
　　Or far Altama's filver waters glide!

Lo from the groves, th' afpiring cliffs that fhade,
　　Afcending pines the furging ocean brave,
Rife in tall mafts, the floating canvas fpread,
　　And rule the dread dominions of the wave!

Where her clear rivers pour the mazy tide,
　　The laughing lawns in full luxuriance bloom,
The golden harveft fpreads her wanton pride,
　　The flow'ry garden breathes a glad perfume.

Her potent voice fhall hufh the ftorms of fate,
　　Where the meads bloffom or the billows roar;
And cities, gay with fumptuous domes of ftate,
　　Stretch their bright turrets on the founding fhore.

There mark that Coast, which seats of wealth surround,
  That haven, rich with many a flowing sail,
Where mighty ships, from earth's remotest bound,
  Float on the chearly pinions of the gale.

There BOSTON smiles, no more the sport of scorn,
  And meanly prison'd by thy fleets no more ;
And far as ocean's billowy tides are borne,
  Lifts her fear'd ensigns of imperial power.

So smile the shores, where lordly Hudson strays,
  (Whose floods fair YORK and proud ALBANIA lave)
Or PHILADELPHIA's happier clime surveys
  Her glist'ring spires in Schuylkyll's lucid wave.

Or southward far extend thy wond'ring eyes,
  Where fertile streams the garden'd vales divide ;
And mid the peopled fields distinguish'd rise
  Virginian tow'rs, and Charlestown's spiry pride.

Genius of arts, of manners and of arms,
  See deck'd with glory and the blooms of grace,
This Virgin-clime unfolds her brighter charms,
  And gives her beauties to thy fond embrace !

Hark, from the glades, and ev'ry list'ning spray,
  What heav'n-born Muses wake th' enraptur'd song !
The vocal shades attune th' enchanting lay,
  And echoing vales harmonious strains prolong.

Thro' the vast series of descending years,
  That lose their currents in th' eternal wave,
Till heav'n's last trump shall rend th' affrighted spheres,
  And ope each empire's everlasting grave ;

Propitious ſkies the joyous field ſhall crown,
  And robe her vallies in perpetual prime,
And ages bleſt of undiſturb'd renown,
  Beam their mild radiance o'er th' imperial clime.

And where is BRITAIN?—In the ſkirt of day,
  Where ſtormy Neptune rolls his utmoſt tide,
Where ſuns oblique diſfuſe a feeble ray,
  And lonely waves the fated coaſts divide;

Seeſt thou yon Iſle, whoſe deſert landſcape yields
  The mournful traces of the fame ſhe bore;
Where matted thorns oppreſs the cultur'd fields,
  And piles of ruin choak the dreary ſhore?—

From thoſe lov'd ſeats, the Virtues ſad withdrew,
  Fro a fell Corruption's bold and venal hand;
Reluctant Freedom wav'd her laſt adieu,
  And Devaſtation ſwept the vaſſal d land.

On her white cliffs, the pillars once of fame,
  Her melancholy Genius ſits to wail;
Drops the fond tear, and o'er her lateſt ſhame,
  Bids dark Oblivion draw her ſable veil.

An ELEGY,

On the death of Mr. BUCKINGHAM ST. JOHN ; *who was drowned in his passage from New-Haven to Norwalk, May 5th,* 1771.

BY THE SAME.

THE world now yeilds to night's returning sway;
 The deeper glooms lead on the solemn hour,
And call my steps, beneath the moon's pale ray,
 To roam in SADNESS on the sea-beat shore.

Now glide the inconstant shadows o'er the plain,
 The broad moon swimming thro the broken clouds,
The gleam of waters brightens on the main,
 And anchor'd navies lift their wavering shrouds.

Deep silence reigns ; save on the moory ground,
 The long reed rustling to the passing gales,
The noise of dashing waves, and hallow sound
 Of rushing winds, that murmur thro the sails.]

Far hence, ye pleasures of a mind at ease,
 The sprightly joys, that rural scenes can yeild,
When spring, led jocund by the softening breeze,
 Wakes the glad morn, and robes the dewy field

Far be the giddy raptures of the gay,
 The midnight joys licentious youth can share,
When ruin, smiling o'er her destin'd prey,
 In sweet allurements hides the deadly snare.

Mine be the mufic of the rolling wave,
   The moonlight fhadows and furrounding gloom ;
Mine the dread haunts of contemplation grave,
   That lift the foul to fcenes beyond the tomb.

Here while deep midnight holds her filent reign,
   And fancy bears the ravifh'd thought along,
Dark melancholy fpreads her airy train,
   And friendfhip calls, and grief infpires the fong. .

As thro thefe mournful glooms I ftretch'd my fight,
   Mid founds of death, that bid the foul attend,
Mid empty forms, and fleeting fhapes of night,
   Slowly I view a white-rob'd fhade afcend,

That fays—" I once was St. John ! from the bounds
   Of unknown realms beneath the dreary wave,
Where ever-reftlefs floods, in nightly rounds,
   Roll their dark furges o'er my watry grave ;

From feats, which ne'er to mortal fight difplay'd,
   The gates of dread eternity furround,
In night conceal'd, and death's impervious fhade,
   My voice afcends : attend the warning found !

Oh thou, attend ! who flufh'd with early bloom,
   In life's new fpring, and vernal fweetnefs gay,
Heedlefs of fate, that muft thy branch entomb,
   Spread'ft thy green bloffoms to the morning ray.

With thee how late, how like, alas ! to thee ;
   To mortal joys, by opening youth beguil'd,
I ftretch'd my airy wifh, and follow'd free,
   Where pleafure triumph'd, and where fancy fmil'd.

Then, while fond hope her glittering pinions fpread,
   * Pointing to climes beyond the diftant wave,
Even then, unnotic'd, o'er my deftin'd head,
   Hung death's dire form, and feal'd me for the grave.

How vain the thought for many a joyous morn,
   To tafte of raptures unallay'd by woe !
At once from life and every pleafure torn,
   From all I wifh'd, and all I lov'd below.

The faithlefs morning, on our opening fails,
   Smil'd out ferene, and fmooth'd our gliding way,
While the gay veffel, fann'd by breathing gales,
   Play'd on the placid bofom of the fea.

When lo, defcending on the darkening wind,
   Burft the dire ftorm,—and feeble to fuftain
The rufhing blafts, in warring fury join'd,
   The frail fkiff finks beneath the furging main. _

And fee, afar the oarlefs boat conveys
   The trembling failors to the diftant fhore ;
Alone, of aid bereft, with one laft gaze,
   I funk in deeps : and funk to rife no more.

In that fad hour, what fearful fcenes arife,
   What pangs diftrefs, what unknown fears difmay !
When future worlds difclofing on our eyes,
   The trembling foul forfakes the kindred day !

------

* *Mr. St. John was meditating a voyage to Europe.*

Before the awful bar, the Almighty throne,
   In dread I've stood the Eternal Judge to see,
And fix d in blifs, or doom'd to endlefs moan,
   Have heard the long, the unrevers'd decree:

Nor earth muft know the reft."——Where art thou now,
   In youthful joys my partner and my friend;
Of thofe bleft hours thy fortune gave below,
   Of all our hopes is this the fatal end?

Ah what avail'd that energy of mind,
   The heights of fcience, and of arts to explore,
That early led where genius unconfin'd,
   Spreads her glad feaft, and opes her claffic ftore!

Ah what avail'd, in earthly blifs fo frail,
   The fame gay-dawning on thy rifing years!
Ah what avail'd,—for what could then avail?—
   Thy friend's deep forrows, or thy country's tears!

In pleafure's paths, by vivid fancy led,
   Mid every hope that blooming worth could raife,
The wings of death with fatal horror fpread,
   Blank'd the bright promife of thy future days.

So, from the louring weft, the darken'd clouds
   Rufh on the fun and dim his orient ray,
And hateful night in glooms untimely fhrouds
   The afcending glories of the vernal day.

Adieu, my friend, fo dear in vain, adieu,
   Till fome fhort days their fleeting courfes roll;
Soon fhall our fteps thine earlier fate purfue,
   Mov'd in the race, and crowding to the goal.

The approaching hour fliall fee the fun no more,
  Wheel his long courfe, or fpread his golden ray ;
Soon the vain dream of mortal life be o'er,
  The brightnefs dawning of celeftial day.

Then join'd in blifs, as once in friendfhip join'd,
  May pitying Heaven our purer fpirits raife,
Each crime atton'd, each virtue well refin'd,
  To pafs a bleft eternity of praife !——

A M B I T I O N.

An E L E G Y.

BY THE SAME.

HENCE, gaudy Flattery, with thy firen fong,
  Thy fading laurels, and thy trump of praife,
Thy magic glafs, that cheats the wondering throng,
  And bids vain men, grow vainer, while they gaze.

For what the gain, tho nature have fupplied
  A tender foul, to feel the fting of pain ?
That fame how poor, that lifts our bafelefs pride,
  And fhews the heights our fteps muft ne'er attain !

E

How vain thofe thoughts that thro creation rove,
  Returning fraught with images of woe!
Thofe gifts how vain that pleafe not thofe we love!
  With grief opprefs'd, how fmall the gain to know!

And oh, that fate, in life's fequefter'd fhade,
  Had fix'd the limits of my filent way,
Far from the fcenes in noify pomp array'd,
  Where hope and fame but flatter to betray.

The lark had call'd me at the birth of dawn,
  My cheerful toils and rural fports to fhare;
Nor, when mild evening glimmer'd on the lawn,
  Had fleep been frighted at the voice of care.

So the foft flocks in harmlefs pleafure ftray,
  Or fport in rapture on the flowery mead,
Enjoy the beauties of the vernal day,
  And no fad prefcience tells them they muft bleed.

Then wild ambition ne'er had fwell'd my heart,
  Nor had my fteps purfued the road to fame;
Then ne'er had flander rais'd the envenom'd dart,
  Nor hung in vengeance o'er my hated name.

Nor views of blifs that never muft be mine,
  Urg'd the fond tear, or fwell'd the burfting figh;
Nor tendereft pangs had bid my foul repine,
  Nor torture warn'd me that my hopes muft die.

Farewell, ye glittering phantoms of the mind,
  The golden vifion, or ambitious dream,
The fickle forms by fairy fancy join'd,
  The pride of laurels and the mufe's theme.

Vain hope, adieu! thou dear deluding cheat,
  Whofe magic charm can burft the bonds of pain;
By thee decoy'd, we clafp the gay deceit,
  And plan the fcenes of future joys in vain.

Come Sadnefs! come, mild fifter of Defpair,
  The helplefs fufferer's laft fupport and friend,
Lead to thofe fcenes that footh the wretch's care,
  Where life's falfe joys, and life itfelf, muft end!

Well pleas'd, I wander o'er the folemn ground,
  Where Death in horror holds his dread domain,
While night fits gloomy in the etherial round,
  And fwimming vapors cloud the dreary plain.

Ye ghofts, the tenants of the evening fkies,
  That fweep in fadnefs o'er the dufky vale,
Enrob'd in mifts, I fee your forms arife;
  I hear your voices founding in the gale!

Of life ye fpeak, and life's fantaftic toys,
  How vain the wifh, that grafps at things below!
How difappointment lours on all our joys,
  And hope bequeaths the legacy of woe!

Ye too, perhaps, while youth fupplied its beam,
  On fancy's pinions foaring to the fky,
Fed your deluded thoughts with many a dream,
  Of love and fame, and future fcenes of joy.

Like your's how foon our empty years fhall fade,
  Paft, like the vapors that in clouds decay,
Paft, like the forms that flit along the fhade,
  Ourfelves as worthlefs, and as vain as they!

Here the kind haven greets our weary fail,
    When the rude voyage of troubled life is o'er,
Safe from the ftormy blaft, the faithlefs gale,
    The gulphs that threaten, and the waves that roar.

The heart no more the pains of love fhall fhare,
    Nor torturing grief the wayward mind enflave,
Thro toil-worn years fatigued with reftlefs care,
    Peace, fought in vain, awaits us in the grave.

Nor peace alone ! death breaks the fullen gloom,
    That dims the portals of eternal day,
Bids the freed foul her nobler powers affume,
    And wing from woes her heaven-directed way.

Fly hence ye fhades ! ye brighter fcenes arife !
    Ye joys celeftial, opening on my view !
Vanifh, ye griefs, that dwell beneath the fkies,
    Ye ftreaming tears, ye fond complaints, adieu !

THE PROPHECY OF BALAAM.

Numbers: Chap. xxiii. 24.

An IRREGULAR ODE. *Written, Anno* 1773.

BY THE SAME.

1

ON lofty Peor's brow,
 That rears its forehead to the fky,
 And fees the airy vapours fly,
And clouds in bright expanfion fail below,
 Sublime the Prophet ftood.
  Beneath its pine-clad fide,
The diftant world her various landfcape yeilds;
Winding vales and lengthening fields,
 Streams in funny maze that flow'd;
  Stretch'd immenfe in profpect wide
  Forefts green in fummer's pride;
 Waving glory gilds the main,
The dazzling fun afcending high;
 While earth's blue verge at diftance dimly feen,
Spreads from the aching fight, and fades into the fky.

II.

Beneath his feet along the level plain,
 The hoft of Ifrael ftretch'd in deep array;
Their tents rofe frequent on the enamell'd green;
 Bright to the winds the colour'd ftreamers play.

Red from the flaughter of their foes,
In awful fteel the embattled heroes ftood;
High o'er the fhaded ark in terror rofe
The cloud, the dark pavilion of their God.
Before the Seer's unwilling eyes,
The years unborn afcend in fight.
He faw their opening morn arife,
Bright in the fun fhine of the favoring fkies;
While from the unfufferable light,
Fled the dire demons of oppofing night.
No more, elate with Stygian aid,
He waves the wand's enchanted power,
And baleful thro the hallow'd glade,
His magic footfteps rove no more.
Fill'd with prophetic fire, he lifts his hand,
O'er the dim hoft in deep array;
And aw'd by Heaven's fupreme command,
Pours forth the rapture of the living lay.

III.

Fair, oh Ifrael, are thy tents!
Bleft the banners of thy fame!
Bleft the dwelling of the faints,
Where their God difplays his name!
Fair as thefe vales, that ftretch their lawns fo wide,
As gardens fmile, in flowery meadows fair,
As rifing cedars on the ftreamlet's fide,
That lift their branches to the fragrant air!
Vain is magic's deadly force,
Vain the dire enchanter's fpell,
Waving wand, or charmed curfe,
Vain the pride, the rage of hell!

From Peor's lofty brow,
. I fee the eternal powers reveal'd,
    And all the lengthen'd plains below
    O'erfhrouded by the Almighty fhield !
God, their guardian God, defcends,
And o'er the favor'd hoft Omnipotence extends.

IV.

And fee, bright Judah's ftar afcending
    Fires the eaft with crimfon day,
Aweful o'er his foes impending,
    Pours wide the lightning of his ray,
And flames deftruction on the oppofing world!
Death's broad banners, dark, unfurl'd,
    Wave o'er his blood-encircled way?
    Scepter'd king of Moab, hear,
        Deeds, that future times await,
    Deadly triumph, war fevere,
        Ifrael's pride, and Moab's fate!
What echoing terrors burft upon my ear!
What aweful forms in ghaftly horror rife!
    Empurpled rage, pale ruin, heart-ftruck fear,
In fcenes of blood afcend, and fkim before my eyes!

V.

Dimly on the fkirt of night
    O'er thy fons the cloud impends,
Louring ftorm with wild affright
    Loud the aftonifh'd ether rends.
Long hofts, emblaz'd with fun-bright fhields appear,
And victory fevere

Sits on their lightening fwords : along the fhores,
· Arm'd with the bolts of fate,
Impending navies wait ;
Above, around, the fhout of ruin roars.
For nought avails, that clad in fpiry pride,
Thy rifing cities glitter'd on the day ;
The vengeful arms wave devaftation wide,
And give thy pompous domes to mouldering flames a prey.

VI.

Edom bows her lofty head ;
Seer fubmits her vanquifh'd bands ;
Amalek, of hofts the dread,
Sinks beneath their wafting hands.
See, whelm'd in fmoky heaps, the ruin'd walls,
Rife o'er thy fons' unhappy grave ;
Low their blafted glory falls ;
Vain the pride that could not fave !
Ifrael's fwords arreft their prey ;
Back to fwift fate thy frighted ftandards turn ;
Black defolation rolls along their way ;
War fweeps in front, and flames behind them burn :
And death, and dire difmay,
Unfold their univerfal grave, and ope the mighty urn.

The DOWNFALL of BABYLON.

An Imitation of sundry passages in the thirteenth and fourteenth
Chapters of the Prophecy of Isaiah, and the eighteenth
Chapter of the Revelations of St. John.

Written, anno 1775.

BY THE SAME.

'TWAS now the day, devote to blest repose,
  From realms of darkness, when the Saviour rose,
In Patmos's Isle, with sacred light inspir'd,
The great Apostle from the world retir'd;
Before his eyes eternal wonders roll,
And future visions open on his soul,
Unfolding skies the scenes of fate display,
And Heaven descending in the beam of day.

. He saw with joy the promis'd Church arise,
Fam'd thro the earth, and favor'd from the skies;
A starry crown invests her radiant head,
Around her form the solar glories spread,
Her power, her grace, by circling realms approv'd,
By angels guarded, and by Heaven belov'd:
Till mystic Babel, with blaspheming pride,
For idol forms the eternal power defied;
Then martyr'd blood the holy offering seal'd,
And persecution dyed the carnag'd field,
Religion sunk in superstitious lore,
And Heaven-built temples swam with sainted gore.

F

But not in reft, till virtue fhould expire,
Slept the juft vengeance of eternal ire.
The Seer beheld, till God's avenging hand
Smote the proud foe, and fwept the guilty land;
Then pious rapture triump'd on his tongue,
And infpiration breath'd the exulting fong.

" What fudden fall hath dimm'd thy boafted ray,
Son of the Morn! bright Phofphor of the day!
How funk in death, a victim of the grave,
Thy pride fo vaunting, and thy arm fo brave!
Where now the haughty boaft?"   Above the fkies,
O'er the ftarr'd arch my towering fteps fhall rife,
To Heaven's high walls my glories fhall afcend,
My throne be 'ftablifh'd, and my power extend,
O'er the wide world to ftretch my arm abroad;
A God in fplendor, and in might a God."

Behold from rage the bold oppreffor ceas'd;
Thy glory wan, and all thy treafures wafte!
Eternal wrath, awaken'd o'er thy land,
Tears the weak fceptre from the injurious hand;
Heaven gives its captive fons a kind releafe,
And earth fmiles, joyous, at the fongs of peace.

Lo, at thy fall, in realms of night below,
Hell greets thine entrance to the worlds of woe!
See from their thrones, along the infernal fhade,
Rife the dark fpectres of the mighty dead,
Friends to thy fway, and partners in thy crimes,
Kings once on earth, and tyrants in their times!
" And art thou fall'n?"—their looks of wonder crave—
" Swept, undiftinguifh'd, to the darkfome grave?

O'er thy pale cheek funereal damps are fpread,
And fhrouds of fable wrap thee with the dead ;
What aw'd the world oblivion's fhadows hide,
And glad worms revel on the wrecks of pride.

Is this the Power, whofe once tremendous eye
Shook the wide earth, and dar'd the avenging fky,
Oppofing kingdoms from their fceptres hurl'd,
And fpread fad ruin o'er the vanquifh'd world ?
Is this the Power, that rofe in boafted ftate,
Proud judge of thrones, and arbiter of fate ?
The Power, whofe forceries, us'd in every clime,
Stain'd the dark annals of recording time,
While perfecution taught the infernal lore,
And zeal was fated with the martyr's gore ?—
Lo ! clos'd thine eyes that wont the Heavens to brave,
Expos'd thou ly'ft, an outcaft from the grave ;
No fplendid urn thy funeral duft contains,
Nor one kind turf conceals thy fad remains ;
For thee no marble lifts its tablet high,
Where kings deceas'd in mournful glory lie ;
For juft renown divides thee from the bleft,
Nor decks the clods that lull thy bones to reft."

And fee Deftruction from the Almighty hand,
Sweeps her broad befom o'er thy guilty land ;
Careering flames attend her dreadful way,
And rifing darknefs intercepts the day ;
The dim fun finks in fearful fhades of night,
The moon and planets veil their trembling light,
O'er thy doom'd walls the louring ftorms afcend,
And fate's dread omens mark thy haftening end.

See mid the o'erarching canopy of shade,
An angel-form, in robes of blood array'd,
Lifts his red arm, that bids the tempest rise,
Wing'd with the etherial vengeance of the skies;
And calls the wintry winds, that all around,
Roll on the storms, and sweep the delug'd ground,
And far beneath, where direful earthquakes sleep,
Bursts the dark chambers of the affrighted deep!
Lo! Heaven avenging pours the fiery tide;
Thy whelm'd walls sink, thy tottering turrets slide,
Thy glittering domes sulphureous torrents lave,
And doom thy seats, a desart and a grave!

For there no more shall gay assemblies meet,
Crowd thy full marts, and throng thy spacious street;
No more the bridegroom's cheerful voice shall call
The viol, sprightly in the sounding hall;
No more the lamp shall yeild her cheerful light,
Gild thy lone roofs and sparkle thro the night.
Each morn shall view thy defolated ground,
With falling domes and shatter'd spires around,
And clad in weeds, in wild confusion thrown,
The marble trophy, and the sculptur'd stone.
No future age thy glories shall recall,
Thy turrets lift, or build thy defart wall;
Where the gilt palace pierc'd the admiring skies,
The owl shall stun thee with funereal cries,
The baleful dragon thro thy gardens rove,
And wolves usurp the confecrated grove.
No shepherd there the wandering flock shall spread,
Nor, tir'd, repofe beneath the tented shed;

No ftranger there with devious footfteps ftray,
Where circling horrors guard the fated way ;
Eternal Ruin rears her ftandard wide,
And vengeance triumphs o'er the realms of pride."

THE SPEECH OF
PROTEUS TO ARISTÆUS,
CONTAINING THE STORY OF ORPHEUS AND EURIDICE ;
Tranflated from the fourth Book of Virgil's Georgics.

A Collegiate Exercife : Written, Anno 1770.

BY THE SAME.

A GOD púrfues thee with immortal hate,
By crimes provok'd that prompt the wrath of fate.
In guiltlefs woe the haplefs Orpheus died,
And calls the powers to avenge his injur'd bride.

Along the ftreams, with flying fteps fhe ftrove,
To fhun the fury of thy lawlefs love ;
Unhappy fair ! nor on the fated way
Saw the dire fnake that ambufh'd for her prey.

Her fifter Dryades wail'd the fatal wound ;
The lofty hills their melting cries refound ;
Then wept the rocks of Rhodope, the towers
Of high Pangæus, and the Rhefian fhores ;
The mournful founds the Attic lands convey,
And Hebrus rolls in fadden'd waves away.

He, on his lyre, essay'd with tuneful art,
To sooth the ceaseless anguish of his heart;
Thee, his fair bride, to lonely grief a prey,
Thee sung at rising, and at falling day:
Then sought the realms of death and Stygian Jove,
Thro black'ning horrors of the infernal grove,
Mid direful ghosts, and powers of deep despair,
Unknown to pity, and unmov'd by prayer.
From hell's dark shores, to Orpheus' melting song,
On every side the gloomy nations throng;
Thin, airy shades, pale spectres void of light,
Like fancied forms that glide athwart the night.
As flitting birds in summer's chequer'd shade,
Dance on the boughs, and flutter thro the glade,
Or seek the woods when night descends amain,
And pours in storms along the wintry plain:
Men, matrons, round the sweet musician press'd,
The spotless maidens, and the youths unblest,
Snatch'd from their parents' eyes, or doom'd to yeild
To war's dire combats on the bloody field;
Whom the deep fens, that drain the moory ground,
And black Cocytus reedy lake surround,
Where baleful Styx her mournful margin laves,
And deadly Lethe rolls the oblivious waves.

Hell heard the song; and fix'd in deep amaze,
On the sweet bard the snaky Furies gaze;
Grim Cerberus hung entranc'd; and ceas'd to reel
The giddy circle of Ixion's wheel.

These dangers 'scap'd, he seeks the upper air,
Elate with joy, and follow'd by the fair:

f · · · · Fates impos'd : but doom'd to prove
·   · · dnefs of ill-omen'd love !
C·   ·, or melt at human woe,
A ·.   .e, were venial aught below !
L·g··· · · d at hand ; the Stygian fhades retire ;
With ·v·es wild, and vanquifh d with defire,
His fe·rs forgot, he turn d ; his lovely bride
Given to his hope, with trembling glance efpy'd.
There end his joys, and vanifh d into air
His fancied raptures and his fruitlefs care,—
Broke is the league—and twice tremendous roars
The diftant thunder on the infernal fhores.

What rage, fhe cried, hath dafh'd our joys again,
Pair'd in fad fates, and doom d to endlefs pain.
I hear the voice that calls me back to woes,
My fwimming eyes eternal flumbers clofe.
A laft farewel ! the infernal glooms arife,
And, wrapt in night, my parting fpirit flies ;
Vain my weak arms, extended to reftore
The bridal hand, that muft be thine no more.

She faid, and vanifh'd inftant from his eye,
Like melting fmoke that mingles with the fky.
No kind embrace, his deepening grief to allay,
No farewel word, tho much he wifh'd to fay,
Nor hope remain'd.   Stern Charon now no more
Confents to waft him to the infernal fhore.
Forever fnatch'd from all his foul could love,
What prayers, what tears, what fongs, the Fates could move !
Her, breathlefs, pale, to manfions of the g ···,
The bark bore floating on the ftygian wave.

In gelid caves, with horrid glooms array'd,
Where cloud-topt hills project an awful shade,
Along the margin of the desert shore,
Where lovely Strymon's rushing waters roar,
Seven hapless months he wail'd his fatal love,
His ravish'd bride, and blam'd the hand of Jove.
Stern tygers soften'd at the tuneful sound,
The thickets move, the forests dance around :
So in some poplar's shade, with soothing song,
Sad Philomela mourns her captive young ;
When some rude swain hath found the unfeather'd prey,
Her nest despoil'd, and borne the prize away ;
Thro the long night she breathes her plaintive strain,
The slow, deep moan resounds, and echoes o'er the plain.

Pleasure no more his soul estrang'd could move,
The charms of beauty, or the joys of love.
Alone he stray'd, where wintry Tanais flows,
Thro deserts whiten'd with eternal snows.
Mourn'd his lost bride, the infernal powers' deceit,
And curs'd the vain, illusive, gifts of fate.

When Bacchus' Orgies stain'd the midnight skies,
Their proffers scorn'd, the Thracian matrons rise ;
Their hopeless rage the bleeding victim tore,
His fever'd limbs are scatter'd on the shore ;
Rent from his breathless corse, swift Hebrus sweeps
His gory visage to the distant deeps.

Yet when cold death sate trembling on his tongue,
With fainting soul, Euridice he sung,
Ah dear, ah lost Euridice, he cries,
Euridice, the echoing shore replies.

THE TRIAL OF FAITH.*

BY TIMOTHY DWIGHT, D. D.

PART I.
DANIEL, CHAP. I.

BENEATH the dawn, o'er Babel's fruitful plain,
In proud effulgence mov'd the conquering train.
Full on the fun's broad beam their buckler's ray
Streak'd the glad fields, and gave a mimic day.

G

---

* THIS Poem is reprinted from the New-Haven Gazette, and the Connecticut Magazine, published by Meigs and Dana, for the year 1786;—where it forms three Numbers of a Periodical Paper, undertaken by Dr. Dwight—and is introduced by the following Preface, viz.——" The ' inclofed Poem is handed you for publication. I have ' long thought that the Bible furnished many subjects for ' poetry, far more deserving the ambition and efforts of ' genius, than those to which it is commonly dedicated. I ' do not mean merely that they are subjects more friendly ' to virtue, but to poetry. They are more sublime, novel, ' beautiful, agreeable, and in every way interesting.—— ' Perhaps this experiment may not have been so happily ' made, as to elucidate the truth of this opinion. But as ' it is, it is submitted to the judgment of your readers. ' Should it have the happy influence to induce even one ' perfon of poetical talents, to apply those talents to this ' method of ornamenting his own character, and that of ' his country, I shall think my labours not unhappily di- ' rected."

With fpiry fplendor varying ftandards glow'd ;
In pomp fublime majeftic chieftains rode ;
The filver clarions gave a folemn found,
And cars unnumber'd, thundering fhook the ground.

There JUDAH's fpoils in proud difplay were borne ;
There purple vefture mock'd the rifing morn ;
There facred veffels, rich from Ophir's mine,
Beam'd their ftrong light, and imag'd art divine ;
There mov'd the prince, the queen, the lord, the fage,
And haplefs captive throngs of every age.

High-thron'd, the monarch from his golden car,
Survey'd the trophies of fuccefsful war.
Majeftic, tall, the mighty hero rofe,
Born to command, and dreadful to his foes :
His lofty limbs, enrob'd in rich attire
Of fteel, and gold, were circled round with fire :
His pride, his foul, expanded at the fight,
And his glad eye-balls warm'd with living light.

As o'er the captive train he caft his eyes,
And heard, unmov'd, their mingled groans and cries,
Four youths, companions, filent pafs'd along,
By form diftinguifh'd from the vulgar throng.
Fair o'er them trembled beauty's purple flame ;
Their eyes, as angels', caft a funny beam ;
Sublime their port ; ferene their folemn look ;
By fear unaw'd, by heavieft woes unbroke ;
To ills fuperior ; earth and time above ;
But touch'd with kindred woe, and yearning love.
The monarch gaz'd.—His fierce and hardy mind
Then firft with fweet and tender thoughts refin'd ;

He felt each nerve with ftrange emotion thrill,
And down each cheek new tears in filence fteal.
No more the hoft, no more the fpoils appear'd ;
No more the trump's infpiring voice was heard ;
Fix'd as he gaz'd, to foft compaffion won,
The pomp was buried, and the triumph gone.

To ARIOCH then, his favor'd, faithful flave,
The turning prince his fovereign pleafure gave :
" Seeft thou, my ARIOCH, thofe bright youthful forms ;
" What grace furrounds them, and what beauty warms !
" With what fair pride, magnificently great,
" They move fuperior to their humble fate !
" For arms, for empire, not for bondage made,
" They win my foul, and claim imperial aid.
" Go then, my ARIOCH, go, their fteps purfue ;
" With gentle fympathy their fouls fubdue ;
" Their monarch's favour to their hearts enfure ;
" Win them from grief ; difrobe their rags impure ;
" Their courfe immediate to the palace bend ;
" Let faithful ASHPENAZ their fteps attend ;
" Superior far to all in every grace,
" Among the chofen youths appoint the place."

The monarch fpake. The faithful chief obey'd,
And to the palace ftrait the youths convey'd.
There ASHPENAZ, the eunuch's prince, receiv'd,
To hope reftor'd them, and from want reliev'd.
Cheer'd with kind words, their every wifh obey'd,
And thus, with foft and tender accent, faid :———

" All-lovely youths ! attir'd with every grace,
' The beft, and brighteft, of your haplefs race,

' Think not, from war's dire fcenes, the Affyrian mind,
' To love imp rvious, or to mifery blind.
' Even the great prince, our mighty realm who fways,
' Train'd in fierce wars, and nurs'd in bloody ways,
' Though proudly borne on Conqueft's lofty wings,
' Lord of a world, and king of countlefs kings,
' Yet bade me kindly every want fupply,
' No hope extinguifh, and no joy deny.

　' By his command, on kingly dainties fed,
' Serv'd by his flaves, and in his palace bred,
' In every art, in every myftery train'd,
' By lords approv'd, by royal love fuftain'd.
' Your lives, in peace ferene, fhall glide away,
' New joys returning with returning day.

　' For me, my bofom, not of ftubborn fteel,
' Well knows to love, and long has learn'd to feel.
' Your woes, O Youths, your nation's fate fevere,
' Pierce my fad foul, and prompt the tender tear.
' Each gentle act, that marks a parent's hand,
' From faithful ASHPENAZ affur'd command ;
' From earlieft years, to youths a conftant guide,
' 'Tis joy to blefs them, and to ferve is pride.''

　Thus fpoke the prince. With meek, but folemn grace,
The elder youth return'd this fad addrefs :
' O Prince of Eunuchs, foothing friend of woe !
' Thy gentle folace bids our forrows flow :
' With love, with gratitude, our bofoms burn,
' But, pierc'd with grief, our haplefs nation mourn.
' For ah ! her fons, of every good forlorn,
' Wafte with dire want, or fhrink from piercing fcorn ;

' Or rage, in flaughter bids them weltering roll;
' Or gloomy flavery blafts the wither'd foul;
' Her childlefs mothers fpread the reeking ground;
' Her babes, unpitied, glut the hungry hound;
' Levell'd in duft, her heaven-built Temple lies,
' And SALEM's fmoking ruins fill the fkies.
' More dread thefe fplendors fhew the fearful doom,
' As day more deeply fhades the darkfome tomb :
' Then, mid all joys, permit our hearts to mourn,
' Nor think thy goodnefs meets a bafe return."

 He fpoke.   The prince, to chambers proud and fair,
Led the fad youths, and footh'd their rifing care,
Their graceful forms in fplendid garments drefs'd,
And kindly cheer'd their troubled minds to reft.

 As now all-fragrant fpread the rich repaft,
Cates of all climes, and wines of every tafte;
Deep cares revolving in his troubled breaft,
His chofen friends the elder youth addrefs'd :——

 " O youths, refin'd in fierce affliction's flame,
' Like gold, refulgent with undrofly beam!
' Now new alarms your virtuous minds affail,
' New dangers tempt, and untried foes prevail.
' As icy rocks, by winter beat in vain,
' Yeild to mild funs, and melt in vernal rain,
' So the firm heart, no cruelty could move,
' May lofe each virtue in the beams of love.
' Thofe cates, compos'd of all things rich and rare,
' Cull'd with nice art, and drefs'd with fkilful care,
' From truth's fair path our footfteps foftly charm,
' Our prayers enfeeble, and our faith difarm.

' To pureſt food the ſacred law confin'd,
' The taſte luxurious, and the wandering mind.
' Fix'd be our hearts its high beheſts to obey,
' Nor let vain banquets lure our feet aſtray.
' From humble pulſe ſereneſt peace ſhall ſpring,
' Health nerve the limbs, and lift the mental wing;
' The ſoul, the form, with health and beauty bloom,
' And heaven complacent grant a milder doom."

Thus ſpoke the youth. With ſmiles of pure delight,
In duty's path the aſſenting friends unite,
To heaven the feaſt, the roving wiſh reſign'd,
And gain'd the banquet of the obedient mind.

The courteous prince, by ſoft intreaties led,
Indulg'd their prayer, and gave the humble bread.
Heaven bleſs'd its ſons.—As mid the inferior grove,
Four beauteous pines aſcend the clouds above,
Mid heats, and droughts, and ſtorms, and froſt, and ſnow,
Through the full year with living verdure grow,
O'er every wood, with pride majeſtic, reign,
And wave exulting round the adjacent plain :
In port, in ſtature, thus, with thoughts ſublime,
And worth, ſuperior to the aſſaults of time,
Their gentle manners, great beyond diſguiſe,
Friendly to man, and faithful to the ſkies,
The favour'd captives grew, and learn'd to ſoar
Through all the myſteries of Chaldean lore;
Learn'd how the ſtars in ſolemn ſplendor roll;
How countleſs realms compoſe one mighty whole;
What arts, what mazes, through the ſyſtem run;
How hoſts are marſhall'd, and how fields are won.

THE TRIAL OF FAITH.

BY THE SAME.

PART II.

DANIEL, CHAP. II.

THUS rofe the youths, by lords and kings approv'd,
By earth exalted, and by Heaven belov'd,
When, loft in flumbers as the fovereign lay,
What time fair Phofphor fings the approach of day,
Full to his eyes a vifion rofe fublime,
Big with dread myfteries of afcending time.
Alarm'd, awak'd, he left the thorny bed;
His fleep all vanifh'd, and the vifion fled:
In vain he tried the wonders to reftore,
The fleeted phantom met his eyes no more.

Then deep convulfions fhook his ftormy mind,
That knew no croffes, and no wifh refign'd.
At once he fummon'd all the learn'd and wife,
Skill'd to explain, and artful to difguife,
Practis'd to bode, in words of foothing guile,
New feats, new triumphs, and new realms of fpoil.
And thus the king——"Let every fage and feer,
Dreamer of dreams, and ftar-taught prophet hear!
This night, as funk in fleep, your monarch lay,
When truth's clear dreams attend approaching day,

Before my eyes a folemn vifion rofe,
Clear, full, diftinct, as morn's full fplendor glows;
Fill'd with dread fcenes, with acts of mighty name,
With change of empires, and with years of fame.
I wak'd—I rofe—but all the events of night
Fled from my view, and took their final flight.
Then hear, ye fages; borne by fkill fublime,
Thro' the dark ages of afcending time,
Explore the vifion, make the wonders known;
And tell what changes wait the Affyrian throne."

The Hero fpoke.   Around the fpacious room
The ftrange command diffus'd a folemn gloom;
When thus a hoary fage——" O king divine,
Be endlefs life, and power, and honour thine!
Thy high behefts our hearts delight to obey;
We own thy glory, and we blefs thy fway.
But, O dread Prince, thy vifions to reveal,
Tranfcends the efforts of terreftial fkill.
Could ft thou, by memory's aid, the fcenes reftore,
Eafy thy feers the myftery would explore;
Would teach, for thee what crowns of triumph bloom,
Or what new nations meet the general doom.
The Gods alone, to whofe unbounded eye .
Spread, in clear fight, all realms beneath the fky,
In obvious view the ftars immenfely roll,
Or on fleet pinions roves the wandering foul,
Can bid the eventful fcenes of night return,
Or ope the vanifh'd vifions of the morn.
A new command, a labour yet undone,
Thy will enjoins us, and thy voice makes known,

Nor lord requir'd, nor prophet e'er divin'd,
The secret motions of the mazy mind."

The monarch heard.   With sudden anger bright,
From his fierce eye-balls flash'd a withering light :
Sternly he cried,——"Base, impious wretches, hear
What wrath betides you, and what fate is near.
If, taught by heaven, your hearts the dream divine,
Wealth waits your steps, and crowns before you shine :
Prophets of truth, your race shall then be seen,
Lov'd by the Gods, and precious gifts to men.
But if this feat your purblind skill denies,
Each wretch, who soils the robe of wisdom, dies.
Mock'd by your boasts, my soul, no longer tame,
Shall rouse to sense, and bid just vengeance flame ;
Each pamper'd carcase this right hand shall tear,
Glut the rob'd wolves, and feast the fowls of air.
Your hosts, your houses, give to flames a prey,
And sweep the nuisance from the world away."

He spoke : the seers withdrew.—The realm around,
From voice to voice diffus'd the dismal sound.
From ARIOCH, ASHPENAZ the tidings knew !
With thoughts all anxious to the youths he flew,
Rehears'd the tale——and " You, by worth betray'd,
Must soon," he cried, " be number'd with the dead."
" Fear not, O Prince,"—the elder youth reply'd :
" While heaven commands no ills the just betide.
Virtue refines, beneath affliction's power,
As gold runs beauteous from dissolving ore.
To light the dream shall rise, or, if the sky
Ordains our death, 'tis highest gain to die.

H

Unmov'd, our hearts, that thoufand deaths have known
In Judah's woes, will meet the pangs of one ;
From toil, and grief, and fhame, unpinion'd rife,
And mix with angels in their native fkies.
But hafte, ah hafte, and faithful ARIOCH bring,
E're he commence the vengeance of the king ;
This night, fhall Heaven the vanifh'd fcenes reftore,
And fave the prophets from vindictive power."

The Prince to ARIOCH flew, and, bath'd in tears,
Rehears'd the tale of mingled hopes, and fears.
He came : And pleas'd to ftay the monarch's rage,
Led to the throne the young, unbearded fage.
With mild regard, the foftening fovereign view'd,
While worth, and beauty, half his wrath fubdued,
Heard him, with modeft mien, his hope propofe,
That Heaven, ere morn, the vifion would difclofe,
And bade glad ARIOCH vengeance dire delay,
'Till the wifh'd hour fhould ope the promis'd day.

Thofe hours, the youths confum'd in fafts fevere,
And the pure fervence of effectual prayer.
The God of worlds, to whom, with beam divine,
Fairer than morn the fons of Zion fhine,
With love all bounteous bade the vifion rife,
Dread, full, and clear, to DANIEL's flumbering eyes.

At earlieft dawn, the youths, in bright array,
Toward the new palace bent their early way ;
Through rows of lords, and rows of kings they pafs'd,
While eyes of wonder thoufands on them caft ;
For round the court had fpread the fearful doom,
That mark'd the guiltlefs Magi to the tomb.

Before the throne the beardlefs prophets ftood ;
Round their fair forms the grace of virtue glow'd ;
Pleas'd, the great monarch view'd : With fofter ray,
His eye-balls fmil'd their fiercer flames away ;
His fettling vifage loft its wrathful form,
As Spring looks fair behind a wintery ftorm.

   " O KING of kings?" the elder youth began—
" Thy dread requeft tranfcends the power of man.
In vain thy feers the vifion would regain ;
Like ours, their wifhes, toils, and tears, are vain.
'Tis God alone the wonders can difplay,
The God, who form'd the heaven, the earth, and fea ;
Naked, and clear, before whofe fcarching eye,
The foul, the thoughts, and deep affections lie ;
He brought the eventful vifion to thy fight,
And he again commands it into light.

   " What time the dew of peace around thy bed
The filent flumbers of the morning fpread,
Dread to thine eyes a wonderous image fhone,
Awful in form, in fplendor like the fun.
Its head of flaming gold, its arms and breaft,
Of filver fair, interior worth confefs'd ;
Its thighs and belly glow'd with brazen light ;
Its legs, of iron, mark'd refiftlefs might ;
Its iron feet, commix'd with miry clay,
Difplay'd unfolid power, to time a prey.
When lo ! fpontaneous, from the mountains rent,
A ftone came thundering down, with fwift defcent ;
Full on the form, with mighty force it burft,
Crufh'd all its limbs, and ground its frame to duft ;

Borne by the winds, thou faw'ft its ruins fly,
Like chaff, when whirlwinds fweep the fummer fky.
And as a rifing cloud, but juft beheld,
Approaching, widens o'er the aerial field,
Expands, afcends, and, flow thro ether driven,
Sails thro the immenfe, and fills the bounds of heaven :
So the fmall cliff to rife, and fwell, began,
Spread thro' the fields, the neighbouring groves o'er-ran,
O'er towns, o'er realms, o'er mountains, left the eye,
Uprofe beyond the clouds, and heav'd the boundlefs fky.

  " 'Tis thus, O king! the Lord of Heaven declares,
What fcenes roll onward with the tide of years.
By us, his fovereign voice to thee makes known,
And tells what changes wait the Affyrian throne.

  " Thou art this head of gold : Thy power fublime,
Rules thoufand kings, and fpreads thro every clime.
But foon thy glory haftens to decay,
Soon the bright arms commence a humbler fway :
That too fhall fail ; the brazen kingdom rife,
Like ocean, fpreading to furrounding fkies.
As iron then an empire ftrong fhall fpring,
Subdue each realm, and vanquifh every king :
Beneath its wonderous power, all nature yeilds,
Europe's lone wilds, and Afia's cultur'd fields.
Hence various kings, to art, and force, a prey,
As iron potent, yet diffolv'd like clay :
Unfound, unfolid, fhall their empire rife,
Varying, as clouds their changes in the fkies.
In thofe far diftant days, o'er every land,
Shall God's dread fceptre rear its high command :

Before its power, refifting powers decay ;
Nations, and kings, and empires, melt away;
Through unknown wilds the vaft dominion roll,
Extend its conquering force from pole to pole ;
From morn's far regions reach the fhores of even,
Fill earth, and time, and rear its pomp to heaven.
Thus, King of kings ! the heavens thy dream reftore,
And teach the changes of terreftial power."

   The monarch heard, and look'd, when heavenly flame,
Round the fair youths fhould caft a golden beam ;
Or o'er their limbs inftinctive lightnings run ;
Or rainbow'd pinions lift them to the fun.
Proftrate to earth he fell : and,—" Oh !" he cries,
" Your God is Lord of gods, and worlds, and fkies :
He, only he, could make thefe vifions known ;
Let praife, and glory, wait his heavenly throne."

   To DANIEL, then the raptur'd hero bade
Incenfe be fir'd, and rich oblations paid ;
O'er his prime lords his favourite place ordain'd,
A prince to every king, and every land :
While, high o'er BABEL's realm, his partners fate
In kingly favour, and judicial ftate.

   Where'er they pafs'd, purfuing wonder came ;
The Magi blefs'd, the children lifp'd their name ;
To them were Judah's prayers and bleffings given,
And the poor mark'd them as the fons of Heaven.

THE TRIAL OF FAITH.

BY THE SAME.

PART III.

DANIEL, CHAP. III.

AND now once more, the spacious empire round,
War's fearful clarion ceas'd its shrilling found ;
Her voice harmonious, on subsiding gales,
Sweet peace refounded through the glad'ening vales :
When lo, new fears the faithful friends await,
And other trials lour'd approaching fate.
Long through the monarch's soul the project ran,
(Grateful to proud and heaven-dethroning man)
To bind the soul, the conscience to enchain,
And force one worship through his wide domain.
Fir'd with the fond design, an image fair,
Rich with pure gold, and gem'd with many a star.
He form'd, fair image of the morning sun,
Acknowledg'd guardian of th' Assyrian throne.
To this, his soul decreed mankind should bow,
Each victim burn, and rife each sacred vow,
And bade his mighty lords direct their way
To meet their sovereign, on th' appointed day.
North of proud Babel's walls, from sky to sky,
The plain of Dura left the labouring eye :

There willows wav'd o'er Tygris flowery fide:
There broad Euphrates roll'd his mighty tide.
This the dread fcene the monarch's will ordain'd;
And hither throng'd the lords of many a land.
As now the deftin'd morn her luftre fhed,
Here o'er the fields a hoft immenfely fpread;
Kings, nobles, chieftains, every fage and feer,
And hofts of flaves, and warriors gather'd here.

Bright rofe, in pomp divine, the imperial fun;
Light, life, and joy danc'd round his golden throne;
The heavens unclouded fmil'd a fairer blue;
Reviving beauty cloath'd the world anew;
As on old ocean glows the fun's broad ray,
And lights his glaffy fields with mimic day;
So, kindled by his beams, around the plain,
A new morn trembled o'er the unnumber'd train;
From helms, and fhields, and fteeds, and cars, afpires
A general glory of immingling fires:
The Tygris brighten'd in the golden beam,
And fweeter murmurs foften'd o'er the ftream.
On a tall pedeftal, before them fhone
The facred image of the rifing fun;
In folemn pomp, a hero rofe fublime,
His eye deep piercing through the fcenes of time.
When firft the orb, afcending from the main,
Caft his far level'd beams along the plain,
The form fuperb with every fplendor fhone,
Streak'd the gay fields, and feem'd another fun.
There the deep ruby pour'd a crimfon ray;
The funny topaz fhed a rival day:

Of every hue the mimic rainbow came,
And join'd its varied lights in one tranfcendant flame.
Far round the plain the throng unnumber'd ftood,
And gaz'd in filence on the imag'd god,
When thus the heralds cried, " With reverent ear
Your Monarch's voice, ye kings and nations, hear,
What time the notes of mingled mufic roll,
With magic influence on th' enraptur'd foul,
Before you golden form, ye fuppliants all
Proftrate on earth, with facred homage, fall.

They fpoke : as, borne thro' fome far winding vale,
The voice of ocean leads the fpringing gale ;
More loud, more folemn from the diftant fhore,
The flow, deep murmurs rife, and fwell, and roar ;
Propp'd on his ftaff, the hoary feaman ftands,
And calls back happier times, and other lands ;
Through his limbs thrills the youth-renewing charm,
And fkies, and winds, and waves, his bofom warm :
So fudden, from ten thoufand pipes and ftrings,
Loud, full and clear, the voice of mufic fprings :
O'er the glad plain, the breathing founds exhale,
And fwell, and wanton in the rifing gale ;
Now deep, majeftic in dread pomp they roll ;
Now foftly languifh on the yeilding foul ;
Now folemn awe, now lively zeal infpire,
Wake heavenly dreams, and light romantic fire :
Now funk on earth, the unnumber'd fuppliants lie,
And fmoking altars cloud the fragrant fky.

'Mid the vaft throng, the friends of Daniel ftood,
Nor bent the knee before the golden god.

Alone they ftood ; for at the palace gate,
So the king bade, in judgement Daniel fate,
The Magi faw, and ftraight, by envy led,
Flew to the king, and thus impatient faid ——
(For tho' the youths preferv'd from death their race,
Their bofoms ficken'd at their rivals' place)
O prince ! regardlefs of thy dread decree,
The Jews, fo honor'd, lov'd and blefs'd by thee,
Before yon golden God refufe to bow,
Prefent the prayer, or pay the folemn vow.
They flight thy gods, defpife thy glorious name,
Nor heed the vengeance of the fearful flame.

Fjr'd at the tale, before their fovereign king
He bade fierce guards the fons of Judah bring.
Serene they came.   And dare your hearts, he cries,
Againft the terrors of my anger rife?
Dare ye refufe before yon god to bow,
Prefent the prayer, and pay the folemn vow ?
Then know from me, vain youths, repenting know,
Before you flames of fearful vengeance glow.
Nor hope to 'fcape.   What man, what god can fave,
When I command you to the burning grave ?
Be warn'd ; be wife, your monarch's god adore ;
Nor tempt the dangers of refiftlefs power.

He fpoke.   As cherubs, drefs'd in robes of light,
To earth, on heaven's high errands, wing their flight,
With folemn, fweet, complacent fmile appear,
And bloffom in immortal beauty here ।
So, rofy fplendor purpling o'er his face,
With meekly dignity and matchlefs grace,

I

Whilſt on the king he caſt a heavenly look,
 That half revers'd the ſentence ere he ſpoke.
His lifted eye ſerene with ſolemn pride,
With gentle voice, the elder* youth replied,
Well pleas'd, O prince! our hearts confeſs thy ſway,
And all thy juſt commands with joy obey;
Faithful and patient, every toil ſuſtain,
Unaw'd by danger, and unmov'd by pain.
But the great GOD who form'd the earth and ſeas,
Firſt claims our homage, firſt demands our praiſe:
To him alone our knees in worſhip bend;
To him our praiſes and our prayers aſcend;
His mighty arm his faithful ſons ſhall ſave
From all the terrors of the burning grave;
Or bid the flames with harmleſs fury glow;
Or crown with endleſs bliſs the tranſient woe.
But know, Aſſyrian prince! ſhould ills moſt dire
Rend our rack'd hearts, and bid our lives expire;
Should virtue yeild to unrelenting power,
And heaven forſake us in the dreadful hour;
Still to his throne our ſacred thoughts ſhall riſe,
Nor heed the gods that dwell beneath the ſkies.

 He ſpoke: Again, with ecſtaſies of ire,
The king's full viſage flaſh'd infernal fire;
Fiercely he bade his guards the offenders bind,
And bear them forth, their feet and arms confin'd,
Through the wide hoſt their guilt and fate proclaim,
And light the furnace with a ſeven-fold flame.

* SHADRACH.

The guards obey'd.   As near the feat of woe,
Their eyes beheld the fearful vengeance glow,
They claim'd, with fervent prayers, the pitying ſky,
And fix'd their fouls to fuffer and to die.
Serene, they faw the dark and dreadful fires,
Felt the fierce heat, and ey'd the gloomy ſpires;
Serene, they heard the long, deep murmurs roar,
As diftant, rifing whirlwinds rend the fhore.

Forth to the flames the unfriended youths they caft;
Nor 'fcap'd the eager guards the fcorching blaft:
Far round them fhot a long, infolding ſpire,
And wrap'd them helplefs in the mantling fire.

Mean time the king, the ftorm of vengeance o'er,
His wrath provok'd, his will oppos'd no more,
Felt other thoughts, and paffions more refin'd
Compofe the fettling tumult of his mind.
Softening, he thought on all their conduct paft,
Their virtue fpotlefs, and their wifdom vaft,
The wondrous dream, to them, with Daniel, given,
And all their pillar'd confidence in heaven.
His will they brav'd, of pains nor death afraid;
But ftill with mildeft meeknefs difobey'd;
With fuch firm truth, fuch peaceful words denied,
As fpoke the foul of virtue, not of pride.
Who knows, he whifper'd, but their well taught mind,
Serves nobler gods, with worfhip more refin'd?
Who knows but he who could the dream reftore,
May fave his favourites from the furnace' power?

As thus he fpoke, with wand'ring courfe and flow,
He turn'd his footfteps towards the feat of woe:

'Till, with unguided, heedless feet he came
Where full before him burn'd the difmal flame.
When lo, dread fcenes amaz'd his wilder'd fight:
The youths walk'd peaceful through the horrid light:
Harmlefs around them climb d the circling fpires,
And mild as zephyrs play'd the lambent fires.
Hymns of fweet praife the adoring prophets fung,
And mid hoarfe murmurs raptur'd warblings rung.

He gaz'd : at once, with light and beauty new,
Through the dread cavern fudden fplendor flew ;
A new dawn brighten'd o'er the dreary tomb,
Drown'd the dark flames and quench'd the fullen gloom.
So when the morn's bright face, in fair attire,
Through orient windows ftrikes the wintry fire,
The red flames wither in the etherial ray,
And all their earthly luftre dies away.

He gaz'd ; when lo ! a form of bodied light,
Sprung from the fun and like the parent bright,
In flow and ftately grandeur, trod the fcene,
And the dread cavern fmil d, a Heaven within.   .
Fair ftars his wondrous crown, his ftrange attire
The lucid rainbow's many-co our'd fire ;
Like threads of burnifh'd filver, round his head,
His twinkling locks in folemn glory play'd ;
In pomp divine above his fhoulders borne,
And dipt in rofeate beams of rifing morn,
His long wings waving, fell : beneath his feet,
The unnumber'd ftreams of fpringing light'nings meet.
Full on the friends he beam'd a fun-bright fmile,
Tranfcendent meed of all their faith and toil !

Complacence pure, all thoughts, all minds above,
That op'd the yearnings of redeeming love.
Such smiles salute th' unbodied soul forgiven;
Such smiles improve the sainted race of Heaven;
Such smiles serene, with unextinguish'd ray,
Purpled the opening morn of endless day.
At once soft sounds of gratulation rung;
Strange music play'd, unseen musicians sung;
The solemn sounds with more than mortal fire,
Wav'd with mild warblings, o'er th' etherial lyre:
Marbled, on earth the prostrate monarch lay,
And swoon'd his vanquish'd sense and soul away.

At length resummon'd from the gloomy dead,
His opening eyes beheld the vision fled.
With strong, but plaintive voice, amaz'd he cried,
Sons of the sky and earth's transcendent pride!
Forth from those dreary flames triumphant come,
And quit the mansions of the destin'd tomb.

Forth came the youths; unsing'd their fair attire,
Their limbs unconscious of the potent fire;
The king, the nobles mark'd with solemn gaze,
And sighs and silence own'd their deep amaze.

Round the wide plain the saddening pomp decay'd;
The music died, the vast assembly fled;
The knee unbent, the image ceas'd to adore;
The extinguish'd altars shed perfumes no more;
The golden form apart forsaken stood,
And not a suppliant hail'd the slighted god:
Round the wide circuit brooding silence lay,
And clouds of deepest gloom o'ercast the day.

Then through his boundlefs empire Heaven's great name,
The humbl'd monarch bade his criers proclaim.
To Heaven s great God, they cried, your honors pay,
Let kings and nations own his fovereign fway ;
With power divine to earth his angel came,
And fav'd his prophets from the fevenfold flame.

To Babel's walls return'd the royal train :
Their wonted honors cloth'd the youths again.
With tranfport, Daniel heard his friends relate
Their glorious triumph o'er the deftin'd fate ;
The flames by heavenly power innoxious made ;
The folemn glories on the angel fhed ;
In dreams the labor'd pomp forever gone ;
The tyrant vanquifh'd and his god o'erthrown.

Belov'd, rever'd, the fons of virtue fhin'd,
Heirs of the fkies, and patrons of mankind.
Through all th' Affyrian world their bounty fpread ;
All Judah triumph'd ; all oppreffion fled ;
Their glad approach, inftinctive homage blefs'd ;
Crouds bent before them, lords and kings carefs'd ;
To them the fongs of every realm were given,
And ceafelefs round them glow'd the light of heaven.

ADDRESS

OF THE

GENIUS OF COLUMBIA,

TO THE MEMBERS OF THE CONTINENTAL CONVENTION.

BY THE SAME.

FROM weftern fkies, a cloud of glory came,
   A fmall, dim fpot, a torch of lambent flame ;
Afcending, widening, flow the fkirts unroll'd,
Rainbow'd with fire, and warm'd with glowing gold.
There, borne by fummon'd winds, in pomp fublime,
His look far-piercing down the vaft of time,
Where the long, narrowing vale deferts the eye,
Unbofom'd dimly on the eternal fky,
The Genius fate.   He faw, when faction fpent,
No more with war his darling kingdom rent,
The ftream of kindred blood forbore to flow,
And morn faint trembled o'er the night of woe,
Call'd from each fifter realm, the wife and great,
In Penn's fair walls, and awful council fate ;
Pois'd in their hands, Columbia's mighty fway,
And tottering laws, and rights, and freedom, lay.

   He faw, when fairer than the glow of even,
And bright as vifions of difclofing heaven,
Full in his face a facred fplendor fhone,
And the weft kindled with another fun.

" All hail, my fons," he cried, " my voice attend,
Your country's genius, guardian, guide, and friend :
The counfels mark, that faithful friend fupplies,
Attend, and learn the dictates of the fkies.
Before you, lo! what fcenes of glory fpread,
The faireft, brighteft, nobleft, heaven has made :
Their home, where freedom, fcience, virtue, find,
The laft receffes of opprefs'd mankind.
The immenfe of empire here, amaz'd, defcry,
Where realms are loft, and hidden oceans lie ;
Where Perfia's vaft would fink in fhades conceal'd,
And Rome's proud world diminifh to a field.
See, from the pole, where frozen fountains rife,
And pour their waters under torrid fkies,
Where Rhines and Danubes, rills and ftreamlets play,
To fwell the pomp of Miffifippi's fea ;
Where a zone's breadth majeftic woods extend, .
And other Andes o'er the ftorms afcend ;
Where meadows bound the morn and evening rays ;
Where plains are kingdoms, and where lakes are feas.

See thro all climes the unmeafur'd empire run,
And drink each influence from the lingering fun ;
Pure fkies unbofom'd, days fereneft roll,
And gales of health, from Darien fan the pole.

In each blefs'd clime, to crown induftrious toil,
See every product fpring from every foil, .
Here the fur whitens in the frozen fhade ;
Here flocks unnumber'd crowd the paftur'd glade ;
Here threatening famine double harvefts fcorn—
Europe's rich grains, and India's ufeful corn—

Virginia's fragrant pride, huge fleets convey,
And fields of rice float cumbrous o'er the fea,
While all its wealth, the world of waters yeilds,
And treafures fill the fubterranean fields.
Thefe goods to waft where'er expands the wind,
To blefs and to fuftain the human kind,
See, ftretch'd immenfe from Cancer to the pole,
On either fide contending oceans roll ;
O'er this, all Europe wings her haughty fails ;
O'er that, all India wafts on fpicy gales :
While bays, and ftreams, and lakes, her realms explore,
And land each product at each happy door.

    To fill thefe realms, a generous race behold,
Of happieft genius, and of firmeft mould ;
In thoughts, in arts, in life, in language join'd,
One faith, one worfhip, one politic mind,
Patient, ferene, in toils and dangers dire,
Their nerves of iron, and their fouls of fire :
Call'd from all realms, thefe chofen fons have join'd
Expanfive manners, and a genial mind,
The liberal fentiment, the adventurous thought,
With greatnefs teeming, and with goodnefs fraught ;
Chain'd to no party ; by no fyftem bound ;
Confining merit to no fpeck of ground ;
Nor Britons, Frenchmen, Germans, Swifs, or Huns,
Of earth the natives, and of heaven the fons,
Regarding, loving, all the great and good,
Of every rank, clime, party, fect, and blood.

K

The fwain, with blifs to Europe's climes unknown,
His wife, his houfe, his lands, his flock, his own,
Treads, independent, on the fubject foil,
Prepar'd for every danger, every toil;
Prepar'd to fee antarctic oceans roll,
To circle earth, and fearch the lonely pole;
Or thro the immenfe of fcience wind his way;
Or lift poetic wings beyond the day;
The ridgy front of death for freedom dare,
Or, round all regions, hufh the voice of war.

Heaven from all climes this happy realm conceal'd,
While wolves and Indians roam'd the bloody field,
Till human rule a foft'ning afpect wore,
Till war's black chariot ceas'd to roll in gore,
Till bigot zeal refign'd his fcarlet fway,
And his dread thunders puff'd in fmoke away.

Thus oh how blefs'd the era of her fate,
How bright the morning, and how long the date!
For now each fair improvement of the mind,
Each nobler effort lifts the human kind;
Vaft means of blifs mechanic arts combine;
All liberal arts the rugged foul refine;
Freedom, and right, and law, their reign affu ne,
Stern Power refift, and cheer the world's fad doom;
On nature's ocean, fcience lifts her fails,
Finds other ftars, and catches nobler gales;
While dawning virtue beams from yonder fky,
And brighter funs arife on human joy.

Such fcenes of blifs, ye fages, blefs your eyes:
For men, for realms like thefe, your plans devife.

Be then your counfels, as your fubject, great,
A world their fphere, and time's long reign their date.

Each party-view, each private good, difclaim,
Each petty maxim, each colonial aim ;
Let all Columbia's weal your views expand,
A mighty fyftem rule a mighty land ;
Yourfelves her genuine fons let Europe own,
Not the fmall agents of a paltry town.

Learn, cautious, what to alter, where to mend ;
See to what clofe projected meafures tend.
From preffing wants the mind averting ftill,
Thinks good remoteft from the prefent ill :
From feuds anarchial to oppreffion's throne,
Mifguided nations hence for fafety run ;
And through the miferies of a thoufand years,
Their fatal folly mourn in bloody tears.

Ten thoufand follies thro Columbia fpread ;
Ten thoufand wars her darling realms invade.
The private intereft of each jealous ftate ;
Of rule the impatience, and of law the hate.
But ah ! from narrow fprings thefe evils flow,
A few bafe wretches mingle general woe.
Still the fame mind her manly race pervades,
Still the fame virtues haunt the hallow'd fhades.
But when the peals of war her center fhook,
All private aims the anxious mind forfook.
In danger's iron-bond her race was one :
Each feparate good, each little view unknown.
Now rule, unfyftem'd, drives the mind aftray ;
Now private intereft points the downward way :

Hence civil difcord pours her muddy ftream,
And fools and villains float upon the brim ;
O'er all, the fad fpectator cafts his eye,
And wonders where the gems and minerals lie.

But ne'er of freedom, glory, blifs, defpond :
Uplift your eyes thofe little clouds beyond ;
See there returning funs, with gladdening ray,
Roll on fair fpring to chafe this wintry day.

Tis yours to bid thofe days of Eden fhine :
Firft, then, and laft, the federal bands entwine :
To this your every aim and effort bend :
Let all your efforts here commence and end.

O'er ftate concerns, let every ftate prefide ;
Its private tax controul ; its juftice guide ;
Religion aid ; the morals to fecure ;
And bid each private right thro time endure.

Columbia's interefts public fway demand,
Her commerce, impoft, unlocated land ;
Her war, her peace, her military power ;
Treaties to feal with every diftant fhore ;

To bid contending ftates their difcord ceafe ;
To fend thro all the calumet of peace ;
Science to wing thro every noble flight ;
And lift defponding genius into light.

Thro every ftate to fpread each public law,
Intereft muft animate, and force muft awe.
Perfuafive dictates realms will ne'er obey ;
Sway, uncoercive, is the fhade of fway.

Be then your tafk to alter, aid, amend;
The weak to ftrengthen, and the rigid bend;
The prurient lop; what's wanted to fupply;
And graft new fcions from each friendly fky.

Slow, by degrees, politic fyftems rife;
Age ftill refines them, and experience tries.
This, this alone confolidates, improves;
Their finews ftrengthens; their defects removes;
Gives that confiftence time alone can give;
Habituates men by law and right to live;
To gray-hair'd rules increafing reverence draws;
And wins the flave to love e'en tyrant laws.
But fhould Columbia, with diftracted eyes,
See o'er her ruins one proud monarch rife;
, Should vain partitions her fair realms divide,
And rival empires float on faction's tide;
Lo fix'd opinions 'gainft the fabric rage!
What wars, fierce paffions with fierce paffions wage!
From Cancer's glowing wilds, to Brunfwick's fhore,]
Hark, how the alarms of civil difcord roar!
" To arms," the trump of kindled warfare cries,
And kindred blood fmokes upward to the fkies.
As Perfia, Greece, fo Europe bids her flame,
And fmiles with eye malignant, o'er her fhame.
Seize then, oh! feize Columbia's golden hour;
Perfect her federal fyftem, public power;
For this ftupendous realm, this chofen race,
With all the improvements of all lands its bafe,
The glorious ftructure build; its breadth extend;
Its columns lift, its mighty arches bend!

Or freedom, fcience, arts, its ftories fhine,
Unfhaken pillars of a frame divine ;
Far o'er the Atlantic wild its beams afpire,
The world approves it, and the heavens admire ;
O'er clouds, and funs, and ftars, its fplendors rife,
Till the bright top-ftone vanifh in the fkies."

C O L U M B I A.

BY THE SAME.

COLUMBIA, Columbia, to glory arife,
    The queen of the world, and child of the fkies !
Thy genius commands thee ; with rapture behold,
While ages on ages thy fplendors unfold.
Thy reign is the laft, and the nobleft of time,
Moft fruitful thy foil, moft inviting thy clime ;
Let the crimes of the eaft ne'er encrimfon thy name,
Be freedom, and fcience, and virtue, thy fame.

To conqueft, and flaughter, let Europe afpire ;
Whelm nations in blood, and wrap cities in fire ;
Thy heroes the rights of mankind fhall defend,
And triumph purfue them, and glory attend.
A world is thy realm : for a world be thy laws,
Enlarg'd as thine empire, and juft as thy caufe ;
On Freedom's broad bafis, that empire fhall rife,
Extend with the main, and diffolve with the fkies.

Fair Science her gates to thy fons fhall unbar,
And the eaft fee thy morn hide the beams of her ftar.
New bards, and new fages, unrival'd fhall foar
To fame, unextinguifh'd, when time is no more;
To thee, the laft refuge of virtue defign'd,
Shall fly from all nations the beft of mankind;
Here, grateful to heaven, with tranfport fhall bring
Their incenfe, more fragrant than odours of fpring.

Nor lefs fhall thy fair ones to glory afcend,
And Genius and Beauty in harmony blend;
The graces of form fhall awake pure defire,
And the charms of the foul ev r cherifh the fire;
Their fweetnefs unmingled, their manners refin'd,
And virtue's bright image, inftamp'd on the mind,
With peace, and foft rapture, fhall teach life to glow,
And light up a fmile in the afpect of woe.

Thy fleets to all regions thy pow'r fhall difplay,
The nations admire, and the ocean obey;
Each fhore to thy glory its tribute unfold,
And the eaft and the fouth yeild their fpices and gold,
As the day-fpring unbounded, thy fplendor fhall flow,
And earth's little kingdoms before thee fhall bow,
While the enfigns of union, in triumph unfurl'd,
Hufh the tumult of war, and give peace to the world.

Thus, as down a lone valley, with cedars o'erfpread,
From war's dread confufion I penfively ftray'd—
The gloom from the face of fair heav'n retir'd;
The winds ceas'd to murmur; the thunders expir'd;

Perfumes, as of Eden, flow'd sweetly along,
And a voice, as of angels, enchantingly sung :
" Columbia, Columbia, to glory arise,
The queen of the world, and the child of the skies."

***

The SEASONS Moralized.

BY THE SAME.

BEHOLD the changes of the skies,
　　And see the circling seasons rise ;
Hence, let the moral truth refin'd,
Improve the beauty of the mind.

　Winter, late with dreary reign,
Rul'd the wide, unjoyous plain ;
Gloomy storms with solemn roar
Shook the hoarse, resounding shore.

　Sorrow cast her sadness round,
Life and joy forsook the ground,
Death, with wild imperious sway,
Bade the expiring world decay.

　Now cast around thy raptur'd eyes,
And see the beauteous spring arise ;
See, flow'rs invest the hills again,
And streams re-murmur o'er the plains.

Hark, hark, the joy-infpiring grove
Echoes to the voice of love ;
Balmy gales the found prolong,
Wafting round the woodland fong.

Such the fcenes our life difplays,
Swiftly fleet our rapid days ;
The hour that rolls forever on,
Tells us our years muft foon be gone.

Sullen Death, with mournful gloom
Sweeps us downwards to the tomb ;
Life, and health, and joy decay,
Nature finks, and dies away.

But the foul in gayeft bloom,
Difdains the bondage of the tomb ;
Afcends above the clouds of even,
And, raptur'd, hails her native heaven.

Youth, and peace, and beauty there
Forever dance around the year ;
An endlefs joy invefts the pole,
And ftreams of ceafelefs pleafure roll.

Light, and joy, and grace divine
With bright and lafting glory fhine :
Jehovah's fmiles, with heav'nly ray,
Diffufe a clear, unbounded day.

K

A HYMN,

Sung at the PUBLIC EXHIBITION of the SCHOLARS, belonging to the Academy in Greenfield, May 2d, 1788.

BY THE SAME.

HAIL child of light, returning Spring,
  Fair image, foretafte fweet, of heaven!
In thee our hearts thy Maker fing,
  By whofe bleft bounty thou waft given.

From thee the wintry glooms retire,
  The fkies their pureft beams difplay,
And winds, and fhowers, and funs confpire,
  To clothe the world with life and May.

Hail knowlege, hail, the moral fpring
  That wakes the verdure of the mind!
To man, thy rays indulgent bring
  All fragrant flowers, and fruits refin'd.

Thy progrefs with the morn began,
  Before thee every region fmil'd;
The favage brighten'd into man,
  And gardens bloffom'd in the wild.

All hail fair Virtue, nobleft good,
  The blifs and beauty of the fkies!
By whom, to yonder bleft abode,
  The humble, and the faithful rife.

While here fair Learning smiles benign,
   And Spring leads on the genial year,
From realms of life and peace divine,
   Descend, and bloom, and flourish here.

And O thou fount of good supreme,
   The sun that lights eternal spring,
At once of knowledge source and theme,
   Thee first, and last, our voices sing !

Virtue, in every charm array'd,
   For this dark world, thy sufferings won ;
Those charms thy matchless life display'd,
   When here the incarnate splendor shone.

As dews refresh, as suns revive,
   When clear and cloudless shines the day,
Command our rising race to live,
   And win them from the world away.

With thee, the source of every grace,
   Our song shall end, as it began ;
Our hope, our trust, our joy, and praise,
   The Saviour, and the Friend of Man.

LOOK, lovely maid, on yonder flow'r,
  And see that busy fly,
Made for the enjoyment of an hour,
  And only born to die.

See, round the rose he lightly moves,
  And wantons in the sun,
His little life in joy improves,
  And lives, before 'tis gone.

From this instinctive wisdom, learn,
  The present hour to prize;
Nor leave to-day's supreme concern,
  'Till morrow's morn arise.

Say, lovliest fair, canst thou divine
  That morrow's hidden doom?
Know'st thou, if cloudless skies will shine,
  Or heaven be wrapt in gloom?

Fond man, the trifle of a day,
  Enjoys the morning light,
Nor knows, his momentary play
  Must end, before 'tis night.

The present joys are all we claim;
  The past are in the tomb;
And, like the poet's dream of fame,
  The future never come.

No longer then, fair maid, delay
    The promis'd scenes of bliss;
Nor idly give another day,
    The joys assign'd to this.

If *then* my breast can soothe thy care,
    'Twill *now* that care allay;
If *joy* this hand can yield, my fair,
    'Twill yield that joy to-day.

Quit then, oh quit! thou lovely maid,
    Thy bashful, virgin pride;
To-day the happy plot be laid,
    The bands, to-morrow, tied!

The purest joys shall be our own,
    That e'er to man were giv'n;
And those bright scenes, on earth begun,
    Shall brighter shine in heaven.

THE CRITICS.*

A FABLE.

Written September 1785.

'To every general rule there are exceptions.'—Common Sense.

___

BY THE SAME.

___

'TIS said of every dog that's found,
 Of mongrel, spaniel, cur, and hound;
That each sustains a doggish mind,
And hates the new, sublime, refin'd.
'Tis hence the wretches bay the moon,
In beauty throned at highest noon;
Hence every nobler brute they bite,
And hunt the stranger-dog with spite;
And hence, the nose's dictates parrying,
They fly from meat to feed on carrion.
'Tis also said, the currish soul
The critic race possesses whole;
As near they come, in tho'ts and natures,
As two legg'd can, to four legg'd creatures;
Alike the things they love and blame,
Their voice, and language, much the same.

___

* This Poem is reprinted from *The Gazette of the United States,* of July 13, 1791; where it was first published.

The Mufe this fubject made her theme,
And told me in a morning dream.
Such dreams you fages may decry ;
But Mufes know they never lie.
Then hear, from me, in grave narration,
Of thefe ftrange facts, the ftrange occafion.

In Greece Cynethe's village lay,
Well known to all, who went that way,
For dogs of every kindred famed,
And from true doggifh manners named.
One morn, a greyhound pafs'd the ftreet;
At once the foul-mouth'd conclave met,
Huddling around the ftranger ran,
And thus their fmart *review* began.
" What tramper" with a grinning fneer,
Bark'd out the clumfy cur, " is here ?
No native of the town, I fee ;
Some foreign whelp of bafe degree.
I'd fhew, but that the record's torn,
We true Welfh curs are better born.
His coat is fmooth ; but longer hair
Would more become a dog by far.
His flender ear, how ftrait and floping !
While ours is much improved by *cropping*."

" Right," cried the blood-hound, " that ftrait ear
Seems made for nothing, but to hear ;
'Tis long agreed, thro' all the town,
That handfome ears, like mine, hang down ;
And tho' his body's gaunt, and round,
'Tis no true rawboned gaunt of hound.

How high his nofe the creature carries!
As if on bugs, and flies, his fare is;
I'll teach this ftrutting ftupid log,
To fmell's the bufinefs of a dog."

    " Baugh-waugh!" the fhaggy fpaniel cried,
" What wretched covering on his hide!
I wonder where he lives in winter;
His ftrait, fleek legs too, out of joint are;
I hope the vagrant will not dare
His fledging with my fleece compare.
He never plung'd in pond or river,
To fearch for wounded duck and diver;
By kicks would foon be fet a fkipping,
Nor take, one half fo well a whipping."

    " Rat me," the lap-dog yelp'd, " thro' nature,
Was ever feen fo coarfe a creature?
I hope no lady's fad mifhap
E'er led the booby to her lap;
He'd fright PRIMRILLA into fits,
And rob FOOLERIA of her wits;
A mere barbarian, Indian whelp!
How clownifh, countryifh, founds his yelp!
He never tafted bread and butter,
Nor play'd the petty fquirm and flutter;
Nor e'er, like me, has learn'd to fatten,
On kiffes fweet, and fofteft patting."

    " Some parfon's dog, I vow," whined puppy;
" His rufty coat how fun-burnt! ftop ye!"
The beagle call'd him to the wood.
The bull-dog bellowed, " Zounds! and blood!"

The wolf-dog and the maſtiff were,
The Muſe ſays, an exception here;
Superior both to ſuch foul play,
They wiſh'd the ſtranger well away.

From *ſpleen* the *ſtrictures* roſe to *fury*,
" Villain," growl'd one, " I can't endure you."
" Let's ſeize the truant," ſnarl'd another,
Encored by every foul-mouth'd brother.
" 'Tis done," bark'd all, " we'll mob the creature,
And ſacrifice him to ill-nature."

The greyhound, who deſpiſed their breath,
Still tho't it beſt to ſhun their teeth.
Eaſy he wing'd his rapid flight,
And left the ſcoundrels out of ſight.

Good JUNO, by the ancients holden,
The genuine *notre-dame* of ſcolding,
Sate pleaſed, becauſe there'd ſuch a fuſs been,
And in the hound's place wiſh'd her huſband;
For here, even pleaſure bade her own,
Her ladyſhip was once out-done.
" Hail dogs," ſhe cried, " of every kind!
Retain ye ſtill this ſnarling mind,
Hate all that's good, and fair, and new,
And I'll a goddeſs be to you.

Nor this the only good you prove;
Learn what the fruits of JUNO's love.
Your ſouls, from forms, that creep all four on,
I'll raiſe, by ſyſtem Pythagorean,

M

To animate the human frame,
And gain my favorite tribe a name.
Be ye henceforth (so I ordain)
Critics, the genuine curs of men.
To snarl be still your higheft blifs,
And all your criticifm like this.
Whate'er is great, or juft, in nature,
Of graceful form, or lovely feature ;
Whate'er adorns the ennobled mind,
Sublime, inventive, and refin'd ;
With fpleen, and fpite, forever blame,
And load with every dirty name.
All things of nobleft kind and ufe,
To your own ftandard vile reduce,
And all in wild confufion blend,
Nor *heed* the *fubject*, *fcope*, or *end*.
But chief, when *modeft young beginners*,
'Gainft *critic laws*, by *nature* finners,
Peep out in verfe, and dare to run,
Thro' towns and villages your own,
Hunt them, as when yon ftranger dog
Set all your growling crew agog ;
Till ftunn'd, and fcared, they hide from view,
And leave the country clear for you."

This faid, the goddefs kind careffing,
Gave every cur a double blefling.
Each doggifh mind, tho' grown no bigger,
Henceforth affumed the human figure,
The body walk'd on two ; the mind
To four, ftill chofe to be confin'd ;

Still creeps on earth, still scents out foes,
Is still led onward by the nose;
Hates all the good, it used to hate,
The lofty, beauteous, new, and great;
The stranger hunts with spite quintessent,
And snarls, from that day to the present.

EPISTLE to Col. HUMPHRYES.

GREENFIELD, 1785.

BY THE SAME.

FROM realms, where nature sports in youthful prime,
Where Hesper lingers o'er his darling clime,
Where sunny genius lights his sacred flame,
Where rising science casts her morning beam,
Where empire's final th one in pomp ascends,
Where pilgrim freedom finds her vanish'd friends,
The world renews, and man from eastern fires,
Phœnix divine, again to Heaven aspires,
Health to my friend this happy verse conveys,
His fond attendant o er the Atlantic feas.

Health to my friend let every wish prolong;
Be this the burden of each artless song;
This in the prayer of every morn arise;
Thou angel guardian, waft it to the skies!

His devious courfe let foftering Heaven furvey ;
Nor ills betide, nor foes arreft his way.

Nor health alone——may blifs thy path attend ;
May truth direct thee, and may peace befriend ;
From virtue's fount thy taintlefs actions flow ;
The fhield of confcience blunt the dart of woe ;
To rifing blifs refin'd above alloy,
Where budding wifhes bloffom into joy,
Where glory dwells, where faints and feraphs fing,
Let Heaven, in profpect, tempt thy lifted wing.

Me the fame views, the fame foft tide of cares,
Bear gently onward down the ftream of years,
Still the fame duties call my courfe along ;
Still grows, at times, the pain-deluding fong ;
Still fcenes domeftic earthly joys refine,
Where bleft Maria mingles cares with mine ;
The fame fond circle ftill my life endears,
Where Fairfield's elms, or Stamford's groupe appears ;
Or where, in rural guife, around me fmile
Manfions of peace, and Greenfield's beauteous hill ;
Still to my cot the friend delighted hies,
And one lov'd parent waits beneath the fkies.

To thee, far fummon'd from each native fcene,
With half the breadth of this wide world between,
How blefs'd the news my happy verfe conveys,
Of friends, divided by interfluent feas ?
Health, peace, and competence, their walks furround,
On the bright margin of yon beauteous Sound ;
Where Hartford fees the firft of waters glide,
Or where thy Avon winds his filver tide.

Yet thou muſt mourn a friend,* a brother dear,
And o'er departed merit drop a tear.
Him ſenſe illum'd, the hero's warmth inſpir'd,
Grace taught to pleaſe, and patriot virtue fir'd ;
Alike in peace, in war, at home, abroad,
Worth gain'd him honor, where his footſteps trode ;
Yet all in vain : his laurel'd garlands bloom ;
But waſte their beauty on the untimely tomb.

Meantime, invited o'er the Atlantic tide,
Where arts refin'd allure thy feet aſide,
May'ſt thou, unmov'd by ſplendor's painted charms,
And ſteel'd, when pleaſure ſmiling ſpreads her arms,
The great ſimplicity of ſoul retain,
The humble fear of Heaven, and love of man.
When round thy courſe temptations ſweetly throng,
When warbling ſirens chant the luſcious ſong,
When wealth's fair bubble beams its hues afar,
When grandeur calls thee to her golden car,
When pleaſure opes the boſom bright of joy,
And the dy'd ſerpent gazes to deſtroy ;
Oh ! may the heavenly Guide thy paſſions warm,
Up virtue's hills thy feet reſiſtleſs charm,
Shew thee what crowns reward the glorious ſtrife,
And quicken fainting duty into life.

Oft has thine eyes, with glance indignant ſeen
Columbia's youths, unfolding into men,

---

* Major Elijah Humphreys, brother to Col. Humphreys,
who died in the Weſt-Indies, in 1785.

Their minds to improve, their manners to adorn,
To Europe's climes by fond indulgence borne;
Oft haft thou feen thofe youths, at cuftom's fhrine,
Victims to pride, to folly, and to fin,
Of worth-bereft, of real fenfe forlorn,
Their land forget, their friends, their freedom fpurn;
Each noble caufe, each folid good defert,
For fplendor happinefs, and truth for art;
The plain, frank manners of their race defpife,
Fair without fraud, and great without difguife;
Where, thro the life the heart uncover'd ran,
And fpoke the native dignity of man.

For thefe, the gain let Virtue blufh to hear,
And each fad parent drop the plaintive tear!
Train'd in foul ftews, impoifon'd by the ftage,
Hoyl'd into gaming, Keyfer'd into age,
To fmooth hypocrify by Stanhope led,
To truth an alien, and to virtue dead,
Swoln with an Englifh butcher's four difdain,
Or to a Fribble dwindled from a man,
Homeward again behold the jackdaw run,
And yield his fire the ruins of a fon!

What tho' his mind no thought has e'er perplex'd,
Converfe illum'd, or obfervations vex'd;
Yet here, in each debate, a judge he fhines,
Of all, that man enlarges, or refines;
Religion, fcience, politics, and fong;
A prodigy his parts; an oracle his tongue.
Hift! hift! ye mere Americans, attend;
Ope wide your mouths; your knees in homage bend;

While Curl difclofes to the raptur'd view
What Peter, Paul, and Mofes, never knew;
The light of new-born wifdom fheds abroad,
And adds a * leanto to the word of God.
What Creole wretch fhall dare, with home-made foils,
Attack opinions, brought three thoufand miles;
Senfe, in no common way to mortals given,
But on Atlantic travellers breath'd by Heaven;
A head, *en queue*, by Monfieur Frizzle drefs'd;
Manners, a Paris Taylor's arts inveft;
Pure criticifm, form'd from *acted* plays;
And graces, that would even a Stanhope grace?
Commercial wifdom, merchants here inhale
From him, whofe eye hath feen the unfinifh'd bale;
Whofe feet have pafs'd the fhop, where pins were fold,
The wire was filver'd, and the heads were roll'd!
Conven'd, ye lawyers, make your humbleft leg!
Here ftands the man has feen Lord Mansfield's wig!
Phyficians hufh'd, hear Galen's lips diftil,
From Buchan's contents, all the Art to heal!
Divines, with reverence ceafe your fcripture whims,
And learn this male Minerva's moral fchemes;
Schemes theologic found in Drury-lane,
That prove the bible falfe, and virtue vain!
Heavens! fhall a child in learning, and in wit,
O'er Europe's climes, a bird of paffage flit;

---

* An awkward addition to a dwelling-houfe, very common
in New-England.

There, as at home, his ſtripling ſelf unknown,
By novel wonders ſtupified to ſtone,
Shut from the wiſe, and by no converſe taught,
No well-read day, nor hour of ſerious thought,
His head by pleaſure, vice, and hurry, turn'd,
All prudence trampled, all improvements ſpurn'd;
Shall he, with leſs of Europe in his cap,
Than ſatchell'd ſchool-boy gueſſes from the map,
On every ſubject ſtruttingly decree,
Ken the far ſhore, and ſearch the unfathom'd ſea,
Where learning has her lamp for ages oil'd,
Where Newton ponders, and where Berkeley toil'd?
Of all the plagues, that riſe in human ſhape,
Good Heaven, preſerve us from the travell'd Ape!
* " Peace to all ſuch :" but were there one, whoſe mind
Bold genius wing'd, and converſe pure, reſin'd,
By nature prompted ſcience' realms to roam,
And both her Indies bring with rapture home;
Who men, and manners, ſearch'd with eagle eye,
Exact to weigh, and curious to deſcry;
Himſelf who burniſh'd with the hand of care,
Till kings might boaſt ſo bright a gem to wear;
Should he, deep plung'd in Circe's ſenſual bowl,
Imbrue his native manlineſs of ſoul,
With eye eſtrang'd, from fair Columbia turn,
Her youth, her innocence, and beauty ſcorn;
To that foul harlot, Europe, yield his mind,
Witch'd by her ſmiles, and to her ſnares reſign'd;

----

* Pope's prologue to the Satires.

To nature's bloom prefer the rouge of art,
A tinfell'd outfide to a golden heart,
Show, to the blifs by fimple freedom given,
To virtue, Stanhope, and Voltaire to Heaven;
Who but muft wifh, the apoftate youth to fee?
Who but muft agonize, were Humphreys he?
But all thy foul fhall 'fcape, the efcape to aid,
Fair to thy view be every motive fpread.
Of each gay caufe the dire effects furvey,
And bring the painted tomb difclos'd to day.
Tho' there proud pomp uprears his throne on high;
Tho' there the golden palace lights the fky;
Tho' wealth unfolds her gay, Edenian feats,
Her walk of grandeur, and her wild of fweets;
The ftage, the park, the ring, the dance, the feaft,
Charm the pall'd eye, and lure the loathing tafte;
Yet there fierce war unceafing founds alarms;
Pride blows the trump, and millions rufh to arms;
See fteel and fire extinguifh human good!
See realms manur'd with corfes, and with blood!
At flaughter's fhrine expires the new-born-joy,
And all Jehovah's bounty fiends deftroy.
See the huge jail in gloomy grandeur rife,
Low'r o'er mankind, and mock the tempted fkies!
Hear the chain clank! the burfting groan attend!
And mark the neighboring gibbet's pride afcend.
See earth's fair face infatiate luxury fpoils!
For one poor tyrant, lo, a province toils!
To brothels, half the female world is driven,
Loft to themfelves, and reprobates of heaven.

N

There too refinement glances o'er the mind;
And nought but vice, and outside, is refin'd;
To vice aufpicious, brilliant manners blend,
The waxen faint, and finner, foe and friend,
Melt from the foul each virtue, as they fhine,
And warm the impoifon'd bloffom into fin.
In fair Columbia's realms, how chang'd the plan;
Where all things bloom, but, firft of all things, man!
Lord of himfelf, the independent fwain,
Sees no fuperior ftalk the happy plain:
His houfe, his herd, his harveft, all his own,
His farm a kingdom, and his chair a throne.
Unbleach'd by foul hypocrify, the foul
Speaks in her face, and bids his accents roll;
(Her wings unclipp'd) with fire inftinctive warms,
Strong pulfes feels, and bold conceptions forms;
At nobleft objects aims her flight fupreme,
The purpofe vaft, and enterprize extreme.
Hence round the pole her fons exalt the fail,
Search fouthern feas, and roufe the Falkland whale;
Or on bold pinions hail the Afian fkies,
And bid new ftars in fpicy oceans rife.
Hence in bright arms her chiefs fuperior flame,
Even new triumphant on the fteep of fame,
Where Vernon's Hero mounts the throne fublime,
And fees no rival grace the reign of time.
Hence countlefs honours rifing Med'cine claims;
Hence Law prefents her conftellated names;
The Sacred Science fees her concave bright
Inftarr'd, and beauteous, with the fons of light:

Hence Edwards cheer'd the world with moral day,
And Franklin walk'd, unhurt, the realms where lightnings
Mechanic genius hence exalts his eye,   [play.
All powers to measure, and all scenes descry,
Bids Rittenhouse the heavenly syftem feign,
And Bushnell search the chambers of the main.
Hence too, where Trumbull leads the ardent throng,
Afcending bards begin the immortal fong:
Let glowing friendship wake the cheerful lyre,
Bleft to commend, and pleas'd to catch the fire.
Be theirs the fame, to bards how rarely given!
To fill with worth the part affign'd by Heaven;
Diftinguifh'd actors on life's bufy ftage,
Lov'd by mankind, and ufeful to the age;
While fcien e round them twines her vernal bays,
And fenfe directs, and genius fires their lays.   -
While this fair land commands thy feet to roam,
And, all Columbian, ftill thou plan'ft for home,
From thofe bright fages, with whofe miffion join'd,
Thou feek'ft to build the interefts of mankind,
Experience, wifdom, honour, may'ft thou gain,
The zeal for country, and the love of man.
There thro' the civil fcience may'ft thou run;
There learn how empires are preferv'd, or won;
How arts politic wide dominions fway;
How well-train'd navies bid the world obey;
How war's imperial car commands the plain,
Or rolls majeftic o'er the fubject main;
Thro' earth, how commerce fpreads a fofter fway,
And Gallia's fons negociate realms away.

Then, crown'd with every gift, and grace, return,
To add new glories to the weſtern morn ;
With ſages, heroes, bards, her charms diſplay,
Her arts, arms, virtues, and her happy ſway ;
Bid o'er the world her conſtellation riſe,
The brighteſt ſplendor in the unmeaſur'd ſkies,
Her genial influence thro' all nations roll,
And huſh the ſound of war from pole to pole.

And oh, may he, who ſtill'd the ſtormy main,
And lightly wing'd thee o'er the glaſſy plain,
Thro' life's rough-billow'd ſea, with kinder gales,
With ſkies ſerener, and with happier ſails,
Each ſhoal eſcap'd, afar each tempeſt driven,
And nought but raptures round the enchanted Heaven,
To bliſs, fair ſhore, thy proſperous courſe convey,
And join my peaceful bark, companion of thy way.

THE PROSPECT OF PEACE.*

BY JOEL BARLOW, ESQUIRE.

THE clofing fcenes of Tyrants' fruitlefs rage,
 The opening profpects of a golden age,
The dread events that crown th' important year,
Wake the glad fong, and claim th' attentive ear.

Long has Columbia rung with dire alarms,
While Freedom call'd her injur'd fons to arms ;
While various fortune fir'd th' embattled field,
Conqueft delay'd, and victory ftood conceal'd ;
While clofing legions mark'd their dreadful way,
And millions trembled for the dubious day.

In this grand conflict heaven's Eternal Sire,
At whofe dread frown the fons of guilt expire,
Bade vengeance rife, with facred fury driven,
On thofe who war with Innocence and Heaven.

Behold, where late the trembling fquadrons fled,
Hofts bow'd in chains, and haplefs numbers bled,
In different fields our numerous heroes roufe,
To crop the wreath from Britain's impious brows.

---

* This Poem is reprinted from the 12mo edition, printed
by Thomas and Samuel Green, New-Haven, 1788,—and
was delivered, by the Author, in Yale-College, at the Public Examination of the Candidates for the Degree of Bache-
lor of Arts ; July 23, 1778.

Age following age shall these events relate
'Till Time's old empire yield to destin'd Fate;
Historic truth our guardian chiefs proclaim,
Their worth, their actions, and their deathless fame;
Admiring crouds their life-touch'd forms behold
In breathing canvass, or in sculptur'd gold,
And hail the Leader of the favorite throng,
The rapt'rous theme of some heroic song.

And soon, emerging from the orient skies,
The blissful morn in glorious pomp shall rise,
Wafting fair Peace from Europe's fated coast;
Where wand'ring long, in mazy factions lost,
From realm to realm, by rage and discord driven,
She seemed resolv'd to reascend her heaven.

This Lewis view'd, and reach'd a friendly hand,
Pointing her flight to this far-distant land;
Bade her extend her empire o'er the West,
And Europe's balance tremble on her crest!

Now, see the Goddess mounting on the day,
To these fair climes direct her circling way,
Willing to seek, once more, an earthly throne,
To cheer the globe, and emulate the sun.
With placid look she eyes the blissful shore,
Bids the loud-thundering cannon cease to roar;
Bids British navies from these ports be tost,
And hostile keels no more insult the coast:
Bids private feuds her sacred vengeance feel,
And bow submissive to the public weal;
Bids long, calm years adorn the happy clime,
And roll down blessings to remotest time.

Hail! heaven-born Peace, fair Nurse of Virtue hail!
Here, fix thy sceptre and exalt thy scale;
Hence, thro' the earth extend thy late domain,
'Till Heaven's own splendor shall absorb thy reign!

What scenes arise! what glories we behold!
See a broad realm its various charms unfold;
See crouds of patriots bless the happy land,
A godlike senate and a warlike band;
One friendly Genius fires the numerous whole,
From glowing Georgia to the frozen pole.

Along these shores, amid these flowery vales,
The woodland shout the joyous ear assails;
Industrious crouds in different labours toil,
Those ply the arts, and these improve the soil.
Here the fond merchant counts his rising gain,
There strides the rustic o'er the furrow'd plain,
Here walks the statesman, pensive and serene,
And there the school boys gambol round the green.

See ripening harvests gild the smiling plains,
Kind Nature's bounty and the pride of swains;
Luxuriant vines their curling tendrils shoot,
And bow their heads to drop the clustering fruit;
In the gay fields, with rich profusion strow'd,
The orchard bends beneath its yellow load,
The lofty boughs their annual burden pour,
And juicy harvests swell th' autumnal store.

These are the blessings of impartial heaven,
To each fond heart in just proportion given.
No grasping lord shall grind the neighbouring poor,
Starve numerous vassals to increase his store;

No cringing flave fhall at his prefence bend,
Shrink at his frown, and at his nod attend;
Afric's unhappy children, now no more
Shall feel the cruel chains they felt before,
But every State in this juft mean agree,
To blefs mankind, and fet th' opprefled free.
Then, rapt in tranfport, each exulting flave
Shall tafte that Boon which God and nature gave,
And, fir'd with virtue, join the common caufe,
Protect our freedom and enjoy our laws.

At this calm period, fee, in pleafing view,
Art vies with Art, and Nature fmiles anew:
On the long, winding ftrand that meets the tide,
Unnumber'd cities lift their fpiry pride;
Gay, flowery walks falute th' inraptur'd eyes,
Tall, beauteous domes in dazzling profpect rife;
There thronging navies ftretch their wanton fails,
Tempt the broad main and catch the driving gales;
There commerce fwells from each remoteft fhore,
And wafts in plenty to the fmiling ftore.

To thefe throng'd feats the country wide reforts,
And rolls her treafures to the op'ning ports;
While, far remote, gay health and pleafure flow,
And calm retirement cheers the laboring brow.
No din of arms the peaceful patriot hears,
No parting figh the tender matron fears,
No field of fame invites the youth to rove,
Nor virgins know a harfher found than love.

Fair Science then her laurel'd beauty rears,
And soars with Genius to the radiant stars.
Her glimmering dawn from Gothic darkness rose,
And nations saw her shadowy veil disclose ;
She cheer'd fair Europe with her rising smiles,
Beam'd a bright morning o'er the British isles,
Now soaring reaches her meridian height,
And blest Columbia hails the dazzling light !

Here, rapt in tho't, the philosophic soul
Shall look thro' Nature's parts and grasp the whole.
See Genius kindling at a FRANKLIN's fame,
See unborn sages catch th' electric flame,
Bid hovering clouds the threatening blast expire,
Curb the fierce stream and hold th' imprison'd fire !

See the pleas'd youth, with anxious study, rove,
In orbs excentric thro' the realms above,
No more perplex'd, while RITTENHOUSE appears
To grace the museum with the rolling spheres.

See that young Genius, that inventive soul,
Whose laws the jarring elements control :
Who guides the vengeance of mechanic power,
To blast the watery world and guard the peaceful shore.

And where's the rising Sage, the unknown name,
That new advent'rer in the lists of fame,
To find the cause, in secret nature bound,
The unknown cause, and various charms of sound ?
What subtil medium leads the devious way ;
Why different tensions different sounds convey ;

O

Why harsh, rough tones in grating discord roll,
Or mingling concert charms th' enraptur'd soul.

And tell the cause why sluggish vapors rise,
And wave, exalted, thro' the genial skies ;
What strange contrivance nature forms to bear
The ponderous burden thro' the lighter air.

These last Displays the curious mind engage,
And fire the genius of the rising age ;
While moral tho'ts the pleas'd attention claim,
Swell the warm soul, and wake the virtuous flame ;
While Metaphysics soar a boundless height,
And launch with EDWARDS to the realms of light.

See the blest Muses hail their roseate bowers,
Their mansions blooming with poetic flowers ;
See listening Seraphs join the epic throng,
And unborn JOSHUAS rise in future song.

Satire attend· at Virtue's wakening call,
And Pride and Coquetry and Dulness fall.

Unnumber'd bards shall string the heavenly lyre,
To those blest strains which heavenly themes inspire ;
Sing the rich Grace on mortal Man bestow'd,
The Virgin's Offspring and the *filial God ;*
What love descends from heaven when JESUS dies !
What shouts attend him rising thro' the skies !

See Science now in lovelier charms appear,
Grac'd with new garlands from the blooming Fair.
See laurel'd nymphs in polish'd pages shine,
And Sapphic sweetness glow in every line.

No more the rougher Mufe fhall dare difgrace
The radiant charms that deck the blufhing face;
But riling Beauties fcorn the tinfel fhow,
The powder'd coxcomb and the flaunting beau;
While humble Merit, void of flattering wiles,
Claims the foft glance, and wakes th' enlivening fmiles.
The opening luftre of an angel-mind,
Beauty's bright charms with fenfe fuperior join'd,
Bid Virtue fhine, bid Truth and Goodnefs rife, ·
Melt from the voice, and fparkle from the eyes;
While the pleas'd Mufe the gentle bofom warms,
The firft in genius, as the firft in charms.
Thus age and youth a fmiling afpect wear,
Aw'd into virtue by the leading Fair;
While the bright offspring, rifing to the ftage,
Conveys the blefiings to the future age.

 THESE are the views that Freedom's caufe attend; ·
THESE fhall endure 'till Time and Nature end.
With Science crown'd, fhall Peace and Virtue fhine,   ·
And bleft Religion beam a light divine.
Here the pure Church, defcending from her God,
Shall fix on earth her long and laft abode;
Zion arife, in radiant fplendors drefs'd,
By Saints admir'd, by Infidels confefs'd;
Her opening courts, in dazzling glory, blaze,
Her walls falvation, and her portals praife.   ·

 From each far corner of th' extended earth,
Her gathering fons fhall claim their promis'd birth.
Thro' the drear waftes, beneath the fetting day,
Where prowling natives haunt the wood for prey,

The fwarthy Millions lift their wond'ring eyes,
And fmile to fee the Gofpel morning rife:
Thofe who, thro' time, in favage darknefs lay,
Wake to new light, and hail the glorious day!
In thofe dark regions, thofe uncultur'd wilds,
Frefh blooms the rofe, the peaceful lilly fmiles;
On the tall cliffs unnumber'd *Carmels* rife,
And in each vale fome beauteous *Sharon* lies.

From this fair Mount th' excinded ftone fhall roll,
Reach the far Eaft and fpread from pole to pole;
From one fmall Stock fhall countlefs nations rife,
The world replenifh and adorn the fkies.
Earth's blood ftain'd empires, with their Guide the Sun,
From orient climes their gradual progrefs run;
And circling far, reach every weftern fhore,
'Till earth-born empires rife and fall no more.
But fee th' imperial GUIDE from heaven defcend,
Whofe beams are Peace, whofe kingdom knows no end;
From calm Vefperia, thro' th' etherial way,
Back fweep the fhades before th' effulgent day;
Thro' the broad Eaft, the brightening fplendor driven,
Reverfes Nature and illumines heaven;
Aftonifh'd regions blefs the gladdening fight,
And Suns and Syftems own fuperior light.

As when th' afterial blaze o'er Bethl'em ftood,
Which mark'd the birth-place of th' incarnate God;
When eaftern priefts the heavenly fplendor view'd,
And numerous crouds the wonderous fign purfu'd;
So eaftern kings fhall view th' unclouded day
Rife in the Weft and ftreak its golden way:

That signal spoke a Savior's humble birth,
This speaks his long and glorious reign on earth !

THEN Love shall rule, and Innocence adore,
Discord shall cease, and Tyrants be no more ;
'Till yon bright orb, and those celestial spheres,
In radiant circles, mark a thousand years ;
'Till the grand *fiat* burst th' etherial frames,
Worlds crush on worlds, and Nature sink in flames !
The Church cleft, from smouldering ruins, rise,
And sail triumphant thro' the yielding skies,
Hail'd by the Bridegroom ! to the Father given,
The Joy of Angels, and the Queen of Heaven !

A P O E M,*

Spoken at the PUBLIC COMMENCEMENT at YALE-COL-
LEGE, in NEW-HAVEN, Sept. 12, 1781.

BY THE SAME.

ONCE more, thou facred Seat, the changing year
    Hath circled heaven and bid the day appear,
That opes thy portals, gilds thy fpiry dome,
And calls thy children from their joyous home.

---

    * This Poem is reprinted from the Hartford Edition;
to which the following Advertifement was prefixed.——
" It may not be amifs to inform the fubfcribers for the
" following performance that a copy was not given at
" the time it was requefted, on account of its containing
" feveral paffages taken from a larger work which the au-
" thor has by him, unfinifhed. Upon farther confidera-
" tion however, it is thought not improper to prefent to
" the Public a fpecimen of that work, in this incorrect
" manner, that a conjecture may be formed what fuccefs
" it may meet, when the whole fhall make its appearance.
" The paffages are thofe that refpect the affairs of America
" at large, and the future progrefs of fociety. As to the
" other parts of the Poem which are confined to the ftate
" of education in Connecticut, although the fubject may
" be thought too particular to be relifhed beyond the lim-
" its of a Commencement Auditory, yet if they fhould
" ferve to turn the attention of any part of the Public to
" the real fituation of Yale College, it may juftify the
" publication."

Thro' feven long years hath war's terrific power
Rang'd every town and crimfon'd every fhore,
Purfu'd fair Science from each happy feat,
Rav'd in her domes and forc'd her laft retreat,
And oft, Yalenfia, doom'd thy final fall,
While thy fad Genius trembled tor thy wall.
Now fee, at laft, the venerable train,
Thine elder fons afcend thy courts again !
We joy the reverend, happy throng to fee,
We wake thy own bleft Mufe, and bid her fing to thee.

Long have we liv'd beneath thy nurturing care,
And joy and friendfhip crown'd our labors there ;
No more within thofe blifsful haunts we dwell,
To all thy train we bid a long farewel ;
One gentle grafp, one filent, forrowing tear,
And joys and friends forever difappear ;
Fate calls us hence the world's broad ftage to tread,
Aft a fhort part, and mingle with the dead.
We go——but may thy glory ftill afcend,
Thy fame, thy virtues thro' the world extend ;
Thy future fons, a calm, delightful throng,
As following years fhall lead their fteps along,
To peace, to happinefs, to glory rife,
Shine thro' the earth and brighten in the fkies.
No ruffian force that treads the diftant fhore,
Shall dare invade thy peaceful labors more ;
While the proud foes beneath our ftandards yield,
And our brave brethren claim the crimfon field,
Within thy courts fhall pride and flaughter ceafe,
And genius dignify the walks of peace.

And oh! may some blest hand regard thy cries,
Some great, some liberal benefactor rise,
Whose soul awakes at thy inspiring call,
To lift thy spires, enlarge thy scanty wall,
Who joys to aid the Muse's feeble voice,
And bid bright learning in her sons rejoice,
Bid wealth and dignity thy steps attend,
And rival arts and rival virtues blend,
O'er all the happy land thy beauties shine,
And every joy, and every wish be thine.

Ye patriot worthies, whom these strains assail,
Ye Reverend Sires, and all ye Sons of Yale,
Behold our seat, by former bounty given,
Pride of our land and favorite child of heaven,
Whence liberal arts and liberal thoughts ye drew,
When few her children and her wants were few;
Now see, the narrow bounds can scarce contain
Half the throng'd numbers of her joyous train,
While every friend averts the unconscious eye,
And power, and interest, pass unheeding by.

As late, when war's grim terrors sought repose,
And evening mists and distant fires arose,
Far in a gloomy grove I pensive stray'd,
Where death's pale phantoms walk'd the midnight shade,
Thin clouds of sickening damps, o'er ether driven,
Obscur'd the stars and shut the eye from heaven;
Unwonted sighs within my bosom rose,
Cities o'erturn'd and all my country's woes
Pour'd on my heart; but chief thy feeble cries,
Neglected Science, bade my griefs arise.

I faw, from Briton's Ifle, thy genius flown,
In thefe fair climes to fix a nobler throne,
While here thy fons the peaceful myrtle yield,
To pluck the crimfon laurel of the field.
I faw thy feats to fcenes of flaughter turn'd,
Thy walls defac'd, thy faireft labours burn'd;
E'en Yale, thy lovlieft handmaid, now no more,
Knew the gay fmiles of youth fhe knew before,
Her funds decreas'd, her ftrength, her int'reft fled,
Her friends neglected, and her HOSMER dead.

Now a calm fplendor burft the faddening gloom,
And gales etherial breath'd a glad perfume,
Mild in the midft a form celeftial fhone,
Rob'd in the veftments of the rifing fun;
Tall rofe his ftature, dignity and grace
Mov'd in his limbs and wanton'd in his face,
His folding mantle flow'd in eafy pride,
His harp divine lay ufelefs by his fide,
His locks in curls from myrtle chaplets hung,
And founds melodious melted from his tongue.

" Mortal, attend, behold before thee ftand
Learning's bright Genius, guardian of the land;
Let grief no more awake the piteous ftrain,
Nor think fair Science left her heaven in vain.
Awhile my fkill muft guide the wild affray,
Range the red field and fweep thy foes away,
Soon fhall this arm a milder fceptre bear,
And bleft Yalenfia prove my favorite care.
Mean time her friends her glory fhall attend,
Enlarge her ftores and bid her walls afcend;

P

Bid every art from that pure fountain flow,
All that the Mufe can fing or man can know ;
The various branches various teachers claim,
And univerfal knowledge lift her fame.

And fee ! ere long in that delightful feat,
Her fons and friends, a numerous concourfe, meet ;
Once more to view her, greet her youthful train,
And hear her feeble, faddening voice complain.
Go thou, in pride of youth attend them there,
And thefe commands in ftrains melodious bear.
Say 'tis for them to ftretch the liberal hand,
While war's dread tumults yet involve the land,
Suftain her drooping, rear her radiant eyes,
And bid her future fame begin to rife.
Tell them the wild commotions foon fhall ceafe,
And bleft Columbia hail the charms of peace,
Where reft the future deeds on earth defign'd
To raife, to dignify and blefs mankind.   .

While Europe's numerous courts my caufe attend,
And mutual intereft fix the mutual friend,
Behold, from each far realm, what glories fhine !
Their power, their commerce and their fcience mine.
And here, what roving views before them fpread !
Where this new empire lifts her daring head !
What wide extent her waving enfigns claim !
Lands yet unknown and ftreams without a name.
Where the deep gulph unfolds Floridia's fhore,
To where Ontario bids hoarfe Laurence roar ;
Where Miffifippi's waves their fources boaft,
Where groves and floods and realms and climes are loft,

To where the mild Atlantic's length'ning tide,
Laves numerous towns, and swells their naval pride.
And see! by nature's hand o'er all bestow'd,
The last pure polish of the forming God.
What various grandeur strikes the gladdening eyes!
Bays stretch their arms and mountains lift the skies;
The lakes, unfolding, point the streams their way,
The plains, the hills their lengthening skirts display,
The vales draw forth, fair wave the glimmering wilds,
And all the majesty of nature smiles.

On this broad theatre, unbounded spread,
In different scenes, what countless throngs must tread!
Soon as the new form'd empire, rising fair,
Calms her brave sons now breathing from the war,
Unfolds her harbours, spreads the genial soil,
And welcomes freemen to the chearful toil.
What numerous sages must exalt her name!
What numerous bards must tell the world her fame!
What numerous chiefs beneath my forming care,
Must blaze in arms and ward the waste of war!
While every art and all the graces meet,
To form her thoufands to the cares of State,
To heal pale sickness, bid difeafes ceafe,
And found the tidings of eternal peace.

Those must arife the present age to lead,
And following millions hail the paths they tread.

Such gladdening views will ope the bounteous store,
The grasp of interest and the pride of power,
Yalensia's friends shall thus attend her call,
And youths unnumber'd bless the favorite wall.

And tho' thou feeft the rage of flaughter roll,
And different views thy wayward race controul,
Tho' ftill oppos'd their intereft, and their laws,
And every fceptre leads a different caufe,
Yet thro' the whole the fame progreffive plan,
Which draws, for mutual fuccour, man to man,
From men to tribes, from tribes to nations fpreads,
And private ties to public compact leads,
Shall rife by flow degrees, and ftill extend,
Their power, their intereft, and their paffions, blend;
Their wars grow milder, policies enlarge,
In creafing nations feel the general charge,
Form broad alliances for mutual aid,
Mingle their manners and extend their trade,
Till each remoteft realm, by friendfhip join'd,
Link in the chain and harmonize mankind,
The union'd banner be at laft unfurl'd,
And wave triumphant round the accordant world.

Already now commencing glories rife,
The work begins beneath yon northern fkies;
The Ruffian forefts to the deep advance,
The ports unfold, the glimmering navies dance,
For commerce arm'd, the different powers combine,
And heaven approving aids the bleft defign.
Tho' rival regions ftill the combat wage,
And hold in bickering ftrife the unfettled age,
Yet no rude war, that fweeps the crimfon plain,
Shall dare difturb the labors of the main;
For heaven, impartial to the earth born race,
Bade one broad circling deep their fhores embrace,

Spread to all realms the fame wide, watry way,
Liberal as air and unconfin'd as day,
That every diftant land the wealth might fhare,
Exchange their wants and fill their treafures there,
Their fpeech affimilate, their empires blend,
And laws and mildnefs thro' the world extend.
Raife now thine eye, the haftening years fhall roll,
And thefe glad fcenes delight thy rifing foul."

We then beheld, 'till where in lonely pride,
The far, blue Baltic pours his laboring tide;
At once in gathering fquadrons, from the north,
The mingling ftreamers lead the nations forth;
From different fhores unnumber'd mafts arife,
And wave their peaceful curtains to the fkies;
Broader and broader ftill the wings unfold,
All Europe's coafts the ftreaming pomp behold,
From Gallia's ports, from Albion's hoary height,
United flags are pointed into fight;
Where broad Hifpania's ftrand two oceans lave,
And the rich Tagus mingles with the wave,
The countlefs navies lift their banners wide,
And ftream their glories o'er the foamy tide;
While thro' the glimmering Strait, in long array,
Pour'd from the fleets that croud the midland fea,
The fails look forth and fwell their beauteous pride,
With wider waves and bolder barks to glide;
While far, far diftant, where the watry way
Spreads the blue borders of defcending day,
The mifty fails advance in lengthening fweep,
Pride of the weftern world and daughters of the deep.

From all the bounds that meet the Atlantic wave,
While to our view the crouded fquadrons heave,
In fign of union, each advancing line,
Leads a calm nation, bids their banners join,
Till far as pole from pole, the cloudlike train
Skirts the dim heavens and fhades the whitening main.

We faw, in other feas and other fkies,
With equal pomp unnumber'd ftreamers rife;
Where Afia's ifles and utmoft fhores extend,
Like rifing funs the fheeted mafts afcend,
Sw ep from all ports that cleave the orient ftrand,
Load every ocean, compafs every land,
For peaceful commerce join the friendly train,
No more to combat on the watry plain.

We faw new barks to new difcoveries roll,
Where unknown waves falute each diftant pole;
Far in the north, where feas Pacific pour,
And ope Columbia from the Afian fhore,
The daring fails th' unmeafur'd flight purfue,
And ifles and countlefs nations rife to view.
While fome bold Sage, Columbus like, defign'd
By other ftars and waves to lead mankind,
With confcious pride and philofophic eye,
Treads the lone borders of the fouthern fky,
With perfevering toil the deeps explores,   [fhores.
Till there a new found world extends her length'ning

We faw, from each new realm, new arts afcend,
New manners rife, new wealth and power extend,
Allure the hero, feed the enquiring fage,
Enlarge the genius, dignify the age,

Till laws and empires fwell their rifing reign,
And their own navies whiten on the main.

Such views around us fpread, when thus the guide,
" Thefe are my works that load the fweeping tide ;
Nor lefs my power the walks of fcience claim,
In this fair land to raife her nobleft name.
No more fhall war difturb her peaceful reign,
And call to fields of death her youthful train,
No more her views by wealth and power immur'd,
To rage alone and fcenes of blood inur'd,
To teach the lance to thirft for human gore,
To teach pale Avarice to fwell the ftore,
To teach the milder arts the prize to yield,   .
Teach her own mufe the clangor of the field,
From ruin'd regions fill the voice of fame,
And call celeftial fire to blaze a tyrant's name.
No more in bolder breafts, to dwell confin'd,
And hold her feat in half the human mind,
O'er gentler paffions fpread a harfh controul,
And light the glare of grandeur in the foul ;
But fofter virtues now demand her care,
And her own laurels grace the rifing fair.
Each rival fex to rival arts afpires,
Each aids alike the univerfal quires ;
This bids bold commerce load the laboring main,
Or rear the peaceful harveft of the plain ;
That leads the hours of calm domeftic toil,
And cheers the houfhold with an evening finile,
To each fond heart an equal tafk affign'd,
And equal virtues raife the mutual mind.

While daring thoughts and deeper tracts of truth
Thro' philosophic mazes lead the youth,
The softer arts demand a softer care,
And loves and graces dignify the fair.
While states and empires, policies and laws,
Lure the firm patriot in the bolder cause,
To stem the tide of power or ward the war,
Like me to suffer and like me to dare.
Behold, with equal dignity and grace,
The matron virtues guide her peaceful race ;
A pleasing task her tender bosom warms,
The infant care now smiling in her arms,
Now ripening features, as the form improves,
Speak the dear image of the man she loves ;
She lures the rising wish to thoughts refin'd,
And her own virtues swell the opening mind,
The prattling throng to lisping reason grown,
To ape her loveliness improve their own ;
The sire beholds the living beauties bloom,
Pride of his life and hope of years to come,
Aids every virtue taught by her to rise,
Joins the delightful task, and trains them for the skies.

    Thus different arts their kindred cares employ,
In fields of action or domestic joy,
Then, rising from the useful to the fine,
Their mingling souls with rival glory shine.
From each pure taste consenting graces blend,
When the tall pillars of the dome ascend,
The walls heave stately, arches bend on high,
And full proportion meets the roving eye.

Or when the garden to the impaffion'd heart,
Unfinifh'd lies and afks the rural art,
With juft defign their equal fancies play,
From each alike the rambling beauties ftray,
Till thro' the whole the different fcenes prevail,
Here flows the fountain and there draws the dale,
The laughing lawn, the frowning footlefs grove,
And all the feats of innocence and love.

' Nor lefs their power the living canvas warms,
And breathes the pencil'd paffion into charms;
Heroes and beauties hear the wakening call,
And diftant ages fill the ftoried wall.

Two kindred arts the fwelling ftatue heave,
Wake the dead wax and teach the ftone to live;
The daring chiffel claims the bolder ftrife,
To roufe the fceptred marble into life,
While fairer hands the livelier fire controul,
And into fofter figures fhed the foul.
In hearts attun'd the voice of mufic dwells,
Steals o'er the lip and into paffion fwells,
Swept by th' alternate hand the living lyre,
To mutual rapture wakes the floating fire,
Till all the magic melody of found,
Pours in delightful harmony around.

And when the breath of heaven from Angel quires,
With life divine the joyous Mufe infpires,
In rival bofoms, fee the Goddefs glow!
And bind her bays on each confenting brow.

Ω

The foaring bard awakes the trembling ftring,
Virtues and loves and heavenly themes to fing;
No more of vengeful chiefs and bickering Gods,
Where ocean crimfons and Olympus nods,
Or heavens, convulfing rend the dark profound,
To chain fierce Titans to the groaning ground,
But, fir'd by milder themes, and charms refin'd,
Beam'd from the beauties of the fair one's mind,
His foul awakes the peace infpiring fong,
And life and happinefs the ftrain prolong;
To moral beauties bids the world attend, •
And jarring realms in focial compact blend;
Bids laws extend and commerce ftretch the wing,
Far diftant fhores their barter'd tributes bring;
He fees the nations join, their blifs increafe,
(Leagu'd in his lays) and fings them into peace.
While pleas'd, the Mufe divides her equal care,
And the fame ardor warms the liftening fair;
From his pure breath fhe lights a bolder flame,
The fame her genius and her flight the fame,
In mutual fmiles the borrow'd graces play,
In mutual fweetnefs flide the hours away,
In mutual aid the borrow'd numbers roll,
And fwell'd to rapture breathes the mutual foul.

From their own loves, thus foften'd and refin'd,
The general wifh extends to all mankind,
The neighbour's cares, the family, the friend
Pour on the heart, and in the bofom blend;
The poor, the ftranger find a welcome home,
The vagrant foot is pointed where to roam,

The eye of anguifh, when no help is near,
Looks the fond wifh and finds the mingling tear ;
E'en to their foes their equal goodnefs bends,
And hoftile minds are foften'd into friends.

And when their lays have pour'd the bounteous mind,
In warm benevolence, to all their kind,
They lift the bolder note, the raptures glow,
To loves pure fource whence all her ftreamlets flow.
Rapt into vifion of the bright abode,
From angel harps they catch th' infpiring God ;
Thro' heavens, o'er-canopy'd by heavens, they foar,
Where floods of light in boundlefs beauty pour,
Seraphs and fyftem'd worlds innumerous move,
Link'd in the chain of harmonizing love ;
Thence following down, th' effulgent glory trace,
Which brought falvation to their kindred race.

Thus, on the ftream of life, with gentle fweep,
They roll delightful to the welcome deep,
Where, unconfin'd, their fpirits gently fail,
View happier climes and tafte a purer gale ;
Thro' ether's boundlefs realms together rife,
And claim their kindred manfions in the fkies ;
There fill the rapture of th' adoring throng,
Whofe lays on earth prelude the heavenly fong."

An ELEGY

On the late honorable Titus Hosmer, Esq. one of the Counsellors of the State of Connecticut, a Member of Congress, and a Judge of the Maritime Court of Appeals for the United States of America.

INSCRIBED TO

-Mrs. LYDIA HOSMER,

Relict of the late honorable Titus Hosmer, *Esq.*

As a testimony of the Author's veneration for the many amiable virtues which rendered her the delight and ornament of so worthy a Consort, and still render her an honour to a very numerous and respectable acquaintance.

BY THE SAME.

COME to my soul, O shade of Hosmer, come,
  Tho' doubting senates ask thy aid in vain ;
Attend the drooping virtues round thy tomb,
  And hear a while the orphan'd Muse complain.

The Muse which thy indulgence bade aspire,
  And dare pursue thy distant steps to fame ;
At thy command she first assum'd the lyre,
  And hop'd a future laurel from thy name.

How did thy smiles awake her infant song !
  How did thy virtues animate the lay !
Still shall thy fate the dying strain prolong,
  And bear her voice with thy lost form away.

Come to my foul thou venerable Sage,
  In all the fheeted majefty of night,
Snatch the bold quill, control the noble rage,
  And feize the raptur'd fancy in her flight.

Come in the form that fhadowy fpirits drefs,
  When death's dim veil hath fhrouded all their pride,
While yon tall cloud but emulates thy face,
  Where the lone moon-beam trembles thro' its fide.

Come on the gale that liftening midnight heaves,
  When glare-ey'd phantoms, bending with a bier,
Stalk thro' the mift, afcend the founding graves,
  And wake wild wonders in the ftartled ear.

In this dread fcene no more the wonted fires
  Kindle my breaft, or opé a wifh within,
The foul, diftracted, from herfelf retires,
  And fighs to mingle and to foar with thine.

And where, thou bleft immortal, art thou flown!
  Can thefe deep fhades detain thy willing ear?
Canft thou from loaded breezes hear a groan?
  Or ftain thy fpotlefs mantle with a tear!

Can ought on earth thy flight hath left behind,
  Borne in the mufic of a once lov'd ftrain,
Approach the unbody'd manfion of the mind?
  Or bend one pitying look to earth again?

Can thence no thought to that fair feat defcend?
  The feat once joyous in thy joys below,
Where robes of fable fadnefs now depend,
  And all the ftill folemnities of woe.

Can the dear partner of thy tender years,
  Sad as the mifty fading face of even,
With all the wafted treafure of her tears,
  Avert no fmile nor bribe a care from heaven?

While that young throng, that dear deferted train,
  Where thy lov'd image foften'd fweetnefs wears,
Swell with new tendernefs each following pain,
  And add unnumber'd, undivided cares.

Around the fair one fee their beauties bloom,
  (Or wilt thou not the moving fair one heed?)
How their keen anguifh points the diftant tomb,
  Where all their joys and every hope is fled!

So lonely Cynthia, on her evening throne,
  And all her young-ey'd planetary train,
In languid luftre feek their fire the fun,
  Down the ftill chambers of the weftern main.

Yet that broad fplendor from his nightly race,
  With rifing radiance fhall the day reftore;
Another fpring renews fair nature's face,
  And years and ages die to waken more.

But thou, alas! no more on earth wilt tread,
  Nor one fhort hour thy bleft employments leave,
Tho' the fad knell, that hail'd thee to the dead,
  Had doom'd thy helplefs country to her grave.

Thy country, whofe ftill fupplicating moan,
  Implores thy counfels with an infant cry;
And loads the fame ftern Angel with a groan,
  Which bore thy kindling fpirit to the fky.

Wilt thou (since nothing here can bribe thy ftay,
   And nothing here can tempt thee from on high,
Since tears of innocence muft idly ftray,   ·
   And grateful millions breathe the fruitlefs figh;

Since every tender tie that mortals prize,
   And all that fame's immortal children gain,
Yield to the untimely mandate of the fkies,
   And afk thy kind continuance ftill in vain :)

Wilt thou in feats of blefſednefs above,
   Where cares of empire claim the eternal ear,
Among thy country's guardian feraphs prove
   The hand to cherifh and the heart to hear?

There, while the dread fublimity of foul
   O'er all the ftar-ey'd heaven exalts thy throne,
While worlds beneath immeafurably roll,
   And fhew the well-known circuit of thine own,

Wilt thou remark the bluely-bending fhore?
   Where hills and champaigns ftretch abroad their pride,
Where opening ftreams their lengthieft currents pour,
   And heaps of heroes fwell the crimfon tide.

Wilt thou recognize that confus'd uproar?
   Towns curl'd in fmoaky columns mounting high,
Mix'd with the clarion's defolating roar;
   Rending and purpling all the nether fky.

Amid the tumult, wilt thou fee afar
   Our laurel'd heroes ftriving for the day?
While clouds, unfolding, ope the wings of war,
   Where the grim legions fweep the foes away.

And while their deeds thy bleſt approvance claim,
   While crouds of rival chiefs thy guidance ſhare,
Eenold that firſt, that finiſh'd heir of fame,
   And be the beſt of heroes ſtill thy care.

That hero whoſe illuminating ſword
   Lights death and victory through the darken'd field,
Bids realms and ages waken at his word,
   Their fire, their ſoul, their ſaviour and their ſhield.

Behold that Senate, whoſe delightful ear
   With thy bold eloquence hath often rung,
Where trembling realms, for many a doubtful year,
   Have learnt their ſure ſalvation from thy tongue.

While cares of empires ſit upon their brow,
   And all th' increaſing counſels of an age,
Demand, alike, bold virtue's warmeſt glow,
   And the wide walks of ſcience in the ſage ;

Let thy own wiſdom's ever beaming light
   Illume their well-known dignity of ſoul,
Let thy benevolence their hearts unite,
   And every voice, and every wiſh controul.

Lift the deep curtain from the vale of time,
   Where unborn years their future circles wind,
Where the broad intereſts of a growing clime
   Spread to all realms and regulate mankind.

Unfold to their keen penetrating view,
   What to the infant empire ſhould be known,
That worlds' and ages' happineſs or woe,
   Hang on th' important iſſue of their own.

And fure thou wilt that honor'd realm revere,
   Where firft thine early fteps began their fame,
Where thy lov'd memory, ever doubly dear,
   Awakes a tenderer tribute to thy name.

Canft thou forget, when youthful years began,
   Where opening fcience kindled every grace,
And fmil'd to fee, afcending in the man,
   The friend, the pride, the glory, of his race?

Where civil rights, the dignity of men,
   And all the extenfive privilege of laws,
Roll'd from thy voice or brighten'd from thy pen,
   Compel'd attention and fecur'd applaufe.

Where rifing worth thine early name enroll'd
   Among the firft fam'd fathers of the age,
And bade the untarnifh'd charafters of gold
   Flame in the front of glory's deathlefs page.

Attentive ftill to virtue's noble aim,
   And greatly ftrenuous to advance her caufe,
Lead thou her counfels, animate her fiame,
   Sire of her fons, and guardian of her laws.

And fee! aloft in that fublime retreat,
   Where injur'd rights obtain their laft appeal,
How penfive juftice o'er thy vacant feat,
   With faltering hand fufpends her turning fcale.

If chance fome Hofmer, with an even eye,
   And fkill'd like thee to poize the trembling weight,
Should chear the nymph, thine honor'd place fupply,
   And blefs the nations with a longer date;

R

When from all bounds of this extenfive land,
  Or where wide oceans fpread their coafts abroad,
Dark caufes rife, demanding from his hand,
  Th' impartial deep difcernment of a god;

Then in his breaft may all thy virtues rife,
  And all thy dignity around him fhine,
Then drop thy own bleft mantle from the fkies,
  And make the perfon as the place divine.

He will, my friends——th' unbodied life above,
  With every virtue brighten'd and refin'd,
That glow'd below, with patriotic love,
  The love of happinefs and human kind,

Will burn ferener in a purer fky,
  Where broader views and bolder thoughts unroll,
Where univerfal Being fills the eye,
  And fwells the unbounded wifhes of the foul.

No tender thought by heaven's own breath infpir'd,
  Which taught the gentle bofom here to glow,
Which the warm breaft with patriot ardor fir'd,
  Or ftole the fecret tear for filent woe;

No tender thought by heaven's own will approv'd,
  Can e'er forfake the manfion firft affign'd;
But reaches ftill the object once belov'd,
  And lives immortal in th' immortal mind.

Fix'd in a brighter fphere, with furer aim,
  Tho' greater fcenes his growing views employ,
Yet Hofmer kindles with an Hofmer's flame,
  And his dear country feeds his nobleft joy.

He fees our rifing, all-involving caufe,
  Spread like the morn to every diftant clime,
Awake the mild magnificence of laws,
  And roll down bleffings on the ftream of time.

Nor think, O haplefs fair one, tho' awhile,
  From thy fond arms his happier fpirit rove,
That foaring innocence can ceafe to fmile,
  Or his Seraphic bofom ceafe to love.

In Heaven's own breaft the felf-exiftent fires,
  E'er time began, illum'd th' eternal flame,
Lit from the beam, the Archangellic quires
  Preferve th' unchanging ardor ftill the fame.

And fhall the heaven-born fpirit after death,
  Robb'd of its virtues from its nature fly,
Or lofe in climes of blifs the afpiring breath,
  Which wing'd its paffage to its kindred fky ?

Think, in the chambers of eternal morn,
  Where beauty blooms along the vernal vale,
Where loves and virtues every fmile adorn,
  And hymns of Angels fwell the floating gale ;

Think how his well-known fympathy of foul
  Views every pain thy tendernefs can know ;
Counts the full tears in filence as they roll,
  And learns the tale of every fpeaking woe.

Thou know'ft, while here, he joy'd to give relief,
  To call dark merit to the eye of day,
To rob the filent orphan of her grief,
  And breathe the figh from innocence away.

How did the trembling visage of the poor,
  With grateful glow embolden at his smile !
And learn, well pleas'd, within his wonted door,
  Its joys to cherish, and its cares beguile.

Thou know'st his early wish began to prize
  The bliss that wayward mortals seldom find,
That lifts the frequent suppliant to the skies,
  While answering blessings fill the raptur'd mind.

Know then, fair mourner, from the climes of day,
  (While these drear shades of solitude you tread)
His unseen hand companion of thy way,
  Thro' the dark paths thy wandering steps shall lead.

While all thy virtues rise before the throne,
  And all thy griefs be number'd in his sight,
Those shall refine and ripen with his own,
  And these be hush'd in everlasting night.

Thy children too, his images below,
  Fair as young plants, and smiling as the morn,
With thy own loveliness shall learn to glow,
  And all thy graces brighten and adorn.

Short is the date that virtue from its home,
  In these deep shades, can suffer and refine ;
And when kind heaven relieves it from the doom,
  Ours be the choice to tremble and resign.

Vain were the task, the daring thought were vain,
  To check the sun's bold circuit as he flies ;
Nor think the cling of fondness can detain
  The soaring seraph from his kindred skies.

Then ceafe, fond partner of his earthly joys,
    And leave behind each unavailing care ;
Think what a fcene his happier flight employs,
    And hafte to meet him and to mingle there.

An   Elegy

On the burning of FAIRFIELD, in CONNECTICUT.

Written on the fpot,—anno 1779.

BY COL. DAVID HUMPHREYS.

YE fmoking ruins, marks of hoftile ire,
    Ye afhes warm, which drink the tears that flow,
Ye defolated plains my voice infpire,
    And give foft mufic to the fong of woe !

How pleafant, Fairfield, on th' enraptur'd fight
    Rofe thy tall fpires, and op'd thy focial halls !
How oft my bofom beat with pure delight,
    At yonder fpot, where ftand the darken'd walls !

But there the voice of mirth refounds no more,
    A filent fadnefs through the ftreets prevails,
The diftant main alone is heard to roar,
    And hollow chimnies hum with fullen gales ;

Save where fcorch'd elms th' untimely foliage fhed,
    Which ruftling hovers round the faded green ;
Save where at twilight mourners frequent tread,
    'Mid recent graves o'er defolation's fcene.

How chang'd the blifsful profpect, when compar'd
  Thefe glooms funereal with thy former bloom :
Thy hofpitable rights when Tryon fhar'd,
  Long ere he feal'd thy melancholly doom.

That impious wretch, with coward voice decreed
  Defencelefs domes and hallow'd fanes to duft,
Beheld with fneering fmile the wounded bleed,
  And fpurr'd his bands to rapine, blood and luft.

Vain was the widow's, vain the orphan's cry,
  To touch his feelings or to footh his rage ;
Vain the fair drop that roll'd from beauty's eye,
  Vain the dumb grief of fupplicating age.

Could Tryon hope to quench the patriot flame,
  Or make his deeds furvive in glory's page ?
Could Britons feek of favages the fame,
  Or deem it conqueft thus the war to wage ?

Yes, Britons fcorn the councils of the fkies,
  Extend wide havoc, fpurn the infulted foes !
Th' infulted foes to tenfold vengeance rife,
  Refiftance growing as the danger grows.

Red in their wounds and pointing to the plain,
  The vifionary fhapes before me ftand ;
The thunder burfts, the battle burns again,
  And kindling fires encrimfon all the ftrand.—

Long dufky wreaths of fmoke, reluctant driven,
  In blackening volumes o'er the landfcape bend ;
Here the broad fplendor blazes high to heaven,
  There umber'd ftreams in purple pomp afcend.

In fiery eddies round the tott'ring walls,
  Emitting fparks, the lighter fragments fly;
With frightful crafh the burning manfion falls,
  The works of years in glowing embers lye.

Tryon! behold thy fanguine flames afpire,
  Clouds ting'd with dyes intolerably bright!
Behold well pleaf'd the village wrap'd in fire;
  Let one wide ruin glut thy ravifh'd fight!

Ere fades the grateful fcene, indulge thine eye,
  See age and ficknefs tremuloufly flow,
Creep from the flames—fee babes in torture dye—
  And mothers fwoon in agonies of woe.

Go, gaze, enraptured with the mother's tear,
  The infant's terror, and the captive's pain,
Where no bold bands can check thy curft career;
  Mix fire with blood on each unguarded plain.

Thefe be thy triumphs! this thy boafted fame!
  Daughters of mem'ry, raife the deathlefs fongs!
Repeat through endlefs years his hated name,
  Embalm his crimes and teach the world our wrongs!

AN ELEGY
ON LIEUTENANT DE HART,*
¡Vol. Aid to Gen. Wayne.

BY THE SAME.

WHEN autumn all humid and drear
    With darkneſs and ſtorms in his train
Announcing the death of the year,
    Deſpoil'd of its verdure the plain :
When horror congenial prevail'd,
    Where graves are with fearfulneſs trod,
De Hart by his ſiſter was wail'd,
    His ſiſter thus ſigh'd o'er his ſod :

" Near Hudſon, a fort, on theſe banks,
    " Its flag of defiance unfurl'd :
" He led to the ſtorm the firſt ranks ;
    " On them, iron tempeſts were hurl'd.
" Tranſpierc'd was his breaſt with a ball—
    " His breaſt a red fountain ſupply'd,
" Which, guſhing in waves ſtill and ſmall,
    " Diſtain'd his white boſom and ſide.

" His viſage was ghaſtly in death,
    " His hair, that ſo laviſhly curl'd,
" I ſaw, as he lay on the heath,
    " In blood, and with dew-drops impearl'd.

---

    * This young warrior was killed in the attack on the block-houſe, near Fort Lee, 1780.

" How dumb is the tongue, that could speak
 " Whate'er could engage and delight !
" How faded the rose on his cheek !
 " Those eyes, how envelop'd in night !

" Those eyes, that illumin'd each soul,
 " All darken'd to us are now grown :
" In far other orbits they roll,
 " Like stars to new systems when gone.
" My brother, the pride of the plain,
 " In vain did the graces adorn ;
" His blossom unfolded in vain,
 " To die like the blossom of morn.

" Oh war, thou hast wasted our clime,
 " And tortur'd my bosom with sighs :
" My brother, who fell ere his prime,
 " Forever is torn from my eyes.
" To me, how distracting the storm,
 " That blasted the youth in his bloom !
" Alas, was so finish'd a form
 " Design'd for so early a tomb ?

" How bright were the prospects that shone !
 " Their ruin 'tis mine to deplore—
" Health, beauty, and youth were his own,
 " Health, beauty, and youth are no more.
" No blessings of nature and art,
 " Nor music that charm'd in the song,
" Nor virtues that glow'd in the heart,
 " Dear youth, could thy moments prolong !

S

" Thrice fix times the fpring had renew'd
  " Its youth and its charms for the boy ;
" With rapture all nature he view'd,
  " For nature he knew to enjoy.
" But chiefly his country could charm :
  " He felt—'twas a generous heat—
" With drums and the trumpet's alarm,
  " His pulfes in confonance beat.

" Ye heroes, to whom he was dear,
  " Come weep o'er this forrowful urn,
" Come eafe the full heart with a tear—
  " My hero will never return :
" He died in the dawn of applaufe,
  " His country demanded his breath ;
" Go, heroes, defend the fame caufe,
  " Avenge with your country his death."

So fung on the top of the rocks,
  The virgin in forrow more fair ;
In tears her blue eyes ; and her locks
  Of auburn flew loofe on the air.
I heard, as pafs'd down the ftream ;
  The guards of the foe were in view :—
To enterprize fir'd by the theme,
  I bade the fweet mourner adieu.

MOUNT VERNON:
An Ode.

BY THE SAME.

BY broad Potowmack's azure tide,
 Where Vernon's mount, in fylvan pride,
  Difplays its beauties far,
Great Wafhington, to peaceful fhades,
Where no unhallow'd wifh invades,
  Retir'd from fields of war.

Angels might fee, with joy, the fage,
Who taught the battle where to rage,
  Or fquench'd its fpreading flame,
On works of peace employ that hand,
Which wav'd the blade of high command,
  And hew'd the path to fame.

Let others fing his deeds in arms,
A nation fav'd, and conqueft's charms :
  Pofterity fhall hear,
'Twas mine, return'd from Europe's courts,
To fhare his thoughts, partake his fports,
  And footh his partial ear.

To thee, my friend, thefe lays belong :
Thy happy feat infpires my fong,
  With gay, perennial blooms,
With fruitage fair, and cool retreats,
Whofe bow'ry wildernefs of fweets
  The ambient air perfumes.

Here fpring its earlieft buds difplays,
Here lateft on the leaflefs fprays,
 The plumy people fing;
The vernal fhow'r, the rip'ning year,
Th' autumnal ftore, the winter drear,
 For thee new pleafures bring.

Here lapp'd in philofophic eafe,
Within thy walks, beneath thy trees,
 Amidft thine ample farms,
No vulgar converfe heroes hold,
But paft or future fcenes unfold,
 Or dwell on nature's charms.

What wond'rous era have we feen,
Plac'd on this ifthmus, half between
 A rude and polifh'd ftate!
We faw the war tempeftuous rife,
In arms a world, in blood the fkies,
 In doubt and empire's fate.

The ftorm is calm'd, feren'd the heav'n,
And mildly o'er the climes of ev'n,
 Expands th' imperial day:
" O God, the fource of light fupreme,
" Shed on our dufky morn a gleam,
 " To guide our doubtful way!

" Reftrain, dread pow'r, our land from crimes!
" What feeks, tho' bleft beyond all times,
 " So querulous an age?
" What means to freedom fuch difguft,
" Of change, of anarchy the luft,
 " The ficklenefs and rage?'

So fpake his country's friend, with fighs,
To find that country ftill defpife
　　The legacy he gave—
And half he fear'd his toils were vain,
And much that man would court a chain,
　　And live through vice a flave.

A tranfient gloom o'ercaft his mind:
Yet, ftill on providence reclin'd,
　　The patriot fond believ'd,
That pow'r benign too much had done,
To leave an empire's tafk begun,
　　Imperfectly achiev'd.

Thus buoy'd with hope, with virtue bleft,
Of ev'ry human blifs poffeft,
　　He meets the happier hours;
His fkies affume a lovelier blue,
His profpects brighter rife to view,
　　And fairer bloom his flow'rs.

AN ODE.

ADDRESSED TO LAURA.

────────

BY THE SAME.

────────

OH, lovely Laura, may a youth,
  Infpir'd by beauty, urg'd by truth,
    Difclofe the heart's alarms,
The fire in raptur'd breafts that glows,
Th' impaffion'd pang on love that grows,
    And dare to fing thy charms!

Enough with war my lay has rung;
A fofter theme awakes my tongue;
    'Tis beauty's force divine:
Can I refift that air, that grace,
The harmony of form and face?
    For ev'ry charm is thine.

Of health, of youth th' expanding flufh,
Of virgin fear the flying blufh,
    With crimfon ftain thy cheek:
The bee fuch nectar never fips,
As yield the rofe-buds of thy lips,
    When fweetly thou doft fpeak.

'Tis thine the heavieft heart to cheer,
Thofe accents, drank with eager ear,
    So mufically roll:

Where fwells the breaft, the fnow-white fkin
Scarce hides the fecret thoughts within,
    Nor needs difguife that foul.

With thee, of cloudnefs days I dream ;
Thy eyes, in morning fplendors, beam
    So exquifitely fair—
What tafte ! as o'er thy back and breaft,
In light-brown ringlets neatly dreft
    Devolves a length of hair.

Unblam'd, oh, let me gaze and gaze,
While love-fick fancy fondly ftrays,
    And feafts on many a kifs ;—
For us let tides of rapture roll,
And may we mingle foul with foul,
    In extacies of blifs !

The GENIUS of AMERICA.
A SONG.
Tune,—The watry God, &c.

BY THE SAME.

WHERE fpirits dwell and fhad'wy forms,
    On Andes' cliffs mid black'ning ftorms,
With livid lightnings curl'd :
The awful genius of our clime,
In thunder rais'd his voice fublime,
    And hufh'd the lift'ning world.

" In lonely waves and waftes of earth,
" A mighty empire claims its birth,
    " And heav'n afferts the claim;
" The fails that hang in yon dim fky,
" Proclaim the promis'd era nigh,
    " Which wakes a world to fame.

" Hail ye firft bounding barks that roam,
" Blue-tumbling billows topp'd with foam,
    " Which keel ne'er plough'd before!
" Here funs perform their ufelefs round,
" Here rove the naked tribes embrown'd,
    " Who feed on living gore.

" To midnight orgies, off'ring dire,
" The human facrifice on fire,
    " A heav'nly light fucceeds—
" But, lo! what horrors intervene,
" The toils fevere, the carnag'd fcene,
    " And more than mortal deeds!

" Ye FATHERS, fpread your fame afar,
" 'Tis yours to ftill the founds of war,
    " And bid the flaughter ceafe;
" The peopling hamlets wide extend,
" The harvefts fpring, the fpires afcend,
    " Mid grateful fongs of peace.

" Shall fteed to fteed, and man to man,
" With difcord thund'ring in the van,
    " Again deftroy the blifs?
" Enough my myftic words reveal,
" The reft the fhades of night conceal,
    " In fate's profound abyfs."

An EPISTLE to dr. DWIGHT.*

On board the Courier de l'Europe, July 30, 1784.

BY THE SAME.

FROM the wide watry wafte, where nought but fkies
  And mingling waves falute the aching eyes ;
Where the fame moving circle bounds the view,
And paints with vap'ry tints the billows blue ;
To thee, my early friend! to thee, dear Dwight!
Fond recollection turns, while thus I write ;
While I reflect, no change of time or place,
The impreffions of our friendfhip can efface ;
Nor peace, nor war, tho' chang'd for us the fcene,
Tho' mountains rife, or oceans roll between ;
Too deep that facred paffion was impreft
On my young heart, too deep it mark'd your breaft ;
Your breaft which afks the feelings of your friend,
What chance betides him, or what toils attend?
Then hear the mufe, in fea-born numbers tell
In mind how cheerful, and in health how well ;
And ev'n that mufe will deign to let you know,
What things concur to make and keep him fo.

T.

* For Dr. Dwight's letter to Col. Humphreys, fee
page 75.

We go, protected by fupernal care,
With cloudlefs fkies, and funs ferenely fair;
While o'er the unruffled main the gentle gale
Confenting breathes, and fills each fwelling fail; .
Confcious of fafety in the felf-fame hand,
Which guides us on the ocean or the land.

Of thee, fair bark! the mufe prophetic fings,
" *Europe's fwift Meffenger!* expand thy wings,
" Rear thy tall mafts, extend thine ample arms,
" Catch the light breeze, nor dread impending harms.
" Full oft fhalt thou, if aught the mufe avails,
" Wing the broad deep with fuch delightful gales;
" Full oft to either world announce glad news,
" Of allied realms promote the friendly views;
" So fhall each diftant age affert thy claim,
" And *Europe's Meffenger* be known to fame!"

What tho' this plain fo uniform and vaft,
Illimitably fpreads its dreary wafte;
What tho' no ifles, nor vales, nor hills, nor groves,
Meet the tired eye that round the horizon roves;
Yet, ftill collected in a narrow bound,
Ten thoufand little pleafures may be found.

Here we enjoy accommodations good,
With pleafant liquors, and well-flavor'd food,
Meats nicely fatten'd in Columbian fields,
And lufcious wines, that Gallia's vintage yields,
On which you bards ('twas fo in former days)
Might feaft your wit, and lavifh all your praife.

Within our fhip, well-furnifh'd, roomy, clean,
Come fee the ufes of each different fcene.

Far in the prow, for culinary ufe,
Fires, not poetic, much good cheer produce;
The ovens there our daily bread afford,
And thence the viands load our plenteous board.

See various landfcapes fhade our dining hall,
Where mimic nature wantons round the wall,
There no vain pomp appears, there all is neat,
And there cool zephyrs fanning, as we eat,
Avert the fervors of the noon-tide ray,
And give the mildnefs of the vernal day.

See the great cabin nigh, its doors unfold,
Shew fleeting forms from mirrors fix'd in gold!
O'er painted ceilings brighter profpects rife,
And rural fcenes again delight our eyes:
There oft from converfe or from focial fports,
We drink delight lefs dafh'd than that of courts.

But when more fober cares the hour requires,
Each to his cell of folitude retires;
His bed, his books, his paper, pen and ink,
Prefent the choice, to reft, to read, or think.

Yet what would all avail to prompt the fmile,
Cheer the fad breaft, or the dull hour beguile;
If well-bred paflengers, difcreet and free,
Were not at hand to mix in focial glee?
Such my companions,—fuch the mufe fhall tell,
Him firft, whom once you knew in war fo well,
Our Polifh friend,* whofe name ftill founds fo hard,
To make it rhyme would puzzle any bard;

* General Kofciufzko.

That youth, whom bays and laurels early crown'd,
For virtue, fcience, arts, and arms, renown'd.
Next him, behold, to grace our watry fcene,
An honeft German lifts his generous mien ;
Him Carolina fends to Europe's fhore,
Canals and inland waters to explore ;
From thence return'd, fhe hopes to fee her tide,
In commerce rich, thro' ampler channels glide.
Next comes the bleak Quebec's well-natured fon ;
And laft our naval chief, the friend of fun ;
Whofe plain, frank manners, form'd on fickle feas,
Are cheerful ftill, and always aim to pleafe :
Nor lefs the other chiefs their zeal difplay,
To make us happy as themfelves are gay.

Sever'd from all fociety but this,
Half way from either world we plough the abyfs :
Save the fmall fea-bird and the fifh that flies,
On yon blue waves no object meets my eyes.
Nor has the infidious hook, with lures, beguil'd
Of peopled ocean fcarce a fingle child.
Yet lucklefs Dolphin, erft to Arion † true,
Nought could avail thy beauteous, tranfient hue ;
As o'er the deck, in dying pang you roll'd,
Wrapt in gay rain-bows and pellucid gold.

Now fee that wand'rer bird, fatigued with flight
O'er many a watry league, is forc'd to light

---

† Ille fedet, citharamque tenet, pretiumque vehendi
Cantat, et æquoreas carmine mulcet aquas.
Ovid. Faft. 2.

High on the maſt,—the bird our ſeamen take,
Tho' ſcar'd, too tir'd its refuge to forſake :
Fear not ſweet bird, nor judge our motives ill,
No barb'rous man, now means thy blood to ſpill,
Or hold thee cag'd ; ſoon as we reach the ſhore,
Free ſhalt thou fly, and gaily ſing and ſoar !

Another grateful ſight now cheers the eye,
At firſt a ſnow-white ſpot in yon clear ſky ;
Then thro' the optic tube a ſhip appears,
And now diſtinct athwart the billows veers :
Daughter of ocean, made to bleſs mankind !
Go, range wide waters on the wings of wind ;
With friendly intercourſe far climes explore,
Their produce barter, and increaſe their ſtore ;
Ne'er ſaw my eye ſo fair a pageant ſwim,
As thou appear'ſt, in all thy gallant trim !

Amus'd with trivial things, reclin'd at eaſe,
While the ſwift bark divides the ſummer ſeas ;
Your bard (for paſt neglect to make amends)
Now writes to you, anon to other friends.

Anon the ſcene, in Europe's poliſh'd climes,
Will give new themes for philoſophic rhymes,
Ope broader fields for reaſon to explore,
Improvements vaſt of ſcientific lore !

•Thro' nations bleſt with peace, but ſtrong in arms,
Refin'd in arts, and apt for ſocial charms,
Your friend will ſtray, and ſtrive, with ſtudious care,
To mark whate'er is uſeful, great, or rare ;

Search the small shades of manners in their lives,
What policy prevails, how commerce thrives;
How morals form of happiness the base,
How others differ from Columbia's race;
And, gleaning knowlege from the realms he rov'd,
Bring home a patriot heart, enlarg'd, improv'd.

———————

A S O N G.

Translated from the French.

BY THE SAME.

IT rains, it rains, my fair,
   Come drive your white sheep fast:
To shelter quick repair,
   Haste, shepherdess, make haste.

I hear—the water pours,
   With patt'ring on the vines:
See here! see here! it lours—
   See there the lightning shines.

The thunder dost thou hear?
   Loud roars the rushing storm:
Take (while we run, my dear)
   Protection from my arm.

I fee our cot, ah hold!
  Mama and fifter Nance,
To open our fheep-fold,
  Moft cheerily advance.

God blefs my mother dear,
  My fifter Nancy too!
I bring my fweet-heart here,
  To fleep to night with you.

Go, dry yourfelf, my friend,
  And make yourfelf at home—
Sifter, on her attend:
  Come in, fweet lambkirs, come.

Mama, let's take good care
  Of all her pretty fheep;
Her little lamb we'll fpare
  More ftraw whereon to fleep.

'Tis done—now let us hafte
  To her;—you here, my fair!
Undrefs'd, oh what a waift!
  My mother, look you there.

Let's fup; come take this place,
  You fhall be next to me;
This pine-knot's cheerful blaze
  Shall fhine direct on thee.

Come tafte this cream fo fweet,
  This fyllabub fo warm;
Alas! you do not eat:
  You feel ev'n yet the ftorm.

'Twas wrong—I prefs'd too much
   Your fteps, when on the way:
But here, fee here your couch—
   There fleep till dawn of day

With gold the mountain tips :—
   Good night, good night, my dove :
Now let me on your lips,
   Imprint one kifs of love.

Mama and I will come,
   When morn begins to fhine,
To fee my fweet-heart home,
   And afk her hand for mine.

EPITAPH

On a Patient killed by a Cancer Quack.

BY DR. LEMUEL HOPKINS.

HERE lies a fool flat on his back,
    The victim of a Cancer Quack;
Who loft his money and his life,
By plaifter, cauftic, and by knife.
The cafe was this—a pimple rofe,
South-eaft a little of his nofe;
Which daily reden'd and grew bigger,
As too much drinking gave it vigour:
A fcore of goffips foon enfure
Full three fcore diff'rent modes of cure:
But yet the full-fed pimple ftill
Defied all petticoated fkill;
When fortune led him to perufe
A hand-bill in the weekly news;
Sign'd by fix fools of diff'rent forts,
All cur'd of cancers made of warts;
Who recommend, with due fubmiffion,
This cancer-monger as magician;
Fear wing'd his flight to find the quack,
And prove his cancer-curing knack;
But on his way he found another,—
A fecond advertifing brother:

U

But as much like him as an owl
Is unlike every handfome fowl;
Whofe fame had rais'd as broad a fog,
And of the two the greater hog:
Who us'd a ftill more magic plaifter,
That fweat forfooth, and cur'd the fafter.
This doctor view'd, with moony eyes
And fcowl'd up face, the pimple's fize;
Then chriften'd it in folemn anfwer,
And cried, " This pimple's name is CANCER."
" But courage, friend, I fee you're pale,
" My fweating plaifters never fail;
" I've fweated hundreds out with eafe,
" With roots as long as maple trees;
" And never fail'd in all my trials—
" Behold thefe famples here in vials!
" Preferv'd to fhew my wond'rous merits,
" Juft as my liver is—in fpirits.
" For twenty joes the cure is done—"
The bargain ftruck, the plaifter on,
Which gnaw'd the cancer at its leifure,
And pain'd his face above all meafure.
But ftill the pimple fpread the fafter,
And fwell'd, like toad that meets difafter.
Thus foil'd, the doctor gravely fwore,
It was a right rofe-cancer fore;
Then ftuck his probe beneath the beard,
And fhew'd them where the leaves appear'd;
And rais'd the patient's drooping fpirits,
By praifing up the plaifter's merits.—

Quoth he, " The roots now fcarcely flick—
" I'll fetch her out like crab or tick ;
" And make it rendezvous, next trial,
" With fix more plagues, in my old vial."
Then purg'd him pale with jalap draftic,
And next applies th' infernal cauftic.
But yet, this femblance bright of hell
Serv'd but to make the patient yell ;
And, gnawing on with fiery pace,
Devour'd one broadfide of his face—
' Courage, 'tis done,' the doctor cried,
And quick th' incifion knife applied :
That with three cuts made fuch a hole,
Out flew the patient's tortur'd foul!

Go, readers, gentle, eke and fimple,
If you have wart, or corn, or pimple ;
To quack infallible apply ;
Here's room enough for you to lie.
His fkill triumphant ftill prevails,
For DEATH's a cure that never fails.

THE HYPOCRITE's HOPE.

BY THE SAME.

BLEST is the man, who from the womb,
    To faintfhip him betakes,
And when too foon his child fhall come,
    A long confeffion makes.

When next in Broad Church-alley, he
  Shall take his former place,
Relates his paft iniquity,
  And confequential grace.

Declares how long by Satan vex'd,
  From truth he did depart,
And tells the time, and tells the text,
  That fmote his flinty heart.

He ftands in half-way-cov'nant fure;
  Full five long years or more,
One foot in church's pale fecure,
  The other out of door.

Then riper grown in gifts and grace,
  With ev'ry rite complies,
And deeper lengthens down his face,
  And higher rolls his eyes.

He tones like Pharifee fublime,
  Two lengthy prayers a day,
The fame that he from early prime,
  Had heard his father fay.

Each Sunday perch'd on bench of pew,
  To paffing prieft he bows,
Then loudly 'mid the quav'ring crew,
  Attunes his vocal nofe.

With awful look then rifes flow,
  And pray'rful vifage four,
More fit to fright the apoftate foe,
  Then feek a pard'ning power.

Then nodding hears the fermon next,
From prieſt haranguing loud;
And doubles down each quoted text,
From Geneſis to Jude.

And when the prieſt holds forth addreſs,
To old ones born anew,
With holy pride and wrinkled face,
He riſes in his pew.

Good works he careth nought about,
But *faith* alone will ſeek,
While Sunday's pieties blot out
The knaveries of the week.

He makes the poor his daily pray'r,
Yet drives them from his board:
And though to his own good he ſwear,
Thro' habit breaks his word.

This man advancing freſh and fair,
Shall all his race complete;
And wave at laſt his hoary hair,
Arrived in Deacon's ſeat.

There ſhall he all church honours have,
By joyous brethren given—
Till prieſt in fun'ral ſermon grave,
Shall ſend him ſtraight to heaven.

ON GENERAL ETHAN ALLEN.

LO Allen 'fcaped from Britifh jails,
His tufhes broke by biting nails.
Appears in hyperborean fkies,
To tell the world the bible lies.
See him on green hills north afar
Glow like a felf-enkindled ftar,
Prepar'd (with mob-colleding club
Black from the forge of Belzebub,
And grim with metaphyfic fcowl,
With quill juft pluck'd from wing of owl)
As rage cr reafon rife or fink
To fhed his blood, or fhed his ink.
Behold infpired from Vermont dens,
The feer of Antichrift defcends,
To feed new mobs with Hell-born manna
In Gentile lands of Sufquehanna;
And teach the Pennfylvania quaker
High blafphemies againft his maker.
Behold him move ye ftaunch divines!
His tall head buftling through the pines;
All front he feems like wall of brafs,
And brays tremendous as an afs;
One hand is clench'd to batter nofes,
While t'other fcrawls 'gainft Paul and Mofes.

AN ORATION,

Which might have been delivered to the Students in Ana-
tomy, on the late Rupture between the two Schools in
this city.*

THE ARGUMENT.

*ADDRESS—the folly and danger of diffention—the Orator
enumerates the enemies of the fraternity—reminds them
of a late unfeafonable interruption—a night fcene in the
Potter's Field---he laments the want of true zeal in the
brotherhood --and boafts of his own---the force of a ruling
paffion---the earth confidered as a great animal---the paffion of love not the fame in a true fon of Efculapius as in
other men---his own amour---a picture of his miftrefs in
high tafte---fhews his learning in the defcription of her
mouth, arm and hand---his miftrefs dies---his grief---and
extraordinary confolation---his unparallel'd fidelity----he
apologizes for giving this hiftory of his amour---the great
difficulties Anatomifts have to encounter in the prefent times,
arifing from falfe delicacy, prejudice and ignorance---a
ftrong inftance in proof that it was not fo formerly---curi-
ous argument to prove the inconfiftency of the prefent opinions refpecting the practice---he mentions many obftacles
in the road to fcience---and reproaches them for their inteftine broils, at a time when not only popular clamour is
loud, but even the powers of government are exerted againft
them---he then encourages his brethren with hopes of better
times, founded on the eftablifhment of the College of Phyfi-
cians---is infpired with the idea of the future glory of that
inftitution---and prophefies great things.*

FRIENDS and affociates! lend a patient ear,
  Sufpend inteftine broils and reafon hear.
Ye followers of F—— your wrath forbear—
Ye fons of S—— your invectives fpare;

* This Poem is afcribed to the late Hon. Francis Hopkinfon, Efq. L. L. D. Federal Judge for the Diftrict of Penn-

The fierce diffention your high minds purfue
Is fport for others—ruinous to you.

Surely fome fatal influenza reigns,
Some epidemic *rabies* turns your brains—
Is this a time for brethren to engage
In public conteft and in party rage?
Fell difcord triumphs in your doubtful ftrife
And, fmiling, whets her anatomic knife;
Prepar'd to cut our precious limbs away
And leave the bleeding body to decay.—

Seek ye for foes!—alas, my friends, look round,
In ev'ry ftreet, fee num'rous foes abound!
Methinks I hear them cry, in varied tones,
" Give us our father's,—brother's,—fifter's bones."
Methinks I fee a mob of failor's rife—
Revenge!—Revenge! they cry—and damn their eyes—

NOTE,---*continued.*

fylvania, &c. &c.—The occafion of its being written, was
this: A Difpute arofe between the Medical Students who
had attached themfelves to two Anatomical Profeffors, in
the city of Philadelphia. This Difpute was carried on for
a confiderable time, and with great violence. Refolutions
of Committees,—Journals of Meetings,—&c. &c. were
printed; and the town was threatened with a deluge of un-
interefting publications. In this fituation of affairs, Dr.
Hopkinfon took up the pen; and by the well-tim'd raillery
of the following Poem, filenced the contending parties, re-
ftored peace to the Schools, and agreeably entertained the
Lovers of Poetry and Humour.—This Poem is reprinted
from the 4to edition, publifhed by T. Dobfon and T. Lang,
February 1789.

Revenge for comrade Jack, whose flesh, they say,
You mince'd to morsels and then threw away.
Methinks I see a black infernal train—
The genuine offspring of accursed *Cain*—
Fiercely on you their angry looks are bent,
They grin and gibber dangerous discontent,
And seem to say,—" Is there not meat enough?
" Ah! massa cannibal, why eat poor CUFF?"
Ev'n hostile watchmen stand in strong array
And o'er our heads their threat'ning staves display,
Howl hideous discord thro' the noon of night,
And shake their dreadful lanthorns in our sight.

   Say, are not these sufficient to engage
Your high wrought souls eternal war to wage?
Combine your strength these monsters to subdue
No friends of science, and sworn foes to you;
On these,—on these your wordy vengeance pour,
And strive our fading glory to restore.

   Ah! think how, late, our mutilated rites
And midnight orgies, were by sudden frights
And loud alarms profan'd—the sacrifice,
Stretch'd on a board before our eager eyes,
All naked lay—ev'n when our chieftain stood
Like a high priest, prepar'd for shedding blood;
Prepar'd, with wondrous skill, to cut or flash
The gentle sliver or the deep drawn gash;
Prepar'd to plunge ev'n elbow deep in gore
Nature and nature's secrets to explore——
Then a tumultuous cry—a sudden fear—
Proclaim'd the foe—the enraged foe is near—

                    W.

In fome dark hole the hard got corfe was laid,
And we, in wild confufion, fled difmay'd.

Think how, like brethren, we have fhar'd the toil,
When in the Potter's Field* we fought for fpoil;
Did midnight ghofts, and death, and horror, brave,
To delve for fcience in the dreary grave.
Shall I remind you of that awful night
When our compacted band maintain'd the fight
Againft an armed hoft?—fierce was the fray,
And yet we bore our fheeted prize away.
Firm on a horfe's back the corfe was laid,
High blowing winds the winding fheet difplay'd;
Swift flew the fteed—but fill his burthen bore—
Fear made him fleet, who ne'er was fleet before;
O'er tombs and funken graves he cours'd around,
Nor ought refpected confecrated ground.
Mean time the battle rag'd—fo loud the ftrife,
The dead were almoft frighten'd into life;
Tho' not victorious, yet we fcorn'd to yield,
Retook our prize, and left the doubtful field.

In this degen'rate age, alas! how few
The paths of fcience with true zeal purfue?
Some trifling conteft, fome delufive joy,
Too oft the unfteady minds of youth employ.
For me—whom ESCULAPIUS hath infpir'd—
I boaft a foul with love of fcience fir'd;
By one great object is my heart poffeft;
One ruling paffion quite abforbs the reft;

_____

* The Negro burial ground.

In this bright point my hopes and fears unite,
And one purfuit alone can give delight.

To me things are not as to vulgar eyes,
I would all nature's works anatomize:
This world a living monfter feems, to me,
Rolling and fporting in the aerial fea;
The foil encompaffes her rocks and ftones
As flefh in animals encircles bones.
I fee vaft ocean, like a heart in play,
Pant *fyftole* and *diaftole* ev'ry day,
And by unnumber'd *venus* ftreams fupply'd
Up her broad rivers force the *arterial* tide.
The world's great lungs, monfoons and trade-winds fhew
From eaft to weft, from weft to eaft they blow
Alternate refpiration——
The hills are pimples which earth's face defile,
And burning *Ætna*, an eruptive boil:
On her high mountains *hairy* forefts grow,
And *downy* grafs o'erfpreads the vales below;
From her vaft body perfpirations rife,
Condenfe in clouds and float beneath the fkies.
Thus fancy, faithful fervant of the heart,
Transforms all nature by her magic art.

Ev'n mighty LOVE, whofe power all power controuls,
Is not, in me, like love in other fouls;
Yet I have lov'd---and CUPID's fubtle dart
Hath thro' my *pericardium* pierc'd my heart.
Brown CADAVERA did my foul enfnare,
Was all my thought by night, and daily care;
I long'd to clafp, in her tranfcendent charms,
A living fkeleton within my arms.

Long, lank and lean, my CADAVERA ſtood,
Like the tall pine, the glory of the wood ;
Ofttimes I gaz'd, with learned ſkill to trace
The ſharp edg'd beauties of her bony face :
There roſe *Os frontis* prominent and bold,
In deep ſunk *orbits* two large eye-balls roll'd,
Beneath thoſe eye-balls, two arch'd bones were ſeen
Whereon two flabby cheeks hung looſe and lean ;
Between thoſe cheeks, protuberant aroſe,
In form triangular, her lovely noſe,
Like EGYPT's pyramid it ſeem'd to riſe,
Scorn earth, and bid defiance to the ſkies ;
Thin were her lips, and of a ſallow hue,
Her open mouth expos'd her teeth to view ;
Projecting ſtrong, protuberant and wide
Stood *inciſores*- -and on either ſide
The *canine* rang'd, with many a beauteous flaw,
And laſt the *grinders*, to fill up the jaw ;
All in their *alveoli* fix'd ſecure,
Articulated by *gomphoſis* ſure.
Around her mouth perpetual ſmiles had made
Wrinkles wherein the loves and graces play'd ;
There, ſtretch'd and rigid by continual ſtrain,
Appear'd the *zygomatic* muſcles plain,
And broad *montanus* o'er her peeked chin
Extended, to ſupport the heavenly grin.
In amorous dalliance oft I ſtroak'd her arm,
Each riſing muſcle was a riſing charm.
O'er the *flexores* my fond fingers play'd,
I found inſtruction with delight convey'd ;

There *carpus*, *cubitus* and *radius* too
Were plainly felt and manifest to view.
No muscles on her lovely hand were seen,
But only bones envelop'd by a skin.
Long were her fingers and her knuckles bare,
Much like the claw-foot of a walnut chair.
So plain was complex *matacarpus* shewn,
It might be fairly counted bone by bone.
Her slender *phalanxes* were well defin'd,
And each with each by *ginglymus* combin'd.
Such were the charms that did my fancy fire,
And love...chaste scientific love inspire.

At length my CADAVERA fell beneath
The fatal stroke of all subduing death:
Three days in grief...three nights in tears I spent,
And sighs incessant gave my sorrows vent.

Few are the examples of a love so true...
Ev'n from her death I consolation drew,
And in a secret hour approach'd her grave,
Resolv'd her precious corse from worms to save;
With active haste remov'd the incumbent clay,
Seiz'd the rich prize and bore my love away.

Her naked charms now lay before my sight,
I gaz'd with rapture and supreme delight,
Nor could forbear, in extasy, to cry...
Beneath that shrivell'd skin what treasures lie!
Then feasted to the full my amorous soul,
And skinn'd, and cut, and slash'd without controul.

'Twas then I saw, what long I'd wish'd to see,
That heart which panted oft for love and me...

In detail view'd the form I once ador'd,
And nature's hidden myfteries explor'd.

Alas! too truly did the wife man fay
That flefh is grafs, and fubject to decay:
Not fo the bones; of fubftance firm and hard,
Long they remain the Anatomift's reward.
Wife nature, in her providential care,
Did, kindly, bones from vile corruption fpare,
That fons their fathers' fkeletons might have,
And heaven-born fcience triumph o'er the grave.

My true love's bones I boil'd---from fat and lean
Thefe hands induftrious fcrap'd them fair and clean,
And ev'ry bone did to its place reftore,
As Nature's hand had plac'd them long before:
Thefe fingers twifted ev'ry pliant wire
With patient fkill, urg'd on by ftrong defire.
Now what remains of CADAVERA's mine,
Securely hanging in a cafe of pine.

Ofttimes I fit and contemplate her charms,
Her nodding fkull and her long dangling arms,
'Till quite inflam'd with paffion for the dead,
I take her beauteous fkeleton to bed;
There ftretch'd, at length, clofe to my faithful fide
She lies all night,---a lovely, grinning bride.——

Excufe, my friends, this detail of my love,
You muft the intent, if not the tale, approve;
By facts exemplary I meant to fhew
To what extent a genuine zeal will go.

A mind, fo fix'd, will not be drawn afide
By vain diffentions or a partial pride;
But ev'ry hoftile fentiment fubdue,
And keep the ruling paffion ftill in view.

Falfe delicacy---prejudices ftrong,
Which no diftinctions know 'twixt right and wrong,
Againft our noble fcience fpend their rage,
And mark the ignorance of this vulgar age.

Time was, when men their living flefh would fpare,
And to the knife their quiv'ring *nates* bare,
That fkilful furgeons† nofes might obtain
For nofes loft---and cut and come again;---
But now the *living* churlifhly refufe
To give their dead relations to our ufe;
Talk of decorum---and a thoufand whims---
Whene'er we hack their wives' or daughters' limbs;
And yet their tables daily they fupply
With the rich fruits of fad mortality;
Will pick, and gut, and cook a chicken's corfe,
Diffect and eat it up, without remorfe;
Devouring fifh, flefh, fowl, whatever comes,
Nor fear the ghofts of murder'd hecatombs.

Now where's the difference?---to the impartial eye
A leg of mutton and a human thigh
Are juft the fame: for furely all muft own
Flefh is but flefh, and bone is only bone;
And tho' indeed, fome flefh and bone may grow ⎫
To make a monkey---fome to make a beau, ⎬
Still the materials are the fame, we know. ⎭

---

* TALIACOTIUS.

Nor can our anatomic knowledge trace
Internal marks diſtinctive of our race....

Whence, then, theſe loud complaints---theſe hoſts of foes
Combin'd, our uſeful labours to oppoſe?
How long ſhall ſooliſh prejudices reign?
And wnen ſhall reaſon her juſt empire gain?

Ah! full of danger is the up-hill road,
That leads the youth to learning's high abode:
His way thick miſts of vulgar errors blind,
And ſneering ſatire follows cloſe behind;
Sour envy ſtrews the rugged path with thorns,
And lazy ignorance his labour ſcorns.

Is this a time, ye brethren of the knife,
For civil conteſt and internal ſtrife?
When loud againſt us gen'ral clamours cry,
And perſecution lifts her laſh on high?
When government---that many headed beaſt---
Againſt our practice rears her horrid creſt,
And, our nocturnal acceſs to oppoſe,
Around the dead a penal barrier* throws?
To cruſh our ſchools her awful pow'r applies,
And ev'n forbids the gibbet's juſt ſupplies.†

Yet in this night of darkneſs, ſtorms and fears,
Behold one bright benignant ſtar‡ appears---

---

* A Law paſt at New-York, making it penal to ſteal
bodies from the burial ground.

† The wheel-barrow law of Pennſylvania.

‡ The Medical College.

Long may it shine, and, e'er it's course is run,
Increase, in size and splendour, to a sun!---
Methinks I see this sun of future days,
Spread far abroad his *diplomatic* rays---
See life and health submit to his controul,
And, like a planet, *death* around him roll.

Methinks I see a stately fabric rise,
Rear'd on the skulls of these our enemies;
I see the bones of our invet'rate foes
Hang round it's walls in scientific rows.
There solemn sit the learned of the day
Dispensing death with uncontrouled sway,
And by *prescription* regulate with ease
The sudden crisis or the slow disease.

Then shall physicians their millennium find,
And reign the real sov'reigns of mankind:
Then shall the face of this vile world be chang'd,
And nature's healthful laws all new arrang'd---
In min'ral powders all her dust shall rise,
And all her insects shall be Spanish flies:
In medicated potions streams shall flow,
Pills fall in hail-storms, and sharp salts in snow;
In ev'ry quagmire boluses be found,
And slimy cataplasms spread the ground---
Nature herself assume the chymist's part,
And furnish poisons unsublim'd by art.

*Then to our schools shall wealth in currents flow,
Our theatres no want of subjects know;
Nor laws nor mobs th' Anatomist shall dread,
For graves shall freely render up their dead.

X.

PHILOSOPHIC SOLITUDE.

BY WILLIAM LIVINGSTON, ESQ.
Late Governor of the State of New-Jersey, &c. &c.

LET ardent heroes seek renown in arms,
 Pant after fame, and rush to war's alarms ;
To shining palaces let fools resort,
And dunces cringe, to be esteem'd at court :
Mine be the pleasure of a rural life,
From noise remote, and ignorant of strife ;
Far from the painted belle, and white-glov'd beau,
The lawless masquerade, and midnight show :
From ladies, lap-dogs, courtiers, garters, stars,
Fops, fidlers, tyrants, emperors, and czars.

Full in the centre of some shady grove,
By nature form'd for solitude and love ;
On banks array'd with ever-blooming flowers,
Near beauteous landscapes, or by roseate bowers,
My neat, but simple mansion I would raise,
Unlike the sumptuous domes of modern days ;
Devoid of pomp, with rural plainness form'd,
With savage game, and glossy shells adorn'd.

No costly furniture should grace my hall ;
But curling vines ascend against the wall,
Whose pliant branches should luxuriant twine,
While purple clusters swell'd with future wine :
To slake my thirst a liquid lapse distil
From craggy rocks, and spread a limpid rill.

Along my manfion, fpiry firs fhould grow,
And gloomy yews extend the fhady row :
The cedars flourifh, and the poplars rife,
Sublimely tall, and fhoot into the fkies :
Among the leaves, refrefhing zephyrs play,
And crouding trees exclude the noon-tide ray ;
Whereon the birds their downy nefts fhould form,
Securely fhelter'd from the battering ftorm ;
And to melodious notes their choir apply,
Soon as Aurora blufh'd along the fky :
While all around th' enchanting mufic rings,
And ev'ry vocal grove refponfive fings.

 Me to fequefter'd fcenes ye mufes guide,
Where nature wantons in her virgin pride ;
To moffy banks, edg'd round with op'ning flowers,
Elyfian fields and amaranthine bowers,
To ambrofial founts, and fleep-infpiring rills, -
To herbag'd vales, gay lawns, and funny hills.

 Welcome, ye fhades ! all hail, ye vernal blooms !
Ye bow'ry thickets, and prophetic glooms !
Ye forefts, hail ! ye folitary woods !
Love-whifpering groves, and filver-ftreaming floods :
Ye meads, that aromatic fweets exhale !
Ye birds, and all ye fylvan beauties, hail !
Oh how I long with you to fpend my days,
Invoke the mufe, and try the rural lays !

 No trumpets there with martial clangor found,
No proftrate heroes ftrew the crimfon ground ;
No groves of lances glitter in the air,
Nor thund'ring drums provoke the fanguine war :

But white-rob'd Peace, and univerfal Love
Smile in the field, and brighten ev'ry grove:
There all the beauties of the circling year,
In native ornamental pride appear.
Gay, rofy-bofom'd Spring, and April fhow'rs,
Wake, from the womb of earth, the rifing flow'rs:
In deeper verdure, Summer clothes the plain,
And Autumn bends beneath the golden grain;
The trees weep amber; and the whifpering gales
Breeze o'er the lawn, or murmur through the vales:
The flow'ry tribes in gay confufion bloom,
Profufe with fweets, and fragrant with perfume;
On bloffoms bloffoms, fruits on fruits arife,
And varied profpects glad the wand'ring eyes.
In thefe fair feats, I'd pafs the joyous day,
Where meadows flourifh, and where fields look gay;
From blifs to blifs with endlefs pleafure rove,
Seek cryftal ftreams, or haunt the vernal grove,
Woods, fountains, lakes, the fertile fields, or fhades,
Aerial mountains, or fubjacent glades.
There from the polifh'd fetters of the great,
Triumphal piles, and gilded rooms of ftate...
Prime minifters, and fycophantic knaves,
Illuftrious villains, and illuftrious flaves,
From all the vain formality of fools,
And odious tafk of arbitrary rules;
The ruffling cares, which the vex'd foul annoy,
The wealth the rich poffefs, but not enjoy,
The vifionary blifs the world can lend,
Th' infidious foe, and falfe, defigning friend,
The feven-fold fury of Xantippe's foul,
And S.——'s rage, that burns without controul:

I'd live retir'd, contented, and ferene,
Forgot, unknown, unenvied, and unfeen.

Yet not a real hermitage I'd choofe,
Nor wifh to live from all the world reclufe;
But with a friend fometimes unbend the foul,
In focial converfe, o'er the fprightly bowl.
With cheerful W——, ferene and wifely gay,
I'd often pafs the dancing hours away:
He, fkill'd alike to profit and to pleafe,
Politely talks with unaffected eafe;
Sage in debate, and faithful to his truft,
Mature in fcience, and feverely juft;
Of foul diffufive, vaft and unconfin'd,
Breathing benevolence to all mankind;
Cautious to cenfure, ready to commend,
A firm, unfhaken, uncorrupted friend;
In early youth, fair wifdom's paths he trod,
In early youth, a minifter of God,
Each pupil lov'd him, when at Yale he fhone,
And ev'ry bleeding bofom weeps him gone.
Dear A—— too, fhould grace my rural feat,
Forever welcome to the green retreat:
Heav'n for the caufe of righteoufnefs defign'd
His florid genius, and capacious mind:
Oft have I heard, amidft th' adorning throng,
Celeftial truths devolving from his tongue:
High o'er the lift'ning audience feen him ftand,
Divinely fpeak, and graceful ftretch his hand;
With fuch becoming grace and pompous found,
With long-rob'd fenators encircled round,

Before the Roman bar, while Rome was free,
Nor bow'd to Cæfar's throne the fervile knee,
Immortal Tulley plea'd the patriot caufe,
While ev'ry tongue refounded his applaufe.
Next round my board fhould candid S—— appear,
Of manners gentle, and a friend fincere,
Averfe to difcord, party-rage and ftrife,
He fails ferenely down the ftream of life.
With thefe three friends, beneath a fpreading fhade,
Where filver fountains murmur thro' the glade ;
Or in cool grots, perfu'n'd with native flow'rs,
In harmlefs mirth, I'd fpend the circling hours ;
Or gravely talk, or innocently fing,
Or, in harmonious concert, ftrike the trembling ftring.

   Amid fequefter'd bow'rs, near gliding ftreams,
Druids and bards enjoy'd fereneft dreams.
Such was the feat where courtly Horace fung,
And his bold harp immortal Maro ftrung :
Where tuneful Orpheus' unrefifted lay
Made rapid tigers bear their rage away :
While groves, attentive to th' extatic found,
Burft from their roots, and, raptur'd, danc'd around.
Such feats the venerable feers of old
(When blifsful years in golden circles roll'd)
Chofe and admir'd : e'en goddeffes and gods
(As poets feign) were fond of fuch abodes :
Th' imperial confort of fictitious Jove
For fount-full Ide forfook the realms above.
Oft to Idalia, on a golden cloud,
Veil'd in a mift of fragrance, Venus rode :

There num'rous altars to the queen were rear'd,
And love-fick youths their am'rous vows prefer'd,
While fair-hair'd damfels (a lafcivious train)
With wanton rites ador'd her gentle reign.
The filver-fhaft d huntrefs of the woods,
Sought pendant fhades, and bath'd in cooling floods.
In palmy Delos by Scamander's fide,
Or where Cajifter roll'd his filver tide,
Melodious Phœbus fang; the mufes round
Alternate warbling to the heavenly found.
E'en the feign'd monarch of heav'n's bright abode,
High thron'd in gold, of gods the fov'reign god,
Oft time prefer'd the fhade of Ida's grove
To all th' ambrofial feafts, and nectar'd cups above.

Behold, the rofy-finger'd morning dawn,
In faffron rob d, and blufhing o'er the lawn !
Reflected from the clouds, a radiant ftream
Tips with etherial dew the mountain's brim.
Th' unfolding rofes, and the op'ning flow'rs
Imbibe the dew, and ftrew the varied bow'rs,
Diffufe nectareous fweets around, and glow
With all the colours of the fhow'ry bow.
Th' induftrious bees their balmy toil renew,
Buz o'er the field, and fip the rofy dew.
But yonder comes th' iluftrious god of day,
Invefts the eaft, and gilds th' etherial way ;
The groves rejoice, the feather'd nations fing,
Echo the mountains, and the vallies ring.

Hail, orb ! array'd with majefty and fire,
That bids each fable fhade of night retire !

Fountain of light ! with burning glory crown'd,
Darting a deluge of effulgence round !
Wak'd by thy genial and prolific ray,
Nature refumes her verdure, and looks gay :
Frefh blooms the rofe, the drooping plants revive,
The groves reflourifh, and the forefts live.
Deep in the teeming earth, the rip'ning ore
Confeffes thy confolidating pow'r ;
Hence Labour draws her tools, and artifts mould
The fufile filver and the ductile gold ;
Hence war is furnifh'd ; and the regal fhield
Like light'ning flafhes o'er th' illumin'd field.
If thou fo fair with delegated light,
That all heav'n's fplendors vanifh at thy fight ;
With what effulgence muft the ocean glow,
From which thy borrow'd beams inceffant flow !
Th' exhauftlefs fource whofe fingle fmile fupplies
Th' unnumber'd orbs that gild the fpangled fkies !

 Oft' would I view, in admiration loft,
Heav'n's fumptuous canopy, and ftarry hoft ;
With level'd tube, and aftronomic eye,
Purfue the planets whirling thro' the fky :
Immeafurable vault ! where thunders roll,
And forky lightnings flafh from pole to pole.
Say, railing infidel ! canft thou furvey
Yon globe of fire, that gives the golden day,
The harmonious ftructure of this vaft machine,
And not confefs its architect divine !
Then go, vain wretch ! tho' deathlefs be thy foul,
Go, fwell the riot, and exhauft the bowl ;

Plunge into vice—humanity refign—
Go fill the ftie—and briftle into fwine !

None but a pow'r omnipotent and wife
Could frame this earth, or fpread the boundlefs fkies :
He made the whole ; at his omnific call,
From formlefs chaos rofe this fpacious ball,
And one Almighty God is feen in all.
By him our cup is crown'd, our table fpread
With lufcious wine, and life-fuftaining bread.
What countlefs wonders doth the earth contain !
What countlefs wonders the unfathom'd main !
Bedrop'd with gold, there fcaly nations fhine,
Haunt coral groves, or lafh the foaming brine.
Jehovah's glories blaze all nature round,
In heaven, on earth, and in the deeps profound ;
Ambitious of his name, the warblers fing,
And praife their maker, while they hail the fpring ;
The zephyrs breathe it ; and the thunders roar,
While furge to furge, and fhore refounds to fhore.
But man, endu'd with an immortal mind,
His Maker's image, and for heaven defign'd,
To loftier notes his raptur'd voice fhould raife,
And chaunt fublimer hymns to his Creator's praife.

When rifing Phœbus ufhers in the morn,
And golden beams th' impurpled fkies adorn ;
Wak'd by the gentle-murmur of the floods,
Or the foft mufic of the waving woods ;
Rifing from fleep with the melodious quire,
To folemn founds I'd tune the hallow'd lyre.

Y

Thy name, O God! fhould tremble on my tongue,
Till ev'ry grove prov'd vocal to my fong:
(Delightful tafk! with dawning light to fing
Triumphant hymns to heav'n's eternal king.)
Some courteous angel fhould my breaft infpire,
Attune my lips, and guide the warbled wire,
While fportive echoes catch the facred found,
Swell ev'ry note, and bear the mufic round;
While mazy ftreams meand'ring to the main,
Hang in fufpence to hear the heav'nly ftrain,
And, hufh'd to filence, all the feather'd throng
Attentive liften to the tuneful fong.

    Father of light! exahuftlefs fource of good!
Supreme, eternal, felf-exiftent God!
Before the beamy fun difpens'd a ray,
Flam'd in the azure vault, and gave the day;
Before the glimm'ring moon, with borrow'd light,
Shone queen amid the filver hoft of night;
High in the heav'ns, thou reign'dft fuperior Lord,
By fuppliant angels worfhip'd and ador'd.
With the celeftial choir then let me join
In cheerful praifes to the pow'r divine.
To fing thy praife, do thou, O God! infpire
A mortal breaft with more than mortal fire:
In dreadful majefty thou fit'ft enthron'd,
With light encircled, and with glory crown'd;
Thro' all infinitude extends thy reign,
For thee, nor heav'n, nor heav'n of heav'ns contain;
But tho' thy throne is fix'd above the fky,
Thy omniprefence fills immenfity.

Saints, rob'd in white, to thee their anthems bring,
And radiant martyrs hallelujahs sing :
Heaven's univerfal hoft their voices raife
In one eternal chorus, to thy praife ;
And, round thy awful throne, with one accord,
Sing, holy, holy, holy is the Lord.
At thy creative voice, from ancient night,
Sprang fmiling beauty, and yon worlds of light :
Thou fpak'ft—the planetary chorus roll'd,
And all th' expanfe was ftarr'd with beamy gold ;
Let there be light, faid God—light inftant fhone,
And from the orient, burft the golden fun ;
Heav'n's gazing hierarchs, with glad furprife,
Saw the firft morn inveft the recent fkies,
And ftrait th' exulting troops thy throne furround
With thoufand thoufand harps of heav'nly found :
Thrones, powers, dominions, (ever fhining trains !)
Shouted thy praifes in triumphant ftrains :
Great are thy works, they fing ; and, all around,
Great are thy works, the echoing heav'ns refound.
The effulgent fun, infufferably bright,
Is but a beam of thy o'erflowing light ;
The tempeft is thy breath : the thunder hurl'd,
Tremendous roars thy vengeance o'er the world ;
Thou bow'ft the heav'ns, the fmoking mountains nod,
Rocks fall to duft, and nature owns her God ;
Pale tyrants fhrink, the atheift ftands aghaft,
And impious kings in horror breathe their laft.
To this great God alternately I'd pay
The ev'ning anthem, and the morning lay.

For fov'reign gold I never would repine,
Nor with the glitt ring duft of monarchs mine.
What tho' high columns heave into the fkies,
Gay cielings fhine, and vaulted arches rife?
Tho' fretted gold the fculptur'd roof adorn,
The rubies redden, and the jafpers burn!
O what, alas! avails the gay attire
To wretched man, who breathes but to expire!
Oft' on the vileft, riches are beftow'd,
To fhow their meannefs in the fight of God.
High from a dunghill, fee a Dives rife,
And, Titan-like, infult th' avenging fkies:
The crowd, in adulation, calls him Lord,
By thoufands'courted, flatter d and ador'd:
In riot plung'd, and drunk with earthly joys,
No higher thought his grov'ling foul employs:
The poor he fcourges with an iron rod,
And from his bofom banifhes his God.
But oft' in height of wealth and beauty's bloom,
Deluded man is fated to the tomb!
For, lo! he fickens; fwift his colour flies,
And rifing mifts obfcure his fwimming eyes:
Around his bed his weeping friends bemoan,
Extort the unwilling tear, and wifh him gone;
His forrowing heir augments the tender fhow'r,
Deplores his death—yet hails the dying hour.
Ah bitter comfort! Sad relief! to die,
Tho' funk in down, beneath the canopy!
His eyes no more fhall fee the cheerful light,
Weigh'd down by death in everlafting night,
And now the great, the rich, the proud, the gay,
Lie breathlefs, cold—unanimated clay!

He, that juſt now was flatter'd by the crowd
With high applauſe, and acclamations loud—
That ſteel'd his boſom to the orphan's cries,
And drew down torrents from the widow s eyes—
Whom, like a God, the rabble did adore—
Regard him now—and, lo! he is no more.

My eyes no dazzling veſtments ſhould behold,
With gems inſtarr d, and ſtiff with woven gold ;
But the tall ram his downy fleece afford,
To clothe, in modeſt garb, his frugal lord.
Thus the great Father of mankind was dreſt,
When ſhaggy hides compos'd his flowing veſt ;
Doom'd to the cumbrous load, for his offence,
When clothes ſupply'd the want of innocence :
But now his ſons (forgetful whence they came)
Glitter in gems, and glory in their ſhame.

Oft' would I wander thro' the dewy field,
Where cluſt'ring roſes balmy fragrance yield :
Or in lone grots, for contemplation made,
Converſe with angels and the mighty dead ;
For all around unnumber d ſpirits fly,
Waft on the breeze, or walk the liquid ſky,
Inſpire the poet with repeated dreams,
Who gives his hallow'd muſe to ſacred themes,
Protect the juſt, ſerene their gloomy hours,
Becalm their ſlumbers, and refreſh their pow'rs.
Methinks I ſee th' immortal beings fly,
And ſwiftly ſhoot athwart the ſtreaming ſky :
Hark! a melodious voice I ſeem to hear,
And heav'nly ſounds invade my liſt'ning ear !

" Be not afraid of us, innoxious band,
" Thy cell furrounding by divine command;
" Ere while, like thee, we led our lives below,
" (Sad lives of pain, of mifery, and woe!)
" Long by afflicion's boift'rous tempefts toft,
" We reach'd at length the ever blifsful coaft:
" Now in th' embow'ring groves, and lawns above,
" We tafte the raptures of immortal love,
" Attune the golden harp in rofeate bow'rs,
" Or bind our temples with unfading flow'rs.
" Oft' on kind errands bent, we cut the air,
" To guard the righteous, heav'n's peculiar care!
" Avert impending harms, their minds compofe,
" Infpire gay dreams, and prompt their foft repofe.
" When from thy tongue divine hofannas roll,
" And facred raptures fwell thy rifing foul,
" To heav'n we bear thy pray'rs, like rich perfumes;
" Where, by the throne, the golden cenfer fumes;
" And when with age thy head is filver'd o'er,
" And, cold in death, thy bofom beats no more,
" Thy foul, exulting, fhall defert its clay,
" And mount, triumphant, to eternal day."

But to improve the intellectual mind,
Reading fhould be to contemplation join'd.
Firft I'd collect from the Parnaffian fpring,
What mufes dictate, and what poets fing.—
Virgil, as prince, fhou'd wear the laurel'd crown,
And other bards pay homage to his throne;
The blood of heroes now effus'd fo long,
Will run forever purple thro' his fong,

See ! how he mounts toward the bleft abodes,
On planets rides, and talks with demigods !
How do our ravifh'd fpirits melt away,
When in his fong Sicilian fhepherds play !
But what a fplendor ftrikes the dazzled eye,
When Dido fhines in awful majefty !
Embroidered purple clad the Tyrian queen,
Her motion graceful, and auguft-her mien ;
A golden zone her royal limbs embrac'd,
A golden quiver rattled by her waift.
See her proud fteed majeftically prance,
Contemn the trumpet, and deride the launce !
In crimfon trappings, glorious to behold,
Confus'dly gay with interwoven gold !
He champs the bit, and throws the foam around,
Impatient paws, and tears the folid ground.
How ftern Æneas thunders thro' the field !
With tow'ring helmet, and refulgent fhield !
Courfers o'erturn'd, and mighty warriors flain,
Deform'd with gore, lie welt'ring on the plain,
Struck through with wounds, ill-fated chieftains lie,
Frown e'en in death, and threaten as they die.
Thro' the thick fquadrons fee the hero bound !
(His helmet flafhes, and his arms refound !)
All grim with rage, he frowns o'er Turnus' head,
(Re-kindled ire ! for blooming Pallas dead)
Then in his bofom plung'd the fhining blade—
The foul indignant fought the Stygian fhade !

    The far-fam'd bards that grac'd Britannia's ifle,
Should next compofe the venerable pile.

Great Milton firſt, for tow'ring thought renown'd,
Parent of ſong, and fam'd the world around!
His glowing breaſt divine Urania fir'd,
Or God himſelf th' immortal bard inſpir'd,
Borne on triumphant wings he takes his flight,
Explores all heaven, and treads the realms of light:
In martial pomp he clothes th' angelic train,
While warring myriads ſhake the etherial plain.
Firſt Michael ſtalks, high tow'ring o'er the reſt,
With heav'nly plumage nodding on his creſt:
Impenetrable arms his limbs infold,
Eternal adamant, and burning gold!
Sparkling in fiery mail, with dire delight,
Rebellious Satan animates the fight:
Arm.potent they ſink in rolling ſmoke,
All heav'n reſounding, to its centre ſhook.
To cruſh his foes, and quell the dire alarms,
Meſſiah ſparkled in refulgent arms:
In radiant panoply divinely bright,
His limbs incas'd, he flaſh'd devouring light:
On burning wheels, o'er heav'n's cryſtalline road
Thunder'd the chariot of the filial God;
The burning wheels on golden axles turn'd,
With flaming gems the golden axles burn'd.
Lo! the apoſtate hoſt, with terror ſtruck,
Roll back by millions! Th' empyrean ſhook!
Sceptres, and orbed ſhields, and crowns of gold,
Cherubs and ſeraphs in confuſion roll'd;
Till from his hand the triple thunder hurl'd,
Compell'd them, head-long, to th' infernal world.

Then tuneful Pope, whom all the nine infpire,
With fapphic fweetnefs, and pindaric fire,
Father of verfe ! melodious and divine !
Next peerlefs Milton fhould diftinguifh'd fhine.
Smooth flow his numbers, when he paints the grove,
Th' enraptur'd virgins lift'ning into love.
But when the night, and hoarfe-refounding ftorm
Rufh on the deep, and Neptune's face deform,
Rough runs the verfe, the fon'rous numbers roar,
Like the hoarfe furge that thunders on the fhore.
But when he fings th' exhilirated fwains,
Th' embow'ring groves, and Windfor's blifsful plains,
Our eyes are ravifh'd with the fylvan fcene,
Embroider'd fields, and groves in living green ;
His lays the verdure of the meads prolong,
And wither'd forefts bloffom in his fong.
Thames' filver ftreams his flowing verfe admire,
And ceafe to murmur while he tunes his lyre.

   Next fhould appear great Dryden's lofty mufe,
For who would Dryden's polifh'd verfe refufe ?
His lips were moiften'd in Parnaffus' fpring,
And Phœbus taught his laureat fon to fing.
How long did Virgil untranflated moan,
His beauties fading, and his flights unknown ;
Till Dryden rofe, and, in exalted ftrain,
Re-fang the fortune of the god-like man !
Again the Trojan prince, with dire delight,
Dreadful in arms, demands the ling'ring fight;
Again Camilla glows with martial fire,
Drives armies back, and makes all Troy retire.

Z

With more than native luftre, Virgil fhines,
And gains fublimer heights in Dryden's lines.

The gentle Watts, who ftrings his filver lyre
To facred odes, and heav'n's all-ruling Sire;
Who fcorns th' applaufe of the licentious ftage,
And mounts yon fparkling worlds with hallow'd rage,
Compels my thoughts to wing th' heav'nly road,
And wafts my foul, exulting, to my God:
No fabled nine, harmonious bard! infpire
Thy raptur'd breaft with fuch feraphic fire;
But prompting angels warm thy boundlefs rage,
Direct thy thoughts, and animate thy page.
Bleft man! for fpotlefs fanctity rever'd,
Lov'd by the good, and by the guilty fear'd:
Bleft man! from gay, delufive fcenes remov'd,
Thy Maker loving, by thy Maker lov'd,
To God thou tun'ft thy confecrated lays,
Nor meanly blufh to fing Jehovah's praife.
Oh! did, like thee, each laurel'd bard delight
To paint Religion in her native light,
Not then with plays the lab'ring prefs would groan,
Nor Vice defy the pulpit and the throne;
No impious rhymers charm a vicious age,
Nor proftrate Virtue groan beneath their rage:
But themes divine in lofty numbers rife,
Fill the wide earth, and echo thro' the fkies.

These for delight. For profit I would read
The labour'd volumes of the learned dead.
Sagacious Locke, by Providence defign'd,
To exalt, inftruct, and rectify the mind.

The unconquerable fage* whom virtue fir'd,
And from the tyrant's lawlefs rage retir'd,
When victor Cæfar freed unhappy Rome
From Pompey's chains, to fubftitute his own.
Longinus, Livy, fam'd Thucydides,
Quintilian, Plato, and Demofthenes,
Perfuafive Tully, and Corduba's fage,†
Who fell by Nero's unrelenting rage ;
Him‡ whom ungrateful Athens doom'd to bleed,
Defpis'd when living, and deplor'd when dead.
Raleigh I'd read with ever frefh delight,
While ages paft rife prefent to my fight :
Ah man unbleft ! he foreign realms explor'd,
Then fell a victim to his country's fword !
Nor fhould great Derham pafs neglected by,
Obfervant fage ! to whofe deep-piercing eye,
Nature's ftupendous works expanded lie.
Nor he, Britannia, thy unmatch'd renown !
(Adjudg'd to wear the philofophic crown)
Who on the folar orb uplifted rode,
And fcann'd the unfathomable works of God !
Who bound the filver planets to their fpheres,
And trac'd the elliptic curve of blazing ftars !
Immortal Newton ; whofe illuftrious name
Will fhine on records of eternal fame.

By love directed, I would choofe a wife,
To improve my blifs, and eafe the load of life.

---

* Cato.   † Seneca.   ‡ Socrates.

Hail, wedlock! hail, inviolable tye!
Perpetual fountain of domeſtic joy!
Love, friendſhip, honour, truth, and pure delight
Harmonious mingle in the nuptial rite.
In Eden, firſt the holy ſtate began,
When perfect innocence diſtinguiſh'd man;
The human pair, the Almighty pontiff led,
Gay as the morning, to the bridal bed;
A dread ſolemnity the eſpouſals grac'd,
Angels the witneſſes, and God the prieſt!
All earth exulted on the nuptial hour,
And voluntary roſes deck'd the bow'r;
The joyous birds on every bloſſom'd ſpray,
Sung hymeneans to the important day,
While Philomela ſwell'd the ſpouſal ſong,
And Paradiſe with gratulation rung.

Relate, inſpiring muſe! where ſhall I find
A blooming virgin with an angel mind?
Unblemiſh'd as the white-rob'd virgin quire
That fed, O Rome! thy conſecrated fire?
By reaſon aw'd, ambitious to be good,
Averſe to vice, and zealous for her God?
Relate, in what bleſt region can I find
Such bright perfections in a female mind?
What phœnix-woman breathes the vital air
So greatly good, and ſo divinely fair?
Sure not the gay and faſhionable train,
Licentious, proud, immoral, and profane;
Who ſpend their golden hours in antic dreſs,
Malicious whiſpers, and inglorious eaſe.

Lo! round the board a shining train appears
In rosy beauty, and in prime of years!
This hates a flounce, and this a flounce approves,
This shows the trophies of her former loves;
Polly avers, that Sylvia dreſt in green,
When laſt at church the gaudy nymph was ſeen;
Chloe condemns her optics; and will lay
'Twas azure ſattin, interſtreak'd with grey;
Lucy, inveſted with judicial power,
Awards 'twas neither,—and the ſtrife is o'er.
Then parrots, lap dogs, monkeys, ſquirrels, beaux,
Fans, ribands, tuckers, patches, furbeloes,
In quick ſucceſſion, thro' their fancies run,
And dance inceſſant, on the flippant tongue.
And when, fatigu'd with ev'ry other ſport,
The belles prepare to grace the ſacred court,
They marſhal all their forces in array,
To kill with glances, and deſtroy in play.
Two ſkilful maids with reverential fear,
In wanton wreaths collect their ſilken hair;
Two paint their cheeks, and round their temples pour
The fragrant unguent, and the ambroſial ſhower;
One pulls the ſhape-creating ſtays; and one
Encircles round her waiſt the golden zone;
Not with more toil to improve immortal charms,
Strove Juno, Venus, and the queen of arms,
When Priam's ſon adjudg'd the golden prize,
To the refiſtleſs beauty of the ſkies.
At length, equip'd in Love's enticing arms,
With all that glitters, and with all that charms,

The ideal goddeſſes to church repair,
Peep thro' the fan, and mutter o'er a pray'r,
Or liſten to the organ's pompous ſound,
Or eye the gilded images around;
Or, deeply ſtudied in coquettiſh rules,
Aim wily glances at unthinking fools;
Or ſhow the lily hand with graceful air,
Or wound the fopling with a lock of hair:
And when the hated diſcipline is o'er,
And miſſes tortur'd with repent, no more,
They mount the pictur'd coach; and, to the play,
The celebrated idols hie away.

Not ſo the laſs that ſhould my joys improve,
With ſolid friendſhip, and connubial love:
A native bloom, with intermingled white,
Should ſet her features in a pleaſing light;
Like Helen fluſhing with unrival'd charms,
When raptur'd Paris darted in her arms.
But what, alas! avails a ruby cheek,
A downy boſom, or a ſnowy neck!
Charms ill ſupply the want of innocence,
Nor beauty forms intrinſic excellence:
But in her breaſt let moral beauties ſhine,
Supernal grace and purity divine:
Sublime her reaſon, and her native wit
Unſtrain'd with pedantry, and low conceit;
Her fancy lively, and her judgment free
From female prejudice and bigotry:
Averſe to idol pomp, and outward ſhow,
The flatt'ring coxcomb, and fantaſtic beau.

The fop's impertinence fhe fhould defpife,
Tho' forely wounded by her radiant eyes ;
But pay due rev'rence to the exalted mind,
By learning polifh'd, and by wit refin'd,
Who all her virtues, without guile, commends,
And all her faults as freely reprehends.
Soft Hymen's rites her paffion fhould approve,
And in her bofom glow the flames of love :
To me her foul, by facred friendfhip, turn,
And I, for her, with equal friendfhip burn :
In ev'ry ftage of life afford relief,
Partake my joys, and fympathize my grief ;
Unfhaken, walk in Virtue's peaceful road,
Nor bribe her Reafon to purfue the mode ;
Mild as the faint whofe errors are forgiv'n,
Calm as a veftal, and compos'd as heaven.
This be the partner, this the lovely wife,
That fhould embellifh and prolong my life,
A nymph ! who might a fecond fall infpire,
And fill a glowing cherub with defire !
With her I'd fpend the pleafurable day,
While fleeting minutes gayly danc'd away :
With her I'd walk, delighted, o'er the green,
Thro' ev'ry blooming mead, and rural fcene ;
Or fit in open fields damafk'd with flow'rs,
Or where cool fhades imbrown the noon-tide bow'rs.
Imparadis'd within my eager arms,
I'd reign the happy monarch of her charms ;
Oft' on her panting bofom would I lay,
And, in diffolving raptures melt away ;

Then lull'd, by nightingales, to balmy reſt,
My blooming fair ſhould ſlumber at my breaſt.

And when decrepid age (frail mortals' doom)
Should bend my wither d body to the tomb,
No warbling ſyrens ſhould retard my flight
To heavenly manſions of unclouded light.
Tho Death, with his imperial horrors crown'd,
Terrific grinn'd, and formidably frown'd,
Offences pardon'd and remitted ſin,
Should form a calm ſerenity within:
Bleſſing my natal and my mortal hour,
(My ſoul commited to the eternal pow'r)
Inexorable Death ſhould ſmile, for I
Who knew to live, would never fear to die.

DESCRIPTIVE LINES,

*Written at the requeſt of a Friend, upon the ſurrrounding
Proſpect from BEACON-HILL in BOSTON.*

BY PHILENIA, A LADY OF BOSTON.

FAR from this ſpot let ſportive FICTION hie,
    While rapt ATTENTION lifts her ſearching eye,
O'er CHARLESTOWN's *field* each hallow'd view explores,
Sees the *twin* rivers lave the purple ſhores,
Where the high ſoil diſdain'd the trembling flood,
And ſtain'd the white wave with *Britannia's* blood,

While the fierce blaze* its wafting vengeance pours,
Wraps the wide domes, and climbs the afcending towers,
The crimfon eye of frantic SLAUGHTER turn'd,
Where *valour* perifh'd, and where *vict'ry* mourn'd,
And kindred worth unboafting forrow fhed,
As deathlefs WARREN bow'd his patriot head.

Thy Temple, *Charles!* a new-rais'd Phœnix fhines,
Thy far fam'd bridge the fifter-city joins,
Whofe flame-tipt fpires reflect the folar ray,
And ftrew with ftars the azure robe of day;
Here varied MARTS one full EMPORIUM boaft,
Rich with the wealth of ev'ry foreign coaft;
How chang'd the fcene, fince round the dreary glade
The frowning foreft bent its murky fhade!
E'en on this fpot, with green favannas fpread,
Adorn'd by GENIUS, and by PLENTY fed,
The hungry *Savage* dafh'd the foaming flood,
Trac'd the blue rock, and fwept the weedy wood;
Our patient Sires the wild'ring region gain,
Bend the hard oak, the wat'ry valley drain,
'Till down the tide the moving foreft flows,
And where the *defart* howl'd, the polifh'd *City* rofe,
Whofe *crefcent* haven's lib'ral furface fmiles,
Clad in the verdure of unnumber'd ifles,
Where fcepter'd WILLIAM's mafly bulwarks ftand,
The *guard* and *glory* of the fceneful land.

Aa

---

* Alluding to the burning of Charleftown by the Britifh in 1775.

Yon orient heights† their rifted foreheads raife,
And claim the triumph of the VICTOR's praife;
Still lives the morn, when from thofe armed brows,
The SONS OF FREEDOM brav'd their *prifon'd* foes;
While o'er the deep the giant *Terror* bends,
Death's lifted arm his fable dart extends,
The *Dance*‡ no more its graceful charm fupplies,
No more the fcenes of *mimic nature* rife,
Thro' bleeding ranks the deathful dangers roll,
And peals of ruin fhake the foldier's foul;
For him no beauty decks the vernal fields,
But ev'ry breeze a more than winter yields,
Flight all his *hope,* and honor all his *care,*
The warlike Briton learns for once *to fear,*
To the bleak wave refigns his murm'ring hoft,
And quits the fullen fanguinary coaft.
So in the climes, where changeful feafons roll,
Ere threat'ning winter gains his full control,
While ruftling leaves in crumbling ruin lie,
Ting'd with the rainbow's variegated dye,
The *feather'd race* the howling ftorm forefee,
The barren meadow, and the naked tree;
Late to thofe fhores were all their joys confin'd,
Now death and hunger float in ev'ry wind,
With outftretch'd wing they fkim along the main,
And quit the Terrors of an hoftile plain.

---

† Dorchefter heights, the fortifying of which by **Gen-eral WASHINGTON** in March 1776, compelled the Britifh to evacuate the town.

‡ The Ball and the Drama formed the amufements of the Garrifon, during the fiege.

Let yon VAST FANE rear its ionic fide,
The boaft of art, the *great defgner's*|| pride;
There refts in filent cells the holy dead,
There weeping SCIENCE droops her widow'd head,
Since BOWDOIN fleeps, deaf to his country's praife,
Deaf to the heavenly poet's living lays.

What varied charms adorn the circling main,
The peopled ifthmus, and the velvet plain !
Here ruddy HEALTH the grateful foil divides,
There gen'rous COMMERCE cleaves the freighted tides.
How fweet the fragrance of the fylvan fcene,
The rofy arbor, and the bow'ry green !
At eve to climb the mountain's pendent brow,
While at its bafe the boiling waters flow,
See the low fun his rubied globe difplay,
And lean collected on the edge of day !
From cultur'd dales behold the high hills rife
With piny fummits, curtain'd by the fkies!
Down whofe green flopes, in all their pearly pride,
Thro' mantling flowers the glaffy riv'lets glide,
While the flocks whiten thro' the cottag'd vale,
And notes of mufic fill the fcented gale.

Like a new planet mid the vaft ferene,
Lo! rifing HARVARD fwells the extended fcene,
O'er diftant regions fpreads a ray divine,
Bids " other BOWDOINS other WINTHROPS fhine"!
Such QUEEN OF CITIES ! are thy rich demains,
And fuch the realm, where GODLIKE FREEDOM reigns!

|| The celebrated Architect, Mr. Harrifon.

O D E
To the President,
On his visiting the Northern States.

BY THE SAME.

THE Season sheds its mildest ray,
 O'er the blue waves the sun-beams play,
The bending harvest gilds the plain,
The tow'ring veffels prefs the main,
The ruddy ploughman quits his toil,
The pallid mifer leaves his spoil,
And grateful pæans hail the festive year,
Which bids *Columbia's* guardian God appear.

 Hence! DISAPPOINTMENT's anxious eye,
And pale AFFLICTION's ling'ring figh;
Let forrow from the brow be torn,
And ev'ry heart forget to mourn;
Let fmiles of peace their charms difplay
To grace this joy-devoted day,
And, where *that* arm preferv'd the peopled plain,
Shall mild Contentment hold her placid reign.

 Let " *white rob'd choirs*" in beauty gay
With lucid flowrets ftrew the way,
Let Lilachs fcent the purpled lawn,
And rofes emulate the dawn,
Let domes their circling honors fpread,
And wreaths entwine that glorious head;
To thee, GREAT WASHINGTON, each lyre be ftrung,
Thy matchlefs deeds by ev'ry bard be fung!

When FREEDOM rais'd her drooping head,
Thy arm her willing heros led,
When all her hopes, to thee refign'd,
Were refting on thy god-like mind,
How did that foul, to fear unknown,
And feeling for *her* fate alone,
O'er Danger's threat'ning form the faulchion wield,
And tread with dauntlefs ftep the crimfon field!

Not DECIUS—patriot dear to fame!
Not CINCINNATUS—deathlefs name!
Not HE,* who led the Athenian band,
The faviour of a bleeding land,
Could fuch exalted worth difplay,
Nor fhine with fuch unclouded ray.
Of *Age* the HOPE, of *Youth* the LEADING STAR,
The *Soul* of PEACE, the CONQUERING ARM OF WAR.

———————————

* THEMISTOCLES.

INVOCATION to HOPE.

BY THE SAME.

SOOTHER of Life! by whose delusive charm
   This feeling heart resists the pointed woe,
Whose magic power, with fancied joys can warm,
   And wipe the tear which Anguish taught to flow ;

If, thro' the varied griefs my Youth has known,
   No charm but these could raise my votive eye ;
O leave me not, now every blessing's flown,
   Whilst my sad bosom heaves the lengthen'd sigh.

The grated prison, and the lov'd-form'd bower,
   The wretch, whom Disappointment wastes away,
The frugal hut, the gilded dome of power,
   Joy in thy smiles and court thy equal sway.

By thee, the friendless sufferer learns to bear ;
   By thee, the patient heart forgets its woe ;
Thou mak'st Misfortune's iron aspect fair,
   And e'en the frozen cheek of Misery glow.

Leave me no more, as on that fated morn
   When my rash soul the impious deed design'd,
And when, unconscious of thy blest return,
   The foe Despair usurp'd my tortur'd mind.

But yet, bright Goddess! with deceptive smile,
   Come, and a host of Fictions in thy train,
With dreams of peace my wearied heart beguile,
   And sink in fancied bliss the real pain.

PRAYER to PATIENCE.

BY THE SAME.

GODDESS of the steady eye !
  All thy Apathy impart,
From a world of woe I fly,
  Take, oh take me to thy heart !

Lend me all thy healing power,
  Teach me to suppress the groan,
Let me while affliction's lower,
  Turn like NIOBE *to stone.*

Let me to the *sneer* of scorn,
  Still return the placid *smile,*
Calm,—when angry passions frown,
  Silent,—when the rude revile.

Check the Tyrant of the mind,
  Source of *sorrow, Foe* to *thee* ;
Who can peace, or solace find,
  Rack'd by *Sensibility !*

Snatch me from her wasting sway,
  Shield me with thy firmer aid,
Let me still thy voice obey,
  Gentle, peace-preserving maid !

If greater pangs this bosom rend,
  Than ever bosom felt before ;
Further may thy sway extend,
  Greater, deeper be thy power.

Be every *wrong* difarm'd by thee,
  Rob ftern *ppreffion* of his pride,
Bid *Malice* at thy prefence flee,
  Turn *Envy's* venom'd dart afide.

Let hard *Reproach* foft kindnefs feel,
  To cold *Difdain* be pity lent,
From *Anger* wreft his lifted fteel,
  From black *Revenge* his difcontent.

Goddefs of the tearlefs eye!
  Yet give me thy pacific charms;
To thy calm bofom let me fly,
  And find a refuge in thy arms!

L I N E S,

Addreffed to the inimitable Author *of the* Poems *under the*
fignature of Delia Crufca.

BY THE SAME,

ACROSS the vaft Atlantic tide,
  Down *Apalachia's* grafly fide,
What echoing founds the foul beguile,
And lend *the lip of grief* a fmile!
'Tis DELLA CRUSCA'S heavenly fong,
Which floats the weftern fhores along,

Breathing as sweet, as soft a strain,
As kindness to the ear of pain ;
Splendid as noon, as morning clear,
And chaste as evening's pearly tear ;
Where *cold despair* in music flows,
While all the FIRE OF GENIUS glows.

Still thy enchanting powers display,
Still charm me with the magic lay !
The Muses all thy soul inspire,
Apollo tunes thy matchless lyre !
O strike the lustral string again,
And o'er Columbia wast the strain.

Ah ! would o'light my clouded days,
One ray from thy unequall'd blaze,
Might thro my darkning fortunes shine,
And grace me with a note like thine !
But no, BRIGHT BARD, for thee alone
The Muses weave the *laurel crown :*
Ne'er can the *timid, plaintive dove,*
Soar with the DAUNTLESS BIRD OF JOVE;
Nor *silv'ry Hesper's* dewy ray
Beam like the *Golden Orb of Day.*

B b

ALFRED to PHILENIA.*

MY morn of life was bright and fair,
  The diftant mifts of gloomy *Care*,
By *Joy's* light breeze, which daily blew,
Were fcatter'd far beyond the view.
Then bleffings crown'd the happy hours—
Then *Pleafure* ftrew'd my path with flowers;
Then *Virtue* oped an eafy way,
And led my footfteps up to day.
If e'er the *Child* of *Sorrow* mourn'd
My fympathetic bofom burn'd;
The higheft blifs my foul could know,
Was, to relieve the pang of woe.

  Such fcenes my fondeft feelings warm'd—
Such fcenes my earlieft habits form'd;
This dangerous race thro' youth I ran,
And, ruin'd, reach'd the verge of man.

  Alas! fad wretch!—I've wept, and run
At *Pity's* call——to be undone;
Beneath the flowers which ftrew'd my way,
The thorn of keeneft anguifh lay;
Even in the bofs of *Virtue's* fhield,
The fting of torture lay conceal'd.

  Ah, fatal *Love!*——
Now *Hope* has clof'd her fun-bright eye,
And midnight glooms my midday fky;

---

* This, and the three next fucceeding Poems, are extracted from the Columbian Centinel of 1791.

Defpair now heaves his horrid form,
And frowns terrific in the ftorm ;
No ray of blifs now meets my fight,
And my whole foul is wrap'd in night.

Ah, fweeteft *Poetefs* ! thy lay
Can charm the weightieft woes away ;
The foft compaffion of thy feeling breaft,
Can fhed a drop of balm, and lull my foul to reft.

PHILENIA to ALFRED.

ALFRED ! the heaven lent mufe is thine,
    Then bid impetuous forrow ceafe ;
And at the bright *Apollo's* fhrine,
    Recal thy exil'd heart to peace.

Vain is the tear in anguifh fhed,
And vain the pang by paffion fed,
Then to the mufe thy moments give,
And for her deathlefs laurel *live*.

Ne'er hope in carelefs crouds to find
A refuge for thy *lonely* mind,
Think not the fympathetick figh,
The language of the moving eye,
    Will o'er thy with'ring forrows flow ;
Envy will fneer, and *rancour* frown,
Or *ignorant malice* drag thee down,
    And fcorn to folace what it cannot know.

Yet there are *some* to mercy true ;
   And such *my griefs* have found,
   Who o'er each life-deltroying wound,
Shed pity's healing dew.

Such be thy favour'd lot, for they
Will live beyond the fummer day,
Will mid'ft the weeping autumn fmile,
And e'en the wintry wafte beguile ;
Will thy fad breaft from anguifh free,
The friends of gentlenefs and thee.

But, if the flave of love thou art
   Still languifh and *endure*,
For when that ftrikes *the feeling heart*,
   Like death, it has no cure.

ALFRED to PHILENIA.

AND does the heart, by love diftrefs'd,
   " Like death, admit no cure?"
Muft *Alfred's* deeply-torturd breaft,
   " Still languifh, and endure ?"

Ah ! for a moment ftay thy doom,
Nor drive him frantic to the tomb.
Thy fweet, thy all-fubduing lay,
The tempefts of the foul obey—
At thy command its ragings ceafe—
Thou fpeak'ft and ev'ry heart is peace ;
While thron'd fublime above the ftorm,
Thou wear'ft a radiant Seraph's form,

And, fmiling o'er the folemn fcene,
Thy afpect fpeaks a mind ferene.

Know then—o'er *Alfred's* finking foul,
The waves of ceafelefs anguifh roll—
Love has affail'd his yielding heart,
And pierc'd it with his fharpeft dart ;
Time's lenient hand its healing aid denies,
And every hour a heavier pang fupplies.

When life's quick eddies warm'd his youthful heart,
He fell a prey to foft deceptive art—
To DELIA every real charm was given,
And ALFRED lov'd her next to Truth and Heaven.
Unus'd to guile, in love with truth,
And glowing with the fire of youth,
His mind the future profpect view'd,
Where fancy every blefling fhew'd—
The path of blifs expanded lay,
And flowers EDENIAN ftrew'd the way,
While all around the alluring fcene,
Tranfported Friendfhip fmil'd ferene,
And Nature with endearing fmile,
Spread out each gay enchanting wile,
And from the landfcape fcene refin'd,
Brought fweeteft rapture to the mind.

But when this gay delufion flew,
A dreary defart opel to view ;
Where nought but thorns the cheerlefs heath fupplied,
Where Hope fwift fled, and Expectation died.

But ALFRED lives amid a world of night,
Each hour beguiles him of a frefh delight ;

" Chill Penury's" fiends, with angry aspect lour
Round his sad path, and wither every flower,
No gleams of joy pierce thro' the encreasing gloom,
And Peace eludes his grasp, and flies beyond the tomb.

Must ALFRED then, " the slave of Love,"
   " Still languish and endure?"
Can nought the torturing pangs remove
   Is death the only cure?

The world has " friends to mercy true"—
   " Such ALFRED's griefs have found,"
Who in his breast " shed pity's healing dew"—
   But Friendship's pity cannot heal the wound.

PHILENIA TO ALFRED.

"PENRY," no ALFRED! 'tis not thine,
   In thy rich Soul's exhaustless Mine
Abounds more Wealth, than GANGES golden Shores
   E'er on the tawny Chiefs bestow'd,
   When parting from the sacred Flood,
   The falsly, glitt'ring, yellow Sand,
   Spreads Treasure thro' the torrid Land,
   Or tho' from out the burning Soil,
   Drawn by the harden'd Hand of Toil,
   The precious sparkling Drops are plac'd
   Round the slim Zone of Beauty's Waist,
And add new Splendour to some Monarch's Stores.
   Does not the vernal Morning rise
   With Radiance to thy grateful Eyes?

Does not the breezy Flow of Eve
A Tranſport to thy Boſom give?
And ev'ry life-diſſolving Sigh,
Fill thy rapt Soul with Extacy,
When thy loſt Charmer on thy Viſion beams,
And feeds wild Fancy with deluſive Dreams?

Ah! ALFRED, I of Griefs could ſpeak,
'Till at ſoft Pity's call
The iron Tears would fall
In burning Streams down hard Oppreſſion's Cheek.
But no! I quit the heartleſs Lay,
And caſt the unavailing Theme away.

When wand'ring o'er the fragrant Vale,
Soft Warblings wafting thro' the Gale,
Does not thy Soul a Pardon find
For Words unjuſt, and Deeds unkind?
Do not the cruel Herd inſpire
Compaſſion or Diſdain?
Can Scorn's cold Eye thy boſom fire,
To yield one Wrong again?
No! ALFRED, no! the MUSE is thine!
And where her Bounties flow,
All the bright beaming Virtues ſhine,
The warm Affections g'ow.
Then can that Duſt poor Miſers hoard,
Enrich thy wealthy Soul?
Can ſordid Ore one Bliſs afford?
One tyrant Pang controul?

The friendlefs Flatt'rer's fmile to prove,
  To purchafe venal Beauty's Eye,
  To fwell mad Envy's frantic Sigh,
And lofe each Sympathy of Love;
Such are the Joys which Gold can give,
And fuch e'en Mifers may receive,
    But fuch can ne'er be thine.—
The MUSE extends her open Arms,
She courts thee with unbounded Charms,
Her Pencil paints each glowing Scene,
Her Mufick floats along the Green,
By her the laurel'd Virtues live,
She bids degraded Vice, the Blufh of Confcience give.
    Science is her's, and ev'ry Art divine.
    Then like PHILENIA quit the Herd,
      Where Mercy is unknown:
    And be thy votive Prayer preferr'd,
      At great APOLLO's Throne.

Sweet Solitude, kind Nurfe of Song,
Allures me from the joylefs Throng,
Spreads her repofing Breaft to me,   [to thee.
And bids my tunelefs Harp waft long Adieus to cities and

POEM,

Written in Boston, at the commencement of the late Revolution.

By James Allen, of Boston.

FROM realms of bondage and a tyrant's reign,
   Our godlike fathers bore no slavish chain ;
To Pharaoh's face the inspired patriarchs stood,
To seal their virtue, with a martyr's blood :
But lives so precious, such a sacred seed,
The source of empires, heaven's high will decreed :
He snatch'd the saints from Pharaoh's impious hand,
And bade his chosen seek this distant land :
Then to these climes the illustrious exiles sped,
'Twas freedom prompted, and the Godhead led.
Eternal woods the virgin soil defac'd,
A dreary desert, and an howling waste ;
A haunt of tribes no pity taught to spare,
And they oppos'd them with remorseless war,
But heaven's right arm led forth the faithful train,
The guardian Godhead swept the insidious plain,
Till the scour'd thicket amicable stood,
Nor dastard ambush trench'd the dusky wood :
Our sires then earn'd, no more, precarious bread,
Nor midst alarms their frugal meals were spread ;
Fair boding hopes inur'd their hands to toil,
And patriot virtue nurs'd the thriving soil ;

C c

Nor fcarce two ages have their periods run,
Since o'er their culture fmil'd the genial fun;
And now what ftates extend their fair domains
O'er fleecy mountains and luxuriant plains!
Where happy millions their own fields poffefs,
No tyrant awes them, and no lords opprefs;
The hand of rule, divine difcretion guides,
And white-robed virtue o'er her paths prefides,
Each polic'd order venerates the laws,
And each, ingenuous, fpeaks in freedom's caufe;
The Spartan fpirit, nor the Roman name,
The patriot's pride, fhall rival thefe in fame;
Here all the fweets that focial life can know,
From the full font of civil fapience flow;
Here golden Ceres clothes the autumnal plain,
And art's fair emprefs holds her new domain;
Here angel fcience fpreads her lucid wing,
And hark, how fweet the new-born Mufes fing!
Here generous commerce fpreads her liberal hand,
And fcatters foreign bleffings round the land.
Shall meagre Mammon, or proud luft of fway,
Reverfe thefe fcenes? Will heaven permit the day?
Shall in this era all our hopes expire,
And weeping freedom from her fanes retire?
Here, fhall the tyrant ftill our peace purfue,
From the pain'd eye-brow drink the vital dew?
Nor nature's barrier wards, our fathers' foe,
Seas roll in vain, and boundlefs oceans flow?

Stay, Pharaoh,* ftay: that impious hand forbear,
Nor tempt the genius of our fouls too far;

---

* The King of Great-Britain.

How oft, ungracious, in thy thanklefs ftead,
Mid fcenes of death, our generous youth have bled!
When the proud Gaul thy mightieft powers repell'd,
And drove thy legions, trembling, from the field,
We rent the laurel from the victor's brow,
And round thy temples taught the wreath to grow.†
Say, when thy flaughter d bands the defart dy'd,
Where lone Ohio rolls her gloomy tide,
Whofe dreary banks their wafting bones infhrine,
What arm aveng'd them? thanklefs! was it thine?‡
But generous valor fcorns a boafting word,
And confcious virtue reaps her own reward:
Yet confcious virtue bids thee now to fpeak,
Tho' guilty blufhes kindle o'er thy cheek:
If wafting wars and painful toils at length,
Had drain'd our veins, and wither'd all our ftrength,
How could ft thou, cruel, form the vile defign,
And round our neck the wreath of bondage twine?
And if fome lingering fpirit rous'd to ftrife,
Bid ruffian murder drink the dregs of life?
Shall future ages e er forget the deed?
And fhan't, for this, impious Britain bleed?

---

† The taking of Louifbourg in the year 1755, by General Pepperell.

‡ The fame year the King's troops were furprized near the banks of the Ohio; when our illuftrious General Wafhington covered the retreat, and faved the deftruction of the whole army. A body of the French was repulfed at an affault of the provincial lines at the weftward, their General taken prifoner, and their whole army compelled to fly back to Canada.

When comes the period, heaven predeſtines muſt,
When Europe's glories ſhall be whelm'd in duſt,
When our proud fleets the naval wreath ſhall wear,
And o' r her empires hurl the bolts of war,
Unnerv'd by fate, the boldeſt heart ſhall fail,
And, mid their guards, auxiliar kings grow pale ;
In vain ſhall Britain lift her ſuppliant eye,
An alien'd offspring feels no filial tye,
Her tears in vain ſhall bathe the ſoldiers' feet,
Remember, ingrate, Boſton's crimſon'd ſtreet ;§
Whole hecatombs of lives the deed ſhall pay,
And purge the murders of that guilty day.‖

　But why to future periods look ſo far,
What force e'er fac'd us, that we fear'd to dare?
Then can'ſt thou think, e'en on this early day,
Proud force ſhall bend us to a tyrant's ſway?
A foreign foe oppos'd our ſword in vain,*
And thine own troops we've rallied on the plain.†
If then our lives your lawleſs ſword invade,
Think'ſt thou, enſlav'd, we'll kiſs the pointed blade?
Nay, let experience ſpeak, be this the teſt,—
Tis from experience that we reaſon beſt,—

———

§ The Maſſacre of the 5th of March 1770.
‖ The Poet ſeems to have been very prophetic in this beautiful paſſage.
* The extirpation of the Neutrals from Nova-Scotia.
† The Provincials covered the retreat from the French lines at Ticonderoga, when the Britiſh General, Abercrombie, was defeated by the Marquis Montcalm, in 1758.

When firſt the mandate ſhew'd the ſhameleſs plan,
To rank our race beneath the claſs of man,
Low as the brute to ſink the human line,
Our toil our portion, and the harveſt thine,
Modeſt but firm, we plead the ſacred cauſe,
On nature baſ'd, and ſanction'd by the laws;
But your deaf ear the conſcious plea denied,
Some demon counſel'd, and the ſword reply'd;
Your navy then our haven cover'd o'er,
And arm'd battalions treſpaſs'd on our ſhore,
Thro the prime ſtreets, they march'd in war's array:
At noon's full blaze, and in the face of day:
With dumb contempt we paſs'd the ſervile ſhow,
While ſcorn's proud ſpirit ſcowl'd on every brow;
Day after day ſucceſſive wrongs we bore,
Till patience, wearied, could ſupport no more,
Till ſlaughter'd lives our native ſtreets prophan'd,
And thy ſlaves' hand our hallow'd crimſon ſtain'd;
No ſudden rage the ruffian ſoldier tore.
Or drench'd the pavements with his vital gore,
Deliberate thought did all our ſouls compoſe.
Till, veil'd in gloo ſ s, the lowery morning roſe;
No mob then furious urg'd the impaſſion'd fray,
Nor clamorous tumults dinn'd the ſolemn day;
In full convene the city‡ ſenate ſat,
Our fathers' ſpirit rul'd the firm debate:
The freeborn ſoul no reptile tyrant checks,
Tis heaven that dictates when the people ſpeaks;

---

‡ Town-meeting at Faneuil-Hall.

Loud from their tongues the awful mandate broke,
And thus, infpir'd, the facred fenate fpoke;
Ye mifcreant troops, be gone! our prefence fly;
S ay, if ye dare, but if ye dare, ye die!
Ah, too fevere, the fearful chief § replies,
Permit one half, the other, inftant, flies.
No parle, avaunt, or by our fathers' fhades,
Your reeking lives fhall glut our vengeful blades.
Ere morning's light, begone,—or elfe we fwear,
Each flaughter'd corfe fhall feed the birds of air!
Ere morning's light had ftreak'd the fkies with red,
The chieftain yielded, and the foldier fled.
Tis thus experience fpeaks—the teft forbear,
Nor fhew thefe ftates your feeble front of war.
But ftill your navies lord it o'er the main,—
Their keels are natives of our oaken plain;
  E'en the proud maft that bears your flag on high,
  " Grew on our foil, and ripen'd in our fky:
  "Know then thyfelf, prefume not us to fcan,
  Your power precarious, and your ifle a fpan.

  Yet could our wrongs in juft oblivion fleep,
And on each neck reviv'd affection weep,
The brave are generous, and the good forgive,
Then fay you've wrong'd us, and our parent live; ||
But face not fate, oppofe not heaven's decree,
Let not that curfe our mother light on thee.

---

§ The infamous Governor Hutchinfon.

|| Her tyrants were too felf-conceited, and too obftinate,
to take the advice of men of the beft fenfe and underftand-
ing. The confequence has been the eftablifhment of liberty and univerfal commerce in America.

AN INTENDED INSCRIPTION,

Written for the Monument on Beacon-Hill, in Boston, and addressed to the Passenger.

BY THE SAME.

WHERE stretch'd your sail, beneath what foreign sky
 Did lovlier landscapes ever charm your eye?
Could fancy's fairy pencil, Stranger! say,
E'en dipt in dreams, a nobler scene portray?

 Behold yon vales, whose skirts elude your view,
And mountains fading to ærial blue!
Along their bow'ry shades—how healthy toil
Alternate sports, or tends the mellow soil.
See rural towns mid groves and gardens rise,
And eastward,—where the stretching ocean lies,
Lo! our fair capital sublimes the scene,
New *Albion's* pride, and ocean's future queen;
How o'er the tradeful port august she smiles,
Her sea-like haven boasts an hundred isles,
Whence hardy commerce swells the lofty sails
O'er arctic seas, and mocks the polar gales,
Thence tides of wealth the wafting breezes bring,
And hence e'en culture feels its vital spring.

 These scenes our Sires from rugged nature wrought,
Since—what dire wars their patriot race have fought!
Witness yon tracts, where first the Briton bled,
Driv'n by our youth redoubted PIERCY fled:

There BREED afcends, and BUNKER's bleeding fteeps,
Still o'er whofe brow abortive Vict'ry weeps;
What Trophies fince! the gaze of after times,
Fear'd *Freedom's* empire o'er our happy climes!

But hence, fond Stranger, take a nobler view,
See you fhorn elm,* whence all thefe glories grew.
Here, where the armed foe prefumptious trod,
Trampled our fhrines, and even mouth'd our GOD,
His vengeful hand, deep as the parent-root,
Lopt each grown branch, and ev'ry fuckling fhoot;
Becaufe beneath her confecrated fhade
Our earlieft vows to LIBERTY were paid.
High from *her Altar* blew the heaven-caught fire,
While all our wealth o'erhung the kindling pyre.
How at the deed the Nations ftood aghaft,
As on the pile our plighted lives we caft!

O! if an alien from our fair domains,
The blood of *Britain*, haplefs, taint your veins,
Pace o'er that hallow'd ground with awful tread,
And tears, atoning, o'er yon relick fhed;
But if, American! your lineage fprings,
From Sires, who fcorn the pedigree of kings,
A Georgian born you breathe the tepid air,
Or on the breezy banks of *Delaware*,
Or hardy *Hampfhire* claim your haughty birth,
Revere yon root, and kifs its nurt'ring earth:
O be its fibre fed by flowing fprings,
Whence rofe our empire o'er the thrones of kings;

---

* The ftump of Liberty-Tree.

E'en now defcend, adore the dear remain,
Where firft rear'd Liberty's illumin'd fane,
There ad her race, while time's revolve fhall come,
As pilgrims flock to MECCA's idol'd tomb.

ELEGIAC ODE,

Sacred to the Memory of General GREENE.

BY GEORGE RICHARDS, OF BOSTON.

SAY, fhall the birds of ancient Greece an Rome,
    I all the athos of impaffion'd woe,
Mourn with their country, at the hero's tomb,
    And fire a world to emulation's glow?
Shall weeping mufes quit Pierian groves,
    To deck the fod, where reft the good, the brave;
And fhall the warrior, whom an empire loves
    Repofe, unfung, unhonor'd in the grave?

Forbid it, heaven! Columbia claims the fong:
    Tonca d with her griefs, I fweep the plaintive lyre;
To her, to Greene, immortal ftrains belong:
    An angel's pencil, and a feraph's fire.
Whilft facred Truth, from realms of light,
    Shall pour the tide of intellectual day,
And lead my footfteps to the hero's fhrine,
    Where patriots guard, and freemen watch the clay.

Dd

When firſt Britannia bath'd her ſword in gore,
  His ſoul, indignant, ſpurn'd the peaceful ſhade;
Inſtant he arm'd, to brave the Lion's roar,
  And the keen terrors of the Highland blade.
Prompt at his call, to hoſtile fields he led
  The hardy yeomen of his native iſle;*
True ſons of liberty; whom virtue bred,
  Strong for the labors of Herculean toil.

Mild of acceſs, in him, no little pride
  Obſcur'd the greatneſs of a noble mind;
He felt for all; the ſoldier at his ſide
  Brought down the ſweeteſt " milk of human kind."
For council honor'd, in the camp belov'd,
  Sagacious, cool, amid the ſtorm ſerene;
Heroes rever'd, applauding States approv'd,
  And Albion trembled at the name of GREENE.

Oft have his limbs the frozen earth compreſs'd,
  Whilſt round his head the watery torrent pour'd;
Thick clouds the curtains to his couch of reſt,
  Where the bleak wind and midnight hail-ſtorm roar'd.
And oft, advancing with the ſolar ray,
  His banners flam'd to meet the lightning's glare,
In torrid realms of more than burning day;
  Sad haunts of death, and plagues, and putrid air.

There hallow'd truths, inſcrib'd on glory's roll,
  Written in blood on honor's purple veſt,
Shall gallant warriors, born of kindred ſoul,
  With conſcious pride, and martial zeal atteſt.

---

* General GREENE commanded the troops raiſed by the
State of Rhode-Iſland, the firſt campaign of the late war.

Illuftrious men! ye nerv'd his mighty hand,
　Fo crufh the fava_e on the warlike plain;
When to the fouth he wheel'd his conquering baud,
　And broke the iron of oppreflion's chain.

Around the fhores which Hudfon's billows lave,
　His laurel wreaths fhall ever verdant bloom;
And Trenton's cyprefs fhade the hero's grave,
　Whilft penfive Princeton mourns his early tomb.
Auguft abodes! ye heard the trumpet's found;
　Which bade his columns range, h: fquadrons form;
Ye faw his courfers fnuff the embattled ground,
　And Greene, triumphant, rule the vengeful ftorm.

Array'd in tears and garb of fable hue,
　See Brandywine the chieftain's hearfe attend;
And Germantown † lament—and Monmouth, rob'd in
　And Afhley's waters wail their god-like friend.　[yew,
Immortal grounds! the theme of every age,
　Your meaneft duft fhall fpeak the hero's praife;
Here bolted vengeance burft with tenfold rage,
　And there he drove the lightning's rapid blaze.

Nor lefs illuftrious are the banks of Dan,
　Or Guilford's fields, where feats of bold emprife,
Proclaim the genius of the matchlefs man:
　Though all the regions, mark'd by azure fkies,
Ye faw his arms the vollied thunders deal,
　Which check'd Cornwallis in his mid career;
With Tarleton's fword, and Rawdon's murderous fteel,
　And favage Balfour pal'd with guilty fear.

_____

† At Germantown, Monmouth, and in South-Caroli-
na, Gen. GREENE was honored with diftinguifhed command,

Illustrious spots of earth's high favor'd mould!
   What, tho no clarions swell to dire alarms,
And no proud chief, in pomp of burnish'd gold,
   Leads on his troops in the bright glow of arms;
Yet shall the veteran there recount the tale
   Of armies rais'd, uncloth'd, unfed, unpaid,
Who stood the summer's heat, the winter's gale,
   Nor turn'd their bosoms from the tyrant's blade.

Such were the men, who own'd the power of GREENE,
   When the shrill music, lengthening down the line,
Urg'd rank on rank, to try the dubious scene,
   And combat hosts, by d sjots thought divine.
Thrice honor'd chief! the work of death is past,
   Thy task completed, smiling peace descends,
Hush'd is the din, and mute the trumpet's blast,
   And ardent warrior's greet as ancient friends.

Mature in life, with endless honor crown'd,
   Too bright for earth, and fit for purer skies,
Celestial bards his mighty deeds resound,
   Whilst thus, aloud, a prince of angels cries.
" At God's decree, by heaven's high throne, I swear,
   " 'Tis done! tis done! his time shall be no more!
" Thou king of death descend, on wings of air,
   " And waft the hero to his native shore."

The obedient monarch cleft the etherial way,‡
   His golden darts were tipp'd with sacred fire,
He rode the chariot of eternal day,
   And, fleet as lightning, pass'd the applauding choir.

---

‡ General GREENE died of the *Coup de Soleil,* or Stroke
of the Sun.

His radiant form the hero kenn'd afar,
   R solv'd in death to boaft fupernal fame,
He mounted fwift, lafh'd on the burning car,
   And tower'd fublime in robes of folar flame.

According fpirits tun'd the fong of love,
   From heavenly harps was heard triu nphant praife,
Which breath d thrice welcome to the climes above,
   In the mild mufic of harmonious lays.
A paufe enfued ; the melting lyre was ftill,
   And this the voice which trumpets roll'd around.
" Go, fix he hero's throne on glory's hill,
   " And be the chief by mightieft warriors crown'd."

The laurel wreath was borne in Warren's hand,
   The great Montgomery thron'd the immortal GREENE,
The gentle Mercer join d the feftive band,
   And gallant Laurens graced the glorious fcene.
Uncoun'ed veterans throng'd the bleft abodes ;
   Loud fwell d the notes to extacy divine ;
And Spartan heroes, next in rank to Gods,
   Proclaim d, with Wolfe, the palm of merit thine.

THE COUNTRY SCHOOL.†

PUT to the door—the fchool's begun—
    Stand in your places every one,—
Attend,————

.   .   .   .   ?

Read in the bible,—tell the place,—
" *Job twentieth and the feventeenth varfe* —
Caleb, begin. *And—he—fhall—fuck—*
Sir,—Mofes got a pin and ftuck——
Silence,—ftop Caleb—Mofes! here!
What's this complaint? *I didn't, Sir,—*
Hold up your hand,—What is't a pin?
O dear, I won't do fo agin.
Read on. *The increafe of his h--h--horfe—*
Hold: H, O, U, S, E, fpells houfe.
Sir, what's this word? for I can't tell it.
Can't you indeed! Why fpell it. *Spell it.*
Begin yourfelf, I fay. *-Who, I?*
Yes, try. Sure you can fpell it. *Try.*
Go, take your feats and primers, go,
You fha'n't abufe the bible fo.

---

  † This Poem is extracted from the New-Hampfhire Spy,
where it is introduced by the following note:——" Mr.
Ofborne, The following may fill a corner of your Spy, if
there is any thing original, natural or juft, in thus fketching
out a picture of a common Town School, where there are
frequently fuch vaft numbers of every age, fize and fex
fent together, as to create perpetual confufion, diftract an
illiterate mafter, and fruftrate the noble defign of fending
them."

SELECTED POETRY.

Will pray Sir Mafter mend my pen?
Say, Mafter, that's enough.—Here Ben,
Is this your copy? Can't you tell?
Set all your letters parallel.
I've done my fum—'tis juft a groat—
Let's fee it.—*Mafter, m' I g' out?*
Yes,—bring fome wood in—What's that noife?
It isn't I, Sir, it s them boys.——

    Come Billy, read—What's that? *That's A—*
Sir, Jim has fnatch'd my rule away——
Return it, James.—Here, rule with this—
Billy, read on,—*That's crooked S.*
Read in the fpelling-book—Begin—
The boys are out— Then call them in—
My nofe bleeds, mayn't I get fome ice,
And hold it in my breeches?—Yes.
John, keep your feat. *My fum is more—*
Then do't again—Divide by four,
By twelve, and twenty—Mind the rule.
Now fpeak, Manaffah, and fpell tool.
I can't—Well try...*T, W, L.*
Not wafh'd your hands yet, boody, ha?
You had your orders yefterday.
Give me the ferrule, hold your hand.
Oh! Oh! There,---mind my next command.

    The grammar read. Tell where the place is.
C founds like K in cat and cafes.
My book is torn. The next....*Here not---*
E final makes it long---fay note.
What are the ftops and marks, Sufannah?
Small points, Sir.——And how many, Hannah?

Four, Sir. How many, George? You look :
Here's more than fifty in my book.
How's this? Juſt come, Sam? *Why I've been---*
Who knocks? *I don't know, Sir.* Come in.
" Your moſt obedient, Sir?" And yours.
Sit down, Sir. Sam, put to the doors.
What do you bring to tell that's new !
" Nothing, that's either ſtrange or true.
" What a prodigious ſchool ! I m ſure
" You've got a hundred here, or more.
" A word, Sir, if you pleaſe." I will---
You girls, till I come in be ſtill.

 " Come, we can dance to night---ſo you
" Diſmiſs your brain-diſtracting crew,
" And come---For all the girls are there.
" We ll have a fiddle and a player."
Well, mind and have the ſleigh-bells ſent,
I'll ſoon diſmiſs my regiment.

 Silence ! The ſecond claſs muſt read.
As quick as poſſible---proceed.
Not found your book yet? Stand---be fix'd—
The next read, ſtop---the next---the next.
You need not read again, tis well.
Come Tom and Dick, chuſe ſides to ſpell.
Will this word do? Yes, Tom ſpell dunce.
Sit ſtill there all you little ones.
I've got a word, Well, name it. *Gizzard.*
You ſpe l it Sampſon....*G, I, Z.*
Spell conſcience, Jack. *K, O, N,*
S, H, U, N, T, S.....Well done !

Put out the next---*Mine is folks.*
Tim, spell it....*P, H, O, U, X.*
O shocking! Have you all try'd? *No.*
Say Matter, but no matter, go---
Lay by your books---and you, Josiah,
Help Jed to make the morning fire.

THE SPEECH OF HESPER.†

YE fires of nations, call'd in high debate,
. From kindre l realms, to save the sinking state,
A boundless sway on one broad base to rear——
My voice paternal claims your listening ear ;
O'er the wide clime my fostering cares extend,
Your guardian genius and your deathless friend.

When splendid victory on her trophy'd car,
Swept from these shores the last remains of war,

E 2

---

† This Poem forms part of a series of publications, in the Connecticut Magazine, for the years 1786 and 1787,—under the title of " American Antiquities ;" of which it makes the tenth number, and is call d an " Extract from the Anarchiad, book xxiv,"—being prefaced by the following lines, viz.————" At the op ning of this book, and previous to the great and final conflict, which, by what is legible at the close of the Poem, appears to establish the Anarch in his dominion of the new world, Hesper, with a solicitude and energy becoming his high station, and the importance of the subject, makes his last solemn address to his principal counsellors and sages, whom he had convened at Philadelphia."

Bade each glad ftate, that boafts Columbia's name,
Exult in freedom and afcend to fame,
To blifs unbounded ftretch their ardent eyes,
And wealth and empire from their labour rife,
My raptur'd fons beheld the difcord ceafe,
And footh'd their forrows in the fongs of peace.

Shall thefe bright fcenes, with happieft omens born,
Fade like the fleeting vifions of the morn?
Shall this fair fabric from its bafe be hurl'd
And whelm in duft the glories of the world?
Will ye, who faw the heavens tempeftuous lower,
Who felt the arm of irritated power,
Whofe fouls diftending with the wafting flood,
Prepar'd the firm foundations, built in blood,
By difcord fiez'd, will ye defert the plan?
The unfinifh'd Babel of the blifs of man?

Go fearch the field of death, where heroes, loft
In graves obfcure, can tell what freedom coft.
Tho' conqueft fmil'd; there flain amid the croud,
And plung'd promifcuous with no winding fhroud,
No friendly hand their gory wounds to lave,
The thoufands moulder in a common grave.
Not fo thy fon, oh Laurens! gafping lies,
Too daring youth, war's lateft facrifice;
His fnow-white bofom heaves with writhing pain,
The purple drops his fnow-white bofom ftain;
His cheek of rofe is wan, a deadly hue
Sits on his face, that chills with lucid dew.——
There Warren, glorious with expiring breath,
A comely corfe, that fmiles in ghaftly death:

See Mercer bleed——and o'er yon wintry wall,
Mid heaps of flain, fee great Montgomery fall!

Behold thofe veterans worn with want and care,
Their finews ftiffen'd, filver'd o'er their hair,
Weak in their fteps of age, they move forlorn,
Their toils forgotten by the fons of fcorn ;
This hateful truth ftill aggravates their pain,
In vain they conquer'd and they bled in vain.
Go then, ye remnants of inglorious wars,
Difown your marks of merit, hide your fcars,
Of luft, of power, of titled pride accuf'd,
Steal to your graves difhonor'd and abuf'd.

For fee proud Faction waves her flaming brand,
And difcord riots o'er the ungrateful land ;
Lo, to the north a wild adventurous crew
In defperate mobs the favage ftate renew ;
Each felon chief his maddening thoufands draws,
And claims bold licence from the bond of laws ;
In other States the chofen fires of fhame,
Stamp their vile knaveries with a legal name ;
In honor's feat the fons of meannefs fwarm,
And fenates bafe the work of mobs perform,
To wealth, to power the foes of union rife,
While foes deride you and while friends defpife.

Stand forth, ye traitors, at your country's bar,
Inglorious authors of inteftine war ;
What countlefs mifchiefs from their labours rife !
Pens dipp'd in gall and lips infpir'd with lies !
Ye fires of ruin, prime detefted caufe
Of bankrupt faith, annihilated laws,

Of selfish systems, jealous, local schemes,
And union'd empire lost in empty dreams,
Your names expanding with your growing crime
Shall float disgustful down the stream of time,
Each future age applaud the avenging song,
And outrag'd nature vindicate the wrong.

Yes there are men, who, touch'd with heavenly fire,
Beyond the confines of these climes aspire,
Beyond the praises of a transient age,
To live immortal in the patriot page;
Who greatly dare, though warring worlds oppose,
To pour just vengeance on their country's foes.

And lo! the etherial worlds assert your cause,
Celestial aid the voice of virtue draws;
The curtains blue of yon expansion rend,
From opening skies heroic shades descend.
See, rob'd in light, the forms of heaven appear,
The warrior spirits of your friends are near;
Each on his steed of fire (his quiver stor'd
With shafts of vengeance) grasps his flaming sword,
The burning blade waves high, and, dipt in blood,
Hurls plagues and death on discord's faithless brood.

Yet what the hope? the dreams of Congress fade,
The federal union sinks in endless shade,
Each feeble call, that warns the realms around,
Seems the faint echo of a dying sound,
Each requisition wafts in fleeting air,
And not one state regards the powerless prayer.

Ye wanton States, by heaven's best blessings curst,
Long on the lap of softening luxury nurst,

What fickle frenzy raves, what visions strange?
Inspire your bosoms with the lust of change?
An I frames the with to fly from fancy'd ill,
And yield your freedom to a monarch's will?

Go, view the lands to lawless power a prey,
Where tyrants govern with unbounded sway;
See the long pomp in gorgeous state display'd,
The tinsel d guards, the squadron'd horse parade;
See heralds gay with emblems on their vest,
In tissued robes tall beauteous pages drest:
Where moves the pageant, throng unnumber'd slave.
Lords, Dukes, and Princes, titulary knaves
Confus'dly shine, the purple gemm'd with stars,
Sceptres, and globes, and crowns, and ruby' . . rs,
On gilded orbs the thundering chariots roll'd
Steeds snorting fire, and champing bitts of ld,
Prance to the trumpet's voice—while h assumes
A loftier gait, and lifts his neck of plumes.
High on the moving throne, and near the van,
The tyrant rides, the chosen scourge of man;
Clarions, and flutes, and drums, his way prepare,
And shouting millions rend the conscious air;
Millions whose ceaseless toils the pomp sustain,
Whose hour of stupid joy repays an age of pain.

From years of darkness springs the regal line,
Hereditary kings by right divine;
'Tis theirs to riot on all nature's spoils,
For them with pangs unblest the peasant toils,
For them the earth prolific teems with grain,
Theirs, the dread labours of the devious main,

Annual for them the wasted land renews
The gifts oppressive, and extorted dues,
For them, when flaughter spreads the gory plains,
The life-blood gushes from a thousand veins,
While the dull herd, of earth-born pomp afraid,
Adore the power that coward meanness made.

Let Poland tell what woe returning springs,
Where right elective yields the crown to kings !
War guides the choice—each candidate abhorr'd
Founds his firm title on the wasting sword,
Wades to the throne amid the sanguine flood,
And dips his purple in a nation's blood.

Behold, where Venice rears her sea-girt towers,
O'er the vile croud proud oligarchy lowers ;
While each Aristocrate affects a throne,
Beneath a thousand kings the poor plebeians groan.

Nor less abhor'd the certain woe that waits
The giddy rage of democratic states ;
Whose pop'lar breath, high-blown in restless tide,
No laws can temper and no reason guide ;
An equal sway their mind indignant spurns,
To wanton change the bliss of freedom turns,
Led by wild demagogues the factious croud,
Mean, fierce, imperious, insolent and loud,
Nor fame nor wealth nor power nor system draws,
They see no object and perceive no cause,
But feel by turns, in one disasterous hour,
The extremes of licence and the extremes of power.

What madness prompts, or what ill-omen'd fates,
Your realm to parcel into petty states?

Shall lordly Hudfon part contending powers?
And broad Potowmac lave two hoftile fhores?
Muft Allegany's facred fummits bear
The impious bulwarks of perpetual war?
His hundred ftreams receive your heroes flain?
And bear your fons inglorious to the main?
Will ftates cement by feebler bonds allied?
Or join more clofely as they more divide?
Will this vain fchene bid reftlefs factions ceafe?
Check foreign wars or fix internal peace?
Call public credit from her grave to rife?
Or gain in grandeur what they loofe in fize?
In this weak realm can countlefs kingdoms ftart
Strong with new force in each divided part?
While empire's head diffected into four
Gains life by feverance of diminifh'd power?
So when the philofophic hand divides
The full grown polypus in genial tides,
Each fever'd part, inform'd with latent life,
Acquires new vigour from the friendly knife,
O'er peopled fands the puny infects creep,
Till the next wave abforbs them in the deep.

What then remains? muft pilgrim Freedom fly
From thefe lov'd regions to her native fky?
When the fair fugitive the orient chaced,
She fixt her feat beyond the watry wafte;
Her docile fons (enough of power refign'd,
And natural rights in focial leagues combin'd)
In virtue firm, tho' jealous in her caufe,
Gave fenates force and energy to laws,

From ancient habit local powers obey,
Yet feel no reverence for one general fway,
For breach of faith no keen compulfion feel,
And find no intereft in the fœderal weal.
But know, ye avour'd race, one potent head,
Muft rule your ftates, and ftrike your foes with dread,
The finance regulate, the trade controul,
Live thro' the empire, and accord the whole.

   Ere death invades, and night's deep curtain falls,
Thro ruin'd realms the voice of Union calls;
Loud as the trump of heaven thro' darknefs roars,
When gyral gufts entomb Caribbean towers,
When nature trembles thro' the deeps convulft,
And ocean foams from craggy cliffs repulft,
On you fhe calls! attend the warning cry,
" YE LIVE UNITED, OR DIVIDED DIE."

*From the New-Haven Gazette, and Connecticut Magazine,
for 1788.**

TO THE PRINTER.

THE diftrefs which the inhabitants of *Guinea* experience
at the lofs of their children, which are ftolen from them
by the perfons employed in the barbarous traffic of human flefh, is, perhaps, more thoroughly felt than de-
fcribed.   But, as it is a fubject to which every perfon
has not attended, the Author of the following lines hopes
that, poffibly, he may excite fome attention, (while he
obtains indulgence) to an attempt to reprefent the anguifh of a mother, whofe fon and daughter were taken
from her by a Ship's Crew, belonging to a Country
where the GOD of Juftice and Mercy is owned and wor-
fhipped.

———————

66 HELP! oh, help! thou GOD of Chriftians!
    " Save a mother from defpair!
  " Cruel white-men fteal my children!
    " GOD of Chriftians, hear my prayer!

  " From my arms by force they're rended,
    " Sailors drag them to the fea;
  " Yonder fhip, at anchor riding,
    " Swift will carry them away.

F f

———————

* This Poem was originally printed in the above-men-
tioned Paper, February 21ft, 1788, in rather an incorrect
manner.   It is now offered to the public, with the amend-
ment of the errors reprehenfible at its firft appearance.

" There my fon lies, ftripp'd, and bleeding;
  " Faft, with thongs, his hands are bound.
" See, the tyrants, how they fcourge him!
  " See his fides a reeking wound!

" See his little fifter by him;
 , " Quaking, trembling, how fhe lies!
" Drops of blood her face befprinkle;
  " Tears of anguifh fill her eyes.

" Now they tear her brother from her;
  " Down, below the deck, he's thrown;
" Stiff with beating, thro' fear filent,
  " Save a fingle, death-like, groan.

" Hear the little creature begging!"—
  ' Take me, white-men, for your own!
' Spare! oh, fpare my darling brother!
  ' He's my mother's only fon.

' See, upon the fhore fhe's raving:
  ' Down fhe falls upon the fands:
' Now, fhe tears her flefh with madnefs;
  ' Now, fhe prays with lifted hands.

' I am young, and ftrong, and hardy;
  ' He's a fick, and feeble boy;
' Take me, whip me, chain me, ftarve me,
  ' All my life I'll toil with joy.

' Chriftians! who's the GOD you worfhip?
  " Is he cruel, fierce, or good?
' Does he take delight in mercy?
  ' Or in fpilling human blood?

' Ah ! my poor diftracted mother !
    ' Hear her fcream upon the fhore.'—
Down the favage Captain ftruck her,
    Lifelefs on the veffel's floor.

Up his fails he quickly hoifted,
    To the ocean bent his way ;
Headlong plunged the raving mother,
    From a high rock, in the fea.

NEW YEAR's WISH.*

By Dr. — — — — —,

TO you, my young friends, while I write,
    Kind wifhes fpontaneous arife ;
And does ought my rude paffions excite,
    They are hufh'd by benevolent fighs.
A mufe, in the form of a Dove,
    Hovers round, and difpels every fear ;
She bids me each talent improve
    To hail you a HAPPY NEW YEAR !

Her mandates I cheerful obey,
    As her fmiles I would ftrive to procure ;
For the lines that my wifhes convey,
    May her favors in future fecure.

---

* Firft publifhed in No. 85, of the Gazette of the United States ; and originally addreffed, by the author, to
a circle of his female friends.

On you, my young friends, may she smile,
  That your verse may with melody flow ;
And may joy all your sorrows beguile,
  Nor an hour be reserved for woe.

When WINTER shall sternly appear,
  And Nature in gloom be array'd ;
When the Mariner shudders thro' fear,
  Lest his bark should by winds be betray'd ;
Then, in safety, well shelter'd from snow,
  May you all, putting sorrow aside,
In domestic tranquility know
  All the joys of a social fire-side.

When SPRING in young beauty shall smile,
  And charm following charm shall unfold ;
In rapture beholding the while,
  May your portion be pleasures untold.
May each songster that chirps on the spray,
  May each floweret that blows in the field,
For you be more cheerful and gay,
  For you its choice fragrances yield.

When SUMMER shall sultry advance,
  And flocks from their sports shall retire ;
May each youth, who declines the light dance,
  Your charms, and your virtues admire.
May the grape-vine form Arbors of ease,
  While the eglantine skirts them around ;
And then may the fresh balmy breeze
  Waft perfumes from each neighboring ground.

When AUTUMN his treasures shall bring,
   When each fruit tree shall bend with its load;
May your hearts ever gratefully sing,
   The hand that such blessings bestow'd.
Thus sweetly shall time roll away,
   Nor shall you once wish it in haste ;
And the YEAR that commences to-day,
   Far happier shall be than the past.

Then, when WINTERS and SPRINGS shall decay,
   When SUMMERS and AUTUMNS are o'er,
And PHOEBUS, the Prince of the day,
   Shall wake the glad Seasons no more :
To you, each forgeting her mirth,
   May beauty immortal be given ;
May you change the faint joys of this earth,
   For transports uncloying in heaven.

From a Gentleman, to a Lady, who had presented him with a
CAKE HEART.

BY THE SAME.

WITH eager haste I homeward flew
   My precious gift to unfold ;
I saw, and at the flattering view,
   My transports thus I told.

Thou beauteous semblance of the heart
   That warms Lucinda's breast,
Come, and each gentle joy impart
   As to my soul thou'rt press'd.

But ſtill, tho chaſte delight full oft
  To my fond heart you give,
Yet thou, ſay what I will, no ſoft
  Impreſſion canſt receive.

O had Lucinda, lovely fair,
  Deign'd but her own to have given,
The gift I'd cheriſh with that care
  As if 'twere ſent from heaven.

In my own boſom it ſhould lie,
  By no rude paſſion toſs'd ;
And, huſh'd to love, it ſhould ſupply
  The place of mine that's loſt.

———————

From the American Magazine, for May 1788.

UTRUM HORUM MAVIS, ELIGE.

LET ſage diſcretion the gay world deſpiſe ;
  Let dull philoſophers o'er lamps grow wiſe,
Like bees their ſummer providently waſte,
And hoard that treaſure which they ne'er ſhall taſte ;
Let ſtateſmen court the bubble of applauſe,
And ſtaring cry for ſumptuary laws ;
Let peeviſh prelates in devotion kneel,
And curſe that pleaſure which they try to feel ;
Life is a bleſſing, uſe it as you can,
And the beſt purpoſe of that bleſſing ſcan.
All human reaſon is no more than this,
To guide our footſteps in the realms of bliſs ;
While, as in drinking, ſo in life, the will
Muſt bound our joy, and dictate what to fill.—

Live freely then; for if thy life offend
'Tis ne'er too late to alter and amend :
But fhould you hefitate the feafon's loft,
As backward fruits are fubject to the froft.
Then, if true fpirit every hope inflame,
Mark well the leffon of my proffer'd fame.

Firft trace the limits of thy deftin'd fphere :
Here reft thy wifdom, thine ambition here.
'Tis not each clown that triumphs, tho' he dare
Afpire to charm and captivate the fair ;
'Tis not each witling, who the ape difplays,
That ftrikes our fancy, or provokes our praife :
But would you fin, be finful with a grace—
Inaptitude can even vice debafe.
Search then your genius, every bent furvey,
And where fhe prompts be ready to obey.
See thro' this crowd where brilliant profpects rife
The chace how luring, and how rare the prize !
The paths of pleafure to no bounds confin'd,
As in their fhape, are various in their kind.
Fix then thy province, make thy talents good,
And be a fop, a gentleman, or blood.

Happy the *firft*, who ftudious to difpenfe
With all the cumberous pedantry of fenfe,
Knows no ambition but the pride of drefs,
And for that toy can every wilh fupprefs :
Whofe natal bounties, like the fly's, confift
In two fhort words, to flutter and exift.
If to fuch fame thine emulation turn,
Hear his purfuits, and from example learn.

——'Till ten the morn is squander'd in his bed ;
One precious hour's devoted to his head ;
Another's finish'd ere, his dress complete
From top to toe be critically neat ;
Then he struts forth to greet his kindred beaux,
And urge some tardy tradesman for his clothes ;
Or mid the town to saunter and to stare,
And kill an hour or two he knows not where.
In the noon's bustle, vacant and serene,
He deals in bows, his business to be seen :
Perhaps united to some fair he meets,
From shop to shop pursues her thro' the streets ;
For the last fashions stimulate her pride,
And on the modes he's zealous to decide.
Next his foil'd charms he hastens to repair,
To give a finer polish to his hair,
His every grace with every art entwine,
And form his looks more strikingly divine ;
Till the last, noblest pastime of the day,
To his bright zenith summons him away.
There, in the circle of some coterie,
Rous'd by the exhilirating fumes of tea,
View him, triumphant, with unrivall'd fame,
Attract each ogle, and each breast inflame ;
To every sense a magic thrill impart,
And steal thro' all the mazes of the heart.

    Next let us view the Gentleman at ease,
Too rich to toil, too indolent to please ;
Whose days, unharrass'd by desire or woe,
In one smooth stream uninterrupted flow ;

Born to no end, for no one purpofe fit,
A load of vanity, a grain of wit,
Who, far remov'd from every wordly ftrife,
·Lives for himfelf, and fleeps away his life.

If to the *third* thy happier choice incline,
And thy warm genius as a Blood would fhine,
Be the firft caution, in thy bold career,
To fhun low comrades, and a vulgar fphere :——
The great unpunifh'd, from their rank, offend ;
But humbler culprits with the laws contend.——
Then if fome revel, or a midnight joke,
Infult our flumbers, or the watch provoke,
Thy looks can wreft ftern juftice from the fcale,
Sufpend her frowns, and fnatch thee from a jail.
Let dauntlefs fpirit animate thy foul,
No fears reftrain thee, and no threats controul ;
Whether, in hunting, at an arm's expence,
You dafh a furious courfer o'er a fence ;
Or, at the bottle, be thy matchlefs boaft,
To fit the longeft, and to drink the moft :
So fhall thy fame to wonderous heights afcend ;
And every rake fhall hail thee as a friend.

But, if thy foul fuch bafe ambition fpurn,
And in thy breaft a purer fpirit burn,
Leave fuch poor laurels to the brows of Youth ;
And place thy zeal in wifdom and in truth.
Then, in thy way, tho mean temptation rife,
The tafk difcourage, or the world defpife,
Proceed ——

Gg

Until the triumph of thy worth record
That virtue is the fureſt, beſt reward.
The Fop, whoſe merits on his charms depend,
May gain a miſtreſs, but will loſe a friend ;·
The Blood will tell thee, ere he quit the ſtage,
That joy of youth's the miſery of age ;
And the deluded Idler, with rêmorſe,
Will own a *bleſſing* what he fear'd a *curſe* ;
But he whoſe wiſdom, ſuch deſires withſtood,
Unites his pleaſure with his greateſt good,
Knows not misfortune, tho a fair one frown,
His wealth eſcape him, and his friends diſown ;
But, firm in what he is, in what he *may* be, bleſt,
Feels an unvaried ſun-ſhine in his breaſt.

E L L A.   A Norwegian Tale.

BY WILLIAM DUNLAP.

Hiſtory ſays that SIVARD, King of Sweden, entered Norway
with a numerous army, and committed the greateſt en-
ormities, but was at laſt overthrown, his Army routed,
and himſelf ſlain by one of thoſe women whom he had
brutally abuſed.

BETWEEN Norwegian hills, wide ſpreads a plain,
    By Nature form'd for ſport ;
The vet'ran warrior here, and hardy ſwain,
    To annual games reſort.

High o'er their heads was hung the hoary brow,
  Which caſt an ample ſhade ;
From thence theſe words majeſtic ſeem'd to flow—
  " Fierce foes your ſports invade !"

They upward gaze—a warrior ſtruck their ſight ;
  He bore aloft his lance,
All ſheath'd in arms, inſufferably bright,
  Where beamy ſplendours dance.

The weſtern ſun beam round his helmet flies,
  He more than man appears ;
And more than mortal ſeem'd to ſound the voice
  That rang upon their ears.

" Ye ſons of Norway ! hearken to my tale,
  " Your rural games oh ceaſe ;
" Sivard is marching through Dulvellon's vale,
  " Break off the ſports of peace !

" The bloody Sivard leads his conqu'ring Swedes,
  " He riots in our ſhame ;
" The man, the matron, and the infant bleeds—
  " Norway is but a name !

" The huſband ſees—curſe on the tyrant's luſt—
  " He ſees his beauteous bride—
" Her virtue, worth and honour in the duſt—
  " Oh where is Norway's pride !

" Rouſe ! rouſe Norwegians ! ſeize your arms amain,
  " Let helms o'erſhade the brow ;
" Let's meet theſe Swediſh demons on the plain,
  " And lay their triumphs low.

" Oh had you feen what thefe poor eyes have feen!
  'Twas Sivard did the deed—

" Our hoary monarch, and our helplefs queen,
  " I—yes, I faw them bleed.

" Their daughter Ella—no, I will not tell!
  " Norwegians ne'er enquire—

" Ne'er hear it—what the royal maid befel;
  " I fee your fouls on fire.

" Oh feize your fwords, your fpears, your helms and fhields!
  " Oh vindicate your fame!

" Sivard and Sweden glare on Norway's fields;
  " Remember Norway's name."

He faid, tears flow apace---fierce glow the fwains,
  Rage fills each honeft breaft;
In Swedifh blood, to wipe away their ftains
  Was ev'ry thought addrefs'd.

Then red hair'd Rollo, fierce advancing cried
  " Whoe'er thou art, come down!

" We live on hills, to ev'ry toil we're tried,
  " And war is all our own.

" Let Sivard come, we'll meet the tyrant here.
  " But Stranger come thou down."

He came; old Athold gaz'd with look fevere;---
  He gaz'd---but ceas'd to frown.

" Or Athold has forgot his monarch's face,
  " Or fure thou art his fon!

" Eric, of mighty Norway's royal race!"——
  Full quick the tidings run.

With fhouts they prefs to fee the beauteous chief;
  The aged kifs his hand!
On either fide faft roll'd the marks of grief,
  Then Athold fpoke the band——

  " Ye fons of Norway, to your homes repair,
    " There feize the fword and fhield,
  " And ere the morning's purple ftreaks the air,
    " Meet Eric in the field.

  " Oh Prince! do you with aged Athold go,
    " And take refrefhing fleep; .
  " Athold will fing, and footh the rifing woe,
    " Or,---break his harp and weep."——

'Twas night---in Athold's hall each took his place;
  Of other times he fung;
Faft ftream'd the tears adown the hero's face
  And groans refponfive rung.

Bright came the morn! and bright in batter'd arms
  The ruftic vet'rans came;
And many a youth, untried in rough alarms,
  Now hop'd a patriot's name.

They hear'd from far the hum of Sivard's hoft;
  Young Eric ftruck his fhield;
Then high in air his heavy fpear he toft,
  And blaz'd along the field.

Next aged Athold follow'd; Rollo ftrohg;
  Black Calmar lifts his mace;
Culullin, Marco, Streno, rufh along,
  And all the rugged race.

Fierce came the Swede, in ſtrength of numbers proud,
   She ſcorn'd his feeble foe ;
But ſoon the voice of battle roar'd aloud,
   And many a Swede lay low.

Strong Rollo ſtruck the towering Olaus dead,
   Full fifteen bled beſide.
Old Athold cleft the brave Adolphus' head,
   In all his youthful pride.

But Eric ! Eric ! rang'd the field around,
   On Sivard ſtill he cried :
The gaſping Swedes lay heap'd upon the ground---
   Sivard ! the hills reply'd.

In fury Sivard ſeiz'd his ſhining ſhield,
   His mail, his helm and ſpear ;
He mounts his car, he thunders o'er the field ;
   And Norway knows to fear.

Great Rollo falls beneath his dreadful arm,
   His ſteeds are ſtain'd with blood ;
Young Eric ſmil'd to hear the loud alarm,
   And flew to ſtop the flood.

He rag'd, he foam'd,---fierce flew the thirſty ſpear,
   Down fell the foremoſt ſtced :
Aſtoniſh'd Sivard felt unuſual fear———
   " Tyrant, thou'rt doom'd to bleed !"

Up ſprung the youth---deep griding fell the ſword
   Sunk in the Tyrant's brow ;
Faſt fly the Swedes, and leave their hated lord,
   His tow'ring pride laid low.

Now Norway's fons their great deliverer hail,
  But lo! he bleeds! he falls!
Old Athold ftrips the helm and beamy mail,
  And on his Gods he calls.

He lifts the helm, and down the fnowy neck
  Faft falls the filky hair—
" And could thofe limbs, the conquering Sivard check
  Oh Pow'r of great defpair!——"

Life ebbs apace---fhe lifts her languid head,
  She ftrives her hand to wave,
Confefs'd to all, the beauteous Ella faid——
  " Thanks, thanks companions brave."

" Freedom rewards you---naught can Ella give
  " Low, low, poor Ella lies;
" Sivard is dead! and Ella would not live."
  She bleeds, fhe faints, fhe dies.

EULOGIUM on RUM.

BY J. SMITH.

ARISE! ye pimpled, tipling race, arife!
  From ev'ry town and village tavern, come!
Shew your red nofes, and o'erflowing eyes
  And help your poet chant the praife of Rum.
The cordial drop, the morning dram, I fing,
The mid-day toddy, and the evening fling.

Hail, mighty Rum! and by this general name
  I call each species—whiſky, gin, or brandy :
(The kinds are various—but the effects the ſame;
  And ſo I chooſe a name that's ſhort and handy ;
For, reader, know, it takes a deal of time,
To make a crooked word lie ſmooth in rhyme.)

Hail, mighty Rum! thy ſong-inſpiring merit
  Is known to many a bard in theſe our days :
Apollo's drink, they find, is void of ſpirit—
  Mere chicken-broth—inſipid as their lays :
And, pleas'd, they'd give a riv'let—aye a ſea
Of tuneful water, for one quart of thee!

Hail, mighty Rum! how wond'rous is thy pow'r!
  Unwarm'd by thee, how would our ſpirits fail,
When dark December comes, with aſpect four,
  And, ſharp as razor, blows the northern gale!
And yet thour't grateful in that ſultry day,
When raging Sirius darts his fervid ray.

Hail, mighty Rum! to thee the wretched fly :
  And find a ſweet oblivion of their woes;
Lock'd in thy arms, as in the grave, they lie—
  Forget their kindred—and forgive their foes.
And Lethe's ſtream, (ſo much extoll'd by ſome,
In ancient times) I ſhrewdly gueſs, was Rum.

Hail, mighty Rum! what can thy pow'r withſtand!
  E'en lordly Reaſon flies thy dreadful face :
And Health, and Joy, and all the lovely band
  Of ſocial Virtues, ſhun thy dwelling place :
(For in whatever breaſt it rears its throne,
Like Turkiſh monarchs, Rum muſt rule alone.)

When our bold fathers crofs'd the Atlantic wave,
  And here arriv'd—a weak defencelefs band—
Pray, what became of all the tribes fo brave—
  The favage owners of this happy land?
Were they fent headlong to the realms below,
" By doom of battle?" friend, * I anfwer no.

Our fathers were too wife to think of war ;
  They knew the woodlands were not quickly paft:
They might have met with many an ugly fcar—
  Loft many a foretop—and been beat at laft.
But Rum, affifted by his fon, Difeafe,
Perform'd the bufinefs with furprifing eafe.

And would our weftern brethren be lefs proud, or,
  In other words, throw by their gun and drum—
For ducks and fquirrels, fave their lead and powder,
  And fend the tawny rogues fome pipes of rum—
I dare predict, they all would gladly fuck it ;
And ev'ry mother's fon foon *kick the bucket*.

But lo ! the ingratitude of Adam's race !
  Tho' all thefe clever things to Rum we owe—
Gallons of ink are fquirted in his face ;
  And his bruis'd back is bang'd with many a blow ;
Some hounds of note have rung his funeral knell,
And ev'ry puppy joins the gen'ral yell.

So have I feen (the fimile is fine—
  And wonderfully pat—tho' rather old)
When rifing Phœbus fhot his rays benign,
  A flock of fheep come fkipping from the fold ;
                    H h

* This alludes only to Jerfey, Pennfylvania, &c.

Some reftlefs fheep cries baa : and all the throng,
Ewes, rams, lambs, wethers, bellowing pour along,

But fear not, Rum, tho' fiercely they affail,
    And none but I, the bard, thy caufe defend,
Think not thy foes—tho' num'rous—fhall prevail,
    Thy pow'r diminifh, or thy being end :
Tho' fpurn d from table, and the public eye,
In the fnug clofet fafely fhalt thou lie.

And oft, when Sol's proud chariot quits the fky,
    And humbler Cynthia mounts her one-horfe chair,
To that fnug clofet fhall thy vot'ry fly ;
    And, rapt in darknefs, keep his orgies there ;
Lift the full bottle, joyous, to his head,
Then, great as Cæfar, reel fublime to bed.

Burlington, Dec. 7th, 1789.

THE COUNTRY MEETING.*

BY T. C. JAMES.

OF war's tremendous deeds, the din of arms,
    And acts by Fame renown'd, fain would I fing,
But that ambition ne'er my bofom warms,
    Nor would Calliope her fuccour bring
    To bard that foars with too advent'rous wing.

---

* Or friends' place of worfhip.

O Shenſtone! ſweeteſt child of fancy fair,
  Dart one fond ray, and guide the weakeſt quill,
That ever raſhly claim'd thy guardian care,
  To point the high path up the ſlipp'ry hill,
  Where thou thy lyre doſt touch with ſtill improving ſkill.

Themes that have ne'er been poliſh'd into rhyme,
  Wou'd a faint pencil in this verſe pourtray,
If in the fond attempt to gain on time,
  No taunting critic meet me on my way,
  And with theſe accents rude my heart diſmay:
' Vain youth, forbear, by deſp'rate folly mov'd,
  ' Of poetaſters the mean herd to ſwell;
' But mark his ſtrain whom laurell'd Phœbus lov'd,
  ' What Horace, tuneful bard, has ſung ſo well,
  ' How Dædalus's ſon, bold artiſt, headlong fell.'

View yonder ancient dome with trees befet,
  From which no lofty ſpire doth proudly riſe,
Nor hence each week, when congregation's met,
  Are ſtudied hymns e'er wing'd unto the ſkies,
  Nor doth amen from pariſh clerk ariſe.
E'en muſic's lulling charms befeemeth wrong
  To thoſe who did this modeſt temple rear;
For all, who to thoſe lonely confines throng,
  Worſhip in guiſe of ſolemn ſilent prayer;
  Nor can they think that words their ſinful deeds repair.

No pulpit here doth grace the naked wall,
  Nor doth the ſculptor his gay art expreſs:
For thus they teach: ' Religion does not call
  ' For the vain ornaments of ſplendid dreſs,
  ' Nor will meek heaven ſuperfluous grandeur bleſs.'

And wrong they hold it, that the flock fhould pay
  For truths which ought to flow without controul,
Free as the filver dew, or light of day,
  To beam mild virtue on the expanding foul,
  And fpread celeftial fparks, free gift, from pole to pole.

But fee, o'er yonder field, the elder train
  Of village dames their little infants bring,
Who elfe might loiter on the graffy plain,
  And wet their new clothes in yon bubbling fpring,
  Which would their parents' minds with forrow fting.
The fportive urchins oft will fkip away,
  To chafe the partridge from the neighb'ring bufh:
And oft, with balls of well-attemper'd clay,
  Will from its covert fright the trembling thrufh, [hufh.
  Nor mind the matron's careful voice, which would them

Down the flop'd hill the gayer tribe defcend,
  On neighing fteeds, that champ the fteeled bit,
Strait to the fane their pompous way they tend;
  There 'midft their peers in goodly order fit,
  Young fwains for ftrength renown'd, and maids for wit:
Such ftrength as at the mill-door oft is feen
  When Colin lifts the fack of mighty weight;
Such wit as fports in gambols o'er the green,
  And would the ear of nicer townfman grate:
  He'd call it fhocking ftuff, and rude, unfeemly prate.

Yet Humour her abode will deign to fix
  Amidft the lively ruftics of the place,
And with the village hinds will often mix,
  Giving to ev'ry feat a feftive grace,
  And fpreading chearfulnefs o'er ev'ry face.

Let the polite, the polifh'd, blame their joys,
   Whom Nature, unconftrain'd, can never charm:
This is the life which ennui never cloys,
   Nor e'er can fell Ambition work it harm,
     Blowing with hideous blaft its poifonous alarm.

See yonder youth on prancing bay fteed ride,
   While fatisfaction on his broad front beams;
And view his gentle charmer by his fide,
   For whom he wifhes, and of whom he dreams;
     Of heavenly form and mind to him fhe feems.
For her each ev'ning anxiously he culls,
   Of wild flow'rs fair, a nofegay fcented fweet:
For her the chefnut drops its prickly hulls,
   And the wood pigeon yields its fav'ry meat,
    With thoufand tempting gifts which verfe cannot repeat.

And now thro' folding doors, full wide difplay'd,
   The affembly's grave and pious numbers throng,
While well each noify buzzing murmur's ftay'd,
   With the loofe prattling of each infant tongue;
     For oft confufion has from childhood fprung.
See the wife elder's venerable grace,
   Mark with what flow-pac'd dignity he moves;
See ev'ry little eye hangs on his face,
   And over all his features fondly roves,
     For he the junior train affectionately loves.

The village teacher fits with looks profound,
   And marks the ent'ring throng, with eye afkance;
If, as he careful views the dome around,
   He fhould on carelefs pupil's vifage chance,
     He fends him ftraight a play-forbidding glance.

Of looks like thefe he hath a plenteous ftore,
  To fright his ftudents from each frolic mood :
And well they watch to fee his afpect lour,
  Trying each art to avert the baleful wood,
  By fitting wond'rous ftill, and feeming e'en as good.

Silence with Sleep his empire now divides,
  While fome on this, and fome on that fide nod ;
The ploughman ftill his fteers and ploughfhare guides,
  And breaks in pleafing dreams the fancied fod ;
  While the fchool-miftrefs wields the birchen rod.
Others, more wakeful, plan their future deeds,
  While on increafe of wealth their wifhes ftray :
The farmer thus in rapture counts his fteeds,
  And deals to each his part of winter's hay,
  Till fpring renews the grafs, and gives returning May.

Where will not thirft of treach'rous gold approach,
  Since here, e'en here, it holds its wide domain !
From the warm cit who rolls in gilded coach,
  To the dull carter, whiftling o'er the plain,
  Does Plutus, god of fhining lucre, reign.
Happy, thrice happy are th' inftructed few,
  On whom fell Want ne'er lays her harpy claws,
But, far retir'd from 'midft the toiling crew,
  Live in obfervance of wife Nature's laws,
  And learn from her to trace the great Eternal Caufe.

✳
✳✳✳
✳

WRITTEN AT SEA, IN A HEAVY GALE.

BY CAPT. PHILIP FRENEAU.

HAPPY the man who, safe on shore,
　　Now trims, at home, his evening fire ;
Unmov'd he hears the tempest roar,
　　That on the tufted groves expire ;
　　　Alas ! on us they doubly fall,
　　　Our feeble bark must bear them all.

Now to their haunts the birds retreat,
　　The squirrel seeks his hollow tree,
Wolves in their shaded caverns meet,
　　All, all are blest but wretched we—
　　　For, doom'd a stranger to repose,
　　　No rest the unsettled ocean knows.

Whilst o'er the dark abyss we roam,
　　Perhaps whate'er the pilots say,
We saw the sun's descending gloom,
　　No more to see the rising ray ;
　　　But buried low, by far too deep,
　　　On coral beds unpitied sleep !

But what a strange uncoasted strand
　　Is that where death permits no day,
No charts we have to mark that land,
　　No compass to direct the way !
　　　What pilot shall explore that realm,
　　　What new Columbus take the helm !

While death and darknefs both furround,
.   And tempefts rage with lawlefs power,
Of friendfhip's voice I hear no found,
    No comfort in this dreadful hour—
        What friendfhip can in tempefts be,
        What comforts on this angry fea !

The barque accuftom'd to obey,
    No more the trembling pilots guide,
Alone fhe gropes her tracklefs way,
    While mountains burft on every fide.
        Thus fkill and fcience both muft fall,
        And ruin is the lot of all.

——————————

TO ELLA.†

AH! vainly Ella, do I hear
    Thy lute complain, in notes fo clear,
As would feduce an angel's ear ;
That bids me check the fong of praife,
And give to *other themes*, my lays.

To fierce difeafe and grief a prey,
In pain I pafs the lingering day.

——————————

* This, and the fucceeding Poems, figned BIRTHA, are
extracted from the Gazette of the United States ; where
they form part of a poetical Correfpondence, carried on under the fignatures of ELLA and BIRTHA.   We have fe-
lected the following Poems as being moft correct, and moft
worthy of prefervation ; efpecially as they are now offered
to the public with the author's corrections.

No more I raife the fprightly ftrain,
   Or warble the melodious fong,
That fill'd the breaft with envied pain,
   And could the joys of life prolong.

Now, when the *glowing orb* of day,
   Hath funk beneath the weftern wave ;
With melancholy heart I ftray
   To hear the ftream his border lave.

Or like fome pilgrim prefs the yielding grafs,
   And wet my fandals with the nightly dew,
A fprig of laurel breaking as I pafs,
   To *thee* I fay the *honoring branch* is due.

My dangerous courfe along the vale I take,
   Beneath the hanging rock, that feems to fhake
With ev'ry blaft, and threatens on my head
   Its crufhing weight to roll ;
   But my undaunted foul,
Enjoys the fcene, nor feels the chill of terror fpread.

Now, near a cavern dark, and wild,
   With folded arms I ftand,
Like melancholy's gloomy child;
   I heave the fwelling figh ;
   Upon the pafling gale ;
   While from my ever-ftreaming eye ;
    Adown my cheeks, fo wan and pale,
The tears inceffant drop upon my hand.
There I hear the moping owl,
His difmal whoopings roll,

Upon the heavy ear of night,
In founds that would thy foul affright.

But oh! my burfting heart!
So tortur'd by the fang of grief,
In other fcenes would feek relief:
On fancy's rapid wing I'd dart
Where Horror with his ftaring eye,
And upright hair,
Sits gazing on the fiery fky,
When fulphurous lightnings fly,
And fwell the foul to wild defpair.

Where the vex'd wave with mad'ning roar,
Rolls thundering on the craggy fhore,
And aims with ev'ry dreadful fhock,
To burft apart the flinty rock;
When ftill like wretched man! in vain
He ftrives his purpofe to obtain;
Mad to defpair, he flies again
And clamours to his parent main.

BIRTHA.

MAY 21, 1791.

––––––––

TO ELLA.

HARK! while I found my trembling fhell,
    And bid the nymph, fweet Echo tell;
Where on her velvet couch fhe lies,
Hid from the gairifh burning fkies;
How the foul-enlivening found
Of thy enchanting lyre,
Was borne on Ether's waves around,
From each foft-fpeaking wire.

'Twas when befide the wizard ftream,
I faw the fun's laft golden bea n,
With yellow tip the afpiring heads,
Of time-contending oaks, the king of fhades !
I faw the night flies buzzing round,
I heard the beetle's humming found :
My foul to fober thought inclin'd,
Thus ran the current of my mind.

No longer now my cheeks difclofe,
The beauty of the budding rofe ;
No longer, as in former days,
I joy, the fprightly laugh to raife.
O ! then each lovely, fummer's night,
'Twas my enraptured foul's delight,
To tread the lonely filent vale,
And " drink the fpirit of the gale :"

Or when the cloudlefs moon on high,
Beam'd forth her radiance from the fky :
To wander o'er the airy hill,
Where pattering falls the lucid rill ;
And fee the wild flow'rs fhining bright,
Crown'd with the *tears of weeping night.*

But O ! the wondrous change !
Now, it delights me not to range,
The fields and vallies, bright and gay,
With beauties of the *laughing May.*

When the fhrill fpirits of the coming ftorm,
    Their fhrieks of terror pour along the wind ;
And fiercer raging all the grove deform,
    The branches tear, and fhatter down the rind:

When heaven's bright fires defcending from on high,
Flafh awful day along the gloomy fky;
And from their dwellings the hoarfe thunders roar,
And dufky torrents down the vallies pour:
'Tis then my foul enjoys the dreadful hour,
And bows, my God! in rev'rence to thy power.
,Twas thus I mus'd, when borne along the air,
Thy heavenly notes came trembling on my ear;
Sweet as the gentleft fhowers
Of fpring, defcending on the flowers,
When murmuring Zephyr finks to reft,
Soft-fighing on the lily's breaft.

Ah! wouldft thou with thy arm fuftain
My wearied form, and foothe my pain?
And wouldft thou all the lingering Eve,
With thy foft founds my foul relieve?
And haft thou learn'd the healing charm,
The power to bid the tyrant Sicknefs fly?
O! hither come, extend thy potent arm,
And bid the *beam of Hope* ftand fparkling in my eye!

Ah! now, ev'n now, this very hour,
I confefs thy magic power!
Charm'd with thy notes divine,
No more my troubled foul,
O'er fcenes of horror loves to brood,
No more my freezing blood,
In lazy tides doth roll,
Bright in my eye the tears of rapture fhine,
Thro' all my nerves I feel a tremor run,
Now cold as Zembla's fnow, now fervid as the fun.

O! may thy generous fympathifing heart,
Ne'er feel the anguifh of affliction's dart;
May ftreams of earthly treafure on thee flow,
That thou, the pure celeftial joy may'ft know,
To bid the beggar fmile, and cheer his *houfe of woe.*

BIRTHA.

JUNE 4, 1791.

TO ELLA.

AGAIN thy fweetly warbled ftrain,
　Thou leader of the choral train;
Again thy fweeping harp I hear,
That long has charmed my ravifhed ear.

New vigour to my foul thy words impart,
With fofter pleafures touch thy wounded heart:
The moral lore that flows along thy line,
Might well befit a PLINY to rehearfe;
The bold defcriptive beauties of thy Verfe,
Would bright on TITIAN's glowing canvas fhine.

When clofed the blazing eye of day,
And on my downy couch I lay,
Deep mufing on thy moral lore;
The God of Sleep around me threw
His mantle dipt in flumbrous dew;
And thus arofe my fervent pray'r—

O! thou from whom creation fprung!
O! fend from thy bright realms above,
Some faint to cheer me with thy love,
And bid me raife the rapturous fong—

For I have heard thy fpirits who on high
Poffefs the plains of yon cerulean fky;
Have oft, in pity to the mortal race,
Defcending clofed them in their pure embrace;
And whifpering foothing mufic to their breaft,
Charm'd all the tempefts of the foul to reft—
Scarce had the words efcaped my moving tongue,
Yet on my lips the trembling accents hung;
When lo! a form defcending from on high,
On filver plumes thro' yonder orient fky:
Wide flows in circling locks her golden hair,
And plays with every eddying of the air.
Her robes of filmy texture white as fnow,
Around her form in graceful foldings flow.
Her bright blue eyes beam forth a gentle light,
And fix and charm at once the gazer's fight.
When near fhe moved I faw bewitching grace,
And heavenly beauty lighten up her face.
Now by my fide upon the earth fhe ftood,
Her quickened glance warm'd all my chilly blood.
High waving in the air a fky-blue wand,
She bade me follow to yon lofty land;
The path fhe led, with joyous heart I flew,
'Till near the high and verdant hill I drew;
Then turning round fhe took my trembling hand,
And waved again her bright cerulean wand:
Soft as the found of fome angelic lute,
Sweet as the breath of Orpheus' mellow flute.
Her words in rapt'rous warblings pour'd along,
And thrill'd my trembling foul with heavenly fong.
Behold! fhe faid, that lovely country round,
With nature's richeft gifts and beauty crown'd;

There pureſt joy flows thro the circling year,
The happy people know no pain, nor fear ;
Their queen I am, from realms of light I came,
Fair virtue's offspring, *blue-eyed Hope* my name.''
She ceaſed ; then roſe before my raviſh'd ſight,
Enchanting ſcenes in nature's beauty bright ;
Here ſpreads a wide and ever verdant plain,
And waves the yellow life-ſupporting grain :
There grandly riſe the proud aſpiring hills,
Between whoſe rocky chinks ſlide down the rills.
Here in majeſtic beauty towering high,
Shoot verdant groves toward the cloudleſs ſky ;
The feathered warblers hop from ſpray to ſpray,
And hold their tuneful ſtrife till cloſing day ;
Then pours the plaintive Nightingale her notes,
And all night long her melting muſic floats—
Along the walks of thoſe e'er blooming bowers,
Forever ſpring new crops of fragrant flowers.
The priſtine colors of the ſun are ſeen
With countleſs changes waving o'er the green—
Rich ſculptur'd figures form'd of blazing gold,
Attract the eye, and firm the ſenſes hold—
Here *Dove-like Innocence*, engaged in play,
With frolic lambs prolongs the happy day ;
There *Charity* throws forth her copious ſtore,
Till the glad ſuppliants ceaſe to aſk for more :
Here, with celeſtial glory in her eye,
Mild Faith with firmneſs gazes on the ſky,
And *Adoration* pours her ſong of praiſe,
While tears of rapture wander down her face.
There o'er white curling lakes the nodding trees,
Wave ſlowly to the gentle paſſing breeze;

And wildly-grand around deep rocky caves
Return the Echo of the dashing waves.   .
Here chryftal mountains shooting to the sky,
With the bright sun in splendor seem to vie;
Where rise the rugged rocks an awful height!
The sheeting torrent holds my wandering sight:
From steep to steep down dash with thundering roar
The mad'ning waves, and foam along the shore.
" Lo said the maid there burfting from the ground,
A bubbling fountain casts its waters round;
And see behind, where opens yonder bower,
The virtuous souls enjoy the rapturous hour:
There many a harp, and many a breathing flute
Is heard; responding sounds the silver lute;
Whilft ravish'd with the melody of sound
The vocal chorus pour their songs around.
Thus all the bleft their happy days employ,
And each contributes to the other's joy;
Their grateful inc nse rises up to heaven,
And for their praife a double joy is given:
Know thou, she said, whoe'er pursues the path
That leads to *Virtue* and unwavering *Faith*,
Shall hail me Queen! and where they dwell shall rise
A scene like this, enchanting to their eyes;
The spheres shall warble music in their ear,
And all creation harmony appear."
Now ceafed her voice, she clap'd her silver wings,
And rising to the sky thro Ether sings.

                               BIRTHA.

JULY 2, 1791.

THE *Lord of light* has journey'd down the fky,
    And bath'd his courfers in the foaming wave;
    The twinkling ftar of Even too, haftes to lave
Her filver form, and vanifh from my eye.
    Now dufky twilight flings her fombre fhade,
      O'er the bright beauties of the filent vale;
    The afpin trembles not, the verdant blade
    No longer nodding anfwers to the gale.
    Come fweet Reflection! hither penfive maid!
      Direct thy wandering fteps, and on this ftone,
    Worn by no traveller's feet, with mofs o'ergrown,
      Repofe with me in folitude's deep fhade.
      Then fhall I know the height of human blifs,
      And tafte the joy of *other worlds* in this.

                          B I R T H A.

MAY 25th, 1791.

              K k

           END OF SELECTED POETRY.

ORIGINAL POETRY.

AN ELEGY,
WRITTEN IN FEBRUARY 1791.

BY MR. RICHARD ALSOP.

DARK is the hour and lone, o'er icy plains
　The wandering meteors gleam a deadly light;
Wild howls the blaſt amid deſcending rains,
　And forms funereal flit along the night.

Retir'd from ſcenes where Pleaſure's airy wand
　Gilds the light moments with deluſive joy,
Where Mirth exulting leads her feſtive band,
　Far other ſcenes my penſive ſoul employ.

The clouds of death that gloom the baleful year,
　The days of joy, alas, ſo lately fled!
While Friendſhip bids its ſympathetic tear
　Stream in remembrance of the much-lov'd dead.

My friend, but now, of every blifs poſſeſt
　That love connubial can on man beſtow,
When mutual wiſhes warm the mutual breaſt;
　Behold the prey of life-conſuming woe.

Of late, how fair the beauteous proſpect ſhow'd,
　How lovely glittering in the morning's eye;
But long ere noon, like April's painted cloud,
　Or hues that tinge the ſummer's evening ſky,

The fairy hopes that raptur'd Fancy drew,
   The dream of future blifs that fhone fo bright,
On Fate's fwift pinions vanifh'd from the view,
   And funk in fhadows of eternal night.——

What notes of woe in mournful cadence fwell
   Along the Weftern breeze from climes afar,
Mix'd with the dying groan, the favage yell,
   And all the horrid diffonance of war!

And lo! mid gliding fpectres dimly feen,
   Pale as the mifts that Autumn's car furround,
A form fuperior lifts his penfive mien,
   While on his bofom glares the fhadowy wound.

" Behold," he cries, " the band who lately bled,
   " Mid weftern wilds in glorious conflict flain;
" While recreant troops in pale confufion fled,
   " Ignobly left unburied on the plain."——

Far opes the view, fublime in favage pride
   A wild unbounded frowns on Fancy's eye;
Tall rife the trees, and o'er favannahs wide
   The rank grafs trembles to the breeze on high.

With torrent fweep, amid a night of woods
   Where fcarce the fun a livid glimmering lends,
A blood-ftain'd river rolls his foaming floods,
   And o'er the plains in wild meanders bends.

Lo! this the fcene where War, with bloody hand,
   Wav'd his red ftandard o'er the carnag'd ground;
Where wild-eyed Horror led the tawny band,
   And fell the brave with dear-bought laurels crown'd.

Here, grim with gore, beneath the inclement sky,
   Smote by the parching ray and driving rain,
The mangled forms of breathless warriors lie,
   All pale extended on the lonely plain.

In slaughter'd heaps, around promiscuous cast,
   Mid savage chiefs Columbia's sons are spread,
While, breath'd from polar snows, the northern blast
   Shakes its cold pinions o'er the unburied dead.

For them no more shall morning gild the sky,
   No more shall May unveil her radiant charms,
No more shall Joy illume the sparkling eye,
   Or Glory's voice excite the soul to arms.

Near yon grey rock by withering leaves conceal'd,
   Amyntor lies, benevolent and brave ;
Whose duteous hand a father's age upheld,
   And smooth'd his dreary passage to the grave.

Not far, a corse distinguish'd o'er the rest,
   Of noble stature and heroic mien ;
Deep opes the wound that gor'd his manly breast,
   And his pale features wear a smile serene.

Too well alas ! that much-lov'd form I know,
   Those features pale with gory dust o'erspread,
O'er whom has Friendship mourn'd in bitterest woe,
   For whom Affection's tenderest tears are shed.

Still, still in Fancy's view recurs the day
   When war's black demons pour'd their hideous yell,
When left expos'd to savage rage a prey,
   Thy gallant band beside their leader fell.

Opprest with toil, while countless foes surround,
   'I hy arm, thy voice, the fainting troop infpir'd ;
And e'en when finking with the deadly wound,
   'I hy lateft breath their martial ardor fir'd.

Lamented Hero, far from weeping friends !
   No funeral honours to thy corfe were paid,
And no memorial o'er thy grave extends
   To mark the lonely fpot where low thou'rt laid.

Yet what avails to pleafe the fenfelefs clay,
   " The trophied tomb," the monumental buft,
Or recks the fpirit mid the realms of day,
   The empty rites attendant on its duft.

A fa'rer wreath fhall friendfhip's hand beftow,
   A fairer tribute fhall thy fhade receive,
Than all the idle pageantry of woe,
   Than all its pompous monuments can give.

Long, long fhall Memory's ardent eye recall
   Thy worth, thy milder virtues to her view ;
Thy Country long lament her hero's fall,
   And o'er thee Fame her brighteft laurels ftrew.

O'er the lone fpot where refts thy mouldering form,
   Shall opening fpring her mildeft breezes wave ;
And Flora's hand with every fragrant charm
   Deck the foft turf that forms thy verdant grove.

There the Wild-Rofe in earlieft pride fhall bloom,
   There the Magnolia's gorgeous flowers unfold,
The purple Violet fhed its fweet perfume,
   And beauteous Meadia wave her plumes of gold.

Reft much-lov'd Chief with thy Jer——a bleft,
  Amid yon realms of light, yon feats of joy,
Where hufh'd is forrow in perpetual reft,
  And pleafure fmiles unconfcious of alloy.

From that calm fhore with pitying eye furvey
  The varying fchemes of man, the bufy ftrife,
The vain purfuits that fill his " little day,"
  And tofs with ceafelefs ftorms the fea of life.

While feraphs, bending from their thrones of gold,
  With fongs of triumph hymn thy foul to peace;
And to thy raptur'd eye, with fmiles, unfold
  The happy manfions of eternal blifs.

VERSIFICATION

OF A PASSAGE FROM THE FIFTH BOOK OF OSSIAN'S TEMORA.

BY THE SAME.

THE hofts like two black ridges ftood,
  On either fide wild Lubar's ftream;
Here Foldath frown'd a darken'd cloud,
  There Fillan fhone a brightening beam.

Their long fpears glittering in the wave,
  Each hero pour'd his voice afar;
Gaul ftruck the fhield, the fignal gave,
  At once both armies plung'd in war.

Steel pour'd its flashing gleam on steel;
  The fields two rushing torrents glow,
That whitening foam, in mingled swell,
  O'er the dark rock's projecting brow.

He comes, with fame immortal crown'd,
  His faulchion lays the heroes low;
Death rides the shadowy blasts around;
  Thy paths O Fillan warriors strew!

Between two rocks in fissures rent,
  Brave Rothmar stood, the warrior's pride;
Two aged oaks, that winds had bent,
  Their branches spread on either side.

Silent he shades his friends in flight,
  While his dark eyes on Fillan roll;
Fingal beheld the approaching fight,
  And all the father fill'd his soul.

As falls the stone of Loda, hurl'd
  From trembling Drumanard's high cliff,
When angry spirits rock the world;
  So Rothmar fell, blue-shielded chief.

Young Culmin's friendly steps are near,
  His eye the bursting tear o'erflows;
Wrathful he cuts the empty air,
  Ere yet with Fillan's mix his blows.

He first with Rothmar bent the bow,
  Along his own blue-winding streams;
And mark'd the dwelling of the roe,
  As shone the fern with morning beams.

" Why Youth would'ft thou provoke the might
 Of that bright beam, that wafting fire?
Unequal were your fires in fight;
 Retire, Culalluins's fon retire !"

Lone in her hall, his mother cafts
 Her eyes o'er Strutha's wind ng ftreams;
Wrapp'd in a whirlwind's eddying blafts,
 Her fon's thin fpectre faintly gleams.

His dogs ftand howling on the plain,
 Red his fufpended fhield with gore;
" And is my fair-hair'd hero flain?
 Pale does he lie on Ullin's fhore ?"

As pierc'd in fecret lies a hind,
 Panting her wonted ftreams befide;
The hunter views her feet of wind;
 Culalluin's fon thus Fillan eyed.

In a fmall ftream his hair is roll'd,
 His blood flow wanders o'er his fhield;
Still grafps his hand, with dying hold,
 The fword that fail'd in danger's field.

" 'Thou'rt fallen ere thy fame was known,"
 Said Fillan, mufing o'er the flain;
" Elate, in hopes of thy renown,
 Thy father fent thee to the plain.

Perhaps, his ftreams grey bending o'er,
 His dim eyes feek thee on the heath;
In vain,—for ah ! returns no more,
 His fon extended pale in death."

Wide o'er the heath, in terror loft,
　　The flight of Erin Fillan pour'd;
But, man on man, falls Morven's hoft,
　　Before the rage of Foldath's fword.

Undaunted, Dermid meets his courfe;
　　The fons of Cona wake the fight;
But cleft his fhield, by Foldath's force,
　　And far is fpread his people's flight.

The exulting foe with haughty boaft,—
　　" Go Malthos, go to Erin's lord;
And bid him guard blue ocean's coaft,
　　Left Morven's king efcape my fword.

For cold muft Fingal lie in gore,
　　Near fome low fen his tomb fhall rife
Without a fong, while hovering o'er,
　　Half hid in mift, his fpirit flies."

In darkening doubt ftood Malthos bold,
　　He knew the boafter's heart of pride;
Around his gloomy eyes he roll'd,
　　And plung'd in war with fullen ftride.

In Clono's narrow vale, two trees
　　Dark-bending o'er the rolling flood,
Shook their broad branches to the breeze;
　　There Dathno's fon in filence ftood.

The blood is ftreaming from his thigh;
　　A rock fuftains his afhen fpear;
His boffy fhield lies broken nigh;
　　" Why Dermid, why that burfting tear?"

" I hear the battle roar afar,
Alone my people on the plain;
No fhield is mine to ftem the war,
And weak and flow my fteps of pain.

Shall Foldath then prevail in fight?
Ere that in death fhall Dermid lie;
Again ftern chief I'll prove thy might,
Again thy fierceft rage defy."

He feiz'd his fpear the ftrife to join,
When Morni's fon before him ftood;
" Stay Dermid ftay, no fhield is thine,
Thy trembling fteps are mark'd with blood."

" Chief of Strumon give thy fhield,
Oft has it ftemm'd the battle's force;
This arm may yet fuftain the field,
May yet repel yon boafter's courfe.

Behold that ftone, with mofs o'erfpread,
Where fpires the waving grafs fo high;
There low a kindred chief is laid—
And there in night let Dermid lie."

Slowly he rofe the hill's tall brow,
And view'd the troubled field of death;
The gleaming ranks of fight below,
Disjoin'd, and broken o'er the heath.

As fires at diftance, feem by night
Now loft in fmoke, in darknefs drown'd,
Now rear on high their ftreams of light,
As ceafe or blow the winds around;

So met the battle from afar
 Broad-shielded Dermid's eager eye.
Amidst the varying scene of war
 The chief of Morna towers on high;

Like some black ship, in lofty pride,
 Dark rider of the billowy plain;
Wide sporting o'er the echoing tide,
 When winter rules the stormy main.

Dermid with rage beheld his course,
 He rush'd to meet the gloomy foe;
But fails the wounded hero's force,
 And tears of pride his eyes o'erflow.

He founded thrice his bossy shield,
 And thrice on Foldath call'd aloud;
Foldath with joy the chief beheld,
 And lifted high his spear of blood.

As some vast rock whose rugged side
 Is mark'd with streams of many a storm;
So look'd, with wandering blood bedyed
 The gloomy chief of Morna's form.

Each host, appall'd, in terror flies,
 From the contending fierce of Kings.
At once their gleaming points arise,
 With speed of lightning Fillan springs.

The haughty foe, with trembling, view'd,
 That dazzling beam of early fame;
That swift, as issuing from a cloud,
 To save the wounded hero came.

In founding ftrife as on the gale
   Two broad-wing'd eagles fierce contend;
So, on Moilena's far-fpread vale,
   The chiefs in gloomy battle bend.

Low on his fhield is Foldath laid,
   Pierc'd by th' youthful hero's fpear;
Nor o'er the fallen Fillan ftaid,
   But onward roll'd the ftorm of war.

Malthos beheld the warrior low,
   Low laid on Lubar's winding fhore;
His bofom melts in generous woe,
   And hatred fills his foul no more.

He feem'd a rock, down whofe grey fides
   The defart waters trickling ftray;
When flow the failing mift divides,
   And gives its blafted trees to day.

Thus to the dying chief he faid,—
   " Say fhall thy moffy ftone afcend,
Where Ullin's dark green hills are fpread,
   Or Morna's woody vales extend?

There, where the fun looks forth ferene,
   On blue Dalrutho's bordering glades;
Fair Dardulena's fteps are feen,
   Thy daughter, pride of Erin's maids."

" Remembereft thou," the chief reply'd,
   " The maid, becaufe no fon is mine,
To roll the battle's deathful tide,
   And in revenge in arms to fhine?

I am reveng'd, for not in vain
   'Has fhone the lightning of my fpear.
Amidft the tombs of thofe I've flain
   My narrow houfe, O Malthos! rear.

Oft fhall I leave my airy fold,
   To hail the fpot where low they lie;
When, fpread around me, I behold,
   The rank grafs of their graves on high."

His fpirit rufh'd on eddying winds,
   And came to Dardulena's dream;
As, wearied with the chace of hinds,
   She flept by blue Dulrutho's ftream.

Her bow unftrung is near her placed,
   The breezes fold her raven hair;
Each charm of youthful beauty graced
   The love of chiefs, the blue-eyed fair.

From the dark fkirts of Morna's wood,
   Her father's ghoft, pale bending, gleam'd;
At times his bloody form he fhew'd,
   Then hid in fhrouding vapors feem'd.

She rofe in tears, her foul divin'd
   The chief in death was lowly laid;
To her a beam of light he fhin'd.
   When folded in his darkeft fhade.

HABAKKUK, Chap. III.

BY THE SAME.

THE Lord of Hosts from Teman came,
　From Paran's mount the Almighty God,—
The heavens his glory wide proclaim,
　And bent the earth beneath his nod.

As light his awful brightness show'd,—
　There was the hiding of his power;
On burning coals Jehovah trode,
　Dire mov'd the pestilence before.

He stood, and measur'd earth and air,
　He look'd, apart the nations fled,
The eternal mountains scatter'd were,
　And hills perpetual bow'd the head.

I saw when Midian's curtains shook,
　I saw pale Cushan's tents in woe;
Say, did the streams thy wrath provoke?
　Against them did thine anger glow?

Did e'er the deep his God displease,
　That on thy horses thou did'st ride?
Thy path was thro' the troubled seas,
　In heaps roll'd back the astonish'd tide.

The mountains saw, they trembling shook,
　The o'erflowing waters passed by,
The mighty deep in horror spoke,
　And lifted up his hands on high.

The rolling ftars their courfes ftay'd,
    The fun and moon ftood ftill in fear;
Before thine arrows blaze they fled,
    Before the lightning of thy fpear.

With rivers did'ft thou cleave the earth,
    And naked made thy dreadful bow;
Thou march'd in indignation forth,
    And laid in duft the heathen low :

Thou wenteft forth on Ifrael's fide,
    To fave from death thy chofen race;
Thy fword has fmote the heathen's pride,
    And everlafting are thy ways.

Altho' the fig-tree fhall not fhoot,
    Nor grape the withering vine fhall yield,
The olive fhall withhold her fruit,
    And blafted be the herbag'd fie'd;

Tho' in the fold the flock fhall die,
    And in the ftall no herd fhall be,
Yet on the Lord will I rely,
    Yet, O my God! will joy in thee.

RUNIC POETRY.

====

TWILIGHT OF THE GODS;
OR
DESTRUCTION OF THE WORLD.

FROM THE EDDA, A SYSTEM OF ANCIENT SCANDINAVIAN
MYTHOLOGY.

———————

BY THE SAME.

———————

A TIME fhall come, a barbarous time,
   Dark fhadowed o'er with every crime,
When ties of kin fhall ceafe to bind,
In love's foft bands, the human mind :
When fons their fathers' blood fhall pour,
And brother blufh with brother's gore :
When, loft to every tender care,
Not one his deareft friend fhall fpare ;
And man, opprefs'd with bittereft woes,
Wifh the fad fcene of life to clofe.

  Winter, clad in wild array,
Then fhall hold his direft fway ;
The fun withdraw his golden light,
And veil the world in darkeft night ;
The winds with wildeft rage contend ;
The fnow in ceafelefs ftorms defcend ;
The earth in icy fetters bound ;
And defolation glare around.

           Mm

Uncherish'd by one genial ray,
Three such winters pass away.
Portents dire shall then succeed;
The Monsters from their chains be freed:
Dreadful, in his fiery car,
Giant Rymer * rush to war;
The Serpent † roll his hideous train
Deep beneath the billowy main,
Whose lifted waters, wildly swell'd,
Wide o'er the earth shall be impell'd;
In thousands men resign their breath,
And throng the gloomy courts of death;
His prey the screaming eagle seek,
And tear the dead with gory beak;
The Earth in dread convulsions heave;
Its wonted course the river leave;
The tottering mountain headlong borne,
From its deep base resistless torn;
Rent from their roots, whole forests fall;
And one vast ruin spread o'er all.
Floating on the whelming tides,
Fate's black Ship ‡ in triumph rides;

---

* Rymer—One of those Giants who, according to the
Edda, are in continual enmity with the Gods, and shall,
in co-operation with the Evil Genii, eventually overpow-
er them.

† The Great Serpent—or Serpent of Midgard, is said
to have been cast by the Gods into the ocean; where he
soon became of such an enormous size as to encircle the
earth.—Midgard—the Residence, or Fortress of the Deities.—

‡ The Ship of the Gods, or of Fate, in which the Host
of the Evil Genii, &c. arrives.

Perfidious Loke § directs her courfe,
Leader of the giant force.
Fenris || burfts his iron chain ;
Nought his fury can reftrain ;
His noftrils fparkling flames expire ;
His eye-balls flalh terrific fire ;
Urged by rage, by vengeance driven,
He rends the beauteous fun from heaven :
The Serpent floods of venom pours
O'er the wide fea and circling fhores ;
Rocks rufh on rocks, together hurl'd ;
Deftruction triumphs o'er the world ;
From the torn concave of the fky,
The affrighted ftars confus'dly fly ;
The vaults of heaven in funder rend ;
The Evil Genii fwift afcend ;
Pour'd from the fouth, in terrors dire,
Before them moves the Prince of Fire,
Surtur * the Black, in flames array'd—
Shines like the fun his waving blade,
The fign of death ; with him their might
The Serpent, Fenris, Loke, unite ;

———————

§ Loke,—the Evil Being : in the higheft degree malicious and deceitful.

|| Fenris,—or the Wolf,—of all the others a monfter
moft dreaded by the Gods ; who by ftratagem confined him
with a magic chain ; which he breaks at the diffolution of
nature.

* Surtur,—the deftroying Principle ; fuppofed to refide
in the South, in the flaming Gulf of Mufpellheim ; leader
of the Evil Genii, who are to deftroy the Univerfe by Fire.

Succeeds a death-determined hoft,
The hideous Giants of the Froft.
His crooked trumpet Heimdall†† takes,
With potent breath the blaft awakes;
Far heard thro heaven's remoteft bound,
Pours the fhrill clangor of the found;
Loud crows the Cock, the bird divine,
Whofe crefts in golden glory fhine;
Hoarfe from beneath, with difmal cries,
The Herald black of death replies;
Trembles the facred Afh ‡‡ with dread,
And groaning fhakes its lofty head;
All nature's fill'd with wild affright;
The Gods, convened, prepare for fight.
A mid-day fun is Odin §§ bold,
Far beaming in his arms of gold;
Againft the Wolf ‖‖ he bends his courfe,
And Frey * encounters Surturf's force.
The enormous ferpent Thor† affails;
The God's refiftlefs might prevails;

---

†† Heimdall,—the Centinel of Heaven.

‡‡ The Sacred Afh of Ydrafil, under which the Council of the Deities is held.

§§ Odin, the firft and moft powerful of all the Gods.

‖‖ Fenris.

* Frey,—a Deity reprefented as clothed in white; and fuppofed to prefide over the productions of the earth.

† Thor,—the firft of the fons of Odin, and ftrongeft of the Gods; who prefides over the thunder; and whofe office it is to protect the injured and oppreffed.

But fhort his joy, he finks in death,
From the Monfter's venom'd breath.
By each others falchions flain,
Loke and Heimdall prefs the plain.
The fnow-white God §§ refigns his life,
By Surtur flain in furious ftrife.
Rufhing from the dark abodes,
Death denouncing to the Go's,
Hideous howls the Dog of night;
He meets with Tyr |||| in mortal fight;
Long the conteft fierce they wage,
And victims fall of mutual rage.
Goddefs, * weep! thy cares are vain—
Odin falls, by Fenris flain.
Swift to vengeance Vidar ++ flies;
By his hand the monfter dies:
Wild Deftruction, hovering o'er,
Waves her banner dipt in gore;
O'erpower'd the h avenly legions fall,
And Death's dark billows clofe on all.
The gloomy Prince, ‡ with conqneft crown'd,
Dreadful fcatters flames around;
In one wide conflagration driven,
The raging fires afcend to heaven;

---

§§ " The fnow-white God,"—Frey.
|||| Tyr,—a Deity anfwering to the Roman Mars.
* The Goddefs Friga. or Freya,—the Mother of Odin.
++ Vidar, a Son of Odin.
‡ " The gloomy Prince:"—Surtur.—

Sinks the world to ruin's power,
And time itself exifts no more.

Burfting from exiftence' grave,
O'er the bofom of the wave,
Lo! a new-born World unroll'd,
Far more beauteous than the old,
Smiles adorn'd with lovelieft green ;
Spring unfading decks the fcene ;
The eagles, foaring mid the breeze,
Their fifhy prey on mountains feize ;
The earth her fruits fpontaneous yields ;
Rich harvefts glad the uncultured fields ;
Unknown to grief, to torturing pain,
There eternal pleafures reign.
Then, from feats of orient light,
In divineft glories bright,
Comes forth the great, the all-powerful One,*
Incommunicate, alone,——
Who was ere Time began his race,
Or being fill'd the vaft of fpace ;
And, unchangable, fupreme,
Thro endlefs ages is the fame.
There a Palace glows, more bright
Than the fun's meridian light,

---

* This Being is entirely diftinct from Odin, and the other Gods of the Scandinavian Mythology ; who had their
birth foon after the creation of the World, and who perifh with it.

Where the virtuous fhall refide;
And, as pleafure rolls its tide
Un-debafed by pain's alloy,
Know an eternity of joy.

EXTRACT FROM THE

CONQUEST OF SCANDINAVIA;

BEING THE INTRODUCTION OF THE FOURTH BOOK.

BY THE SAME.

ODIN *having defeated the Scandinavians in feveral great bat-*
tles, WOLDOMIR, *the druidical fovereign of Scandinavia,*
reduced to the utmoft diftrefs, obtains the affiftance of
GRYMER, *Prince of the Saraceni,—a Scythian Tribe,—*
the hereditary foe of ODIN; *and having affembled his*
forces on an extenfive plain, near the banks of a river,
prepares to attack the Enemy, who are encamped on the
oppofite fhore.—The prefent Book commences with the Night
preceding the engagement.

NOW Night, in clouds involv'd, her mantle drew,
   And deepeft darknefs veil'd the etherial blue;
Dire heard afar, with wild and hollow roar,
Hoarfe groan'd the woods along the rocky fhore;
Loaded with vapours dank and drizzling rains,
The chill North-eaft fhrill whiftled o'er the plains;
Pale fhone the phantom fires, whofe boding light
In tenfold horror vefts the ftorms of night;

And, wildly yelling thro the dreary shade,
Shriek'd the sad spectres of the unburied dead;
Involv'd in anxious cares, and gloomy thought,
When Mondak's* Son the tent of Ulfo fought.
Ulfo the old, renown'd for magic lore,
From Volga's flood to cold Kamfchatka's shore;
Amid the gloom of Scythian forefts bred,
Where Altai lifts on high his wintry head;
Among a favage race, rapacious, rude,
Wild as the ftorms that tofs the Cafpian flood,
As thunder dreadful, burfting from the cloud,
When Night o'er Altai hangs her fable fhroud.
Olaf his fire, in fields of death renown'd,
As chief in war, the ftern barbarians own'd,
Sprung from that race accurf, whofe demon fway
The hoary Giants of the Froft obey,
The fame ftern foul which mark'd his fires of yore,
The fame fell hate to Woden's laws he bore,
The fame infpir'd the fon, whofe rebel pride
The God derided, and his power defied.
In nature vers'd, to him each plant was known
That blooms mid Scythia's fnows, or Afric's torrid zone;
Each fecret power that earth's dark bofom hides,
That rules in ocean, or in air prefides.
To him had Grymer fent, o'er realms afar,
With coftly gifts, to win him to the war,
When firft imperial Woldomir implor'd,
In Scandinavia's aid, the hero's fword;

---

* Grymer.

Nor lefs impell'd by envious hate, he came,
Of Odin's glory and of Woden's name.

Intent to folve the dark decrees of fate,
In deep enquiry fix'd, the Wizard fate ;
When, Grymer entering, from his feat he preft,
With eager hafte, and thus the Chief addreft.
" Say, at this hour, when o'er the dreary plains,
In all her horrors, Night funereal reigns ;
While fhrieks of terror on the blaft arife,
And the black tempeft howls along the fkies ;
At this untimely hour, what potent caufe
Forth from his tent the Prince of Scythia draws?"

" O Sire of magic !" thus the Prince replied,—
" My Shield in battle, and my counfels' guide,
Full well to thee is known what weight of care
Hangs on the vaft uncertainty of war ;
What anxious fears a leader's peace annoy,
Poffefs his foul, and every thought employ.
The chief who hopes in glory's walks to fhine,
And round his brows the palms of conqueft twine,
When war's dark tempeft fpreads its horrors round,
Not in the bowers of thoughtlefs Eafe is found ;
Not on the lap of Sloth reclines his head,
By proud Prefumption's flattering glare mifled ;—
Which oft the vainly confident betrays,
And lights to ruin with its phantom blaze ;—
But, when the hour of battle hovers near,
Neglects no caution, tho' he knows no fear.
By cares like thefe impell'd, I hither come,
Of reft neglectful, mid the dreary gloom ;

N n

While, wide around, the camp in filence lies,
And flumber feals the wearied foldier's eyes:
For lo! to morrow wakes the rage of fight,
When morning opes the golden gates of light;
To morrow gives my eager arm to dare
This fcourge of Scandia's realms, this peft of war;
Gives me, perchance, that firft of joys to know,
The joy of vengeance on a hated foe.
For that fell hate, which fteel'd our fires of yore,
Which dyed fo oft in blood Jaxartes' fhore,
That hate my breaft with all its rage infpires,
Sublim'd, by rival love, to fiercer fires.
Yes! ftill revenge has fet that day afide,
When, fcorn'd my paffion, and my fuit denied,
Hermanric's daughter gave her heaven of charms,
Detefted thought! to Odin's happy arms.
But tho' my foul delights where Danger rears
His awful creft, amid the ftrife of fpears,
And glows with tranfport in the fierce alarms,
The fhock of battles, and the din of arms;
Tho', in comparifon, the foe are loft
Mid the vaft numbers of our warlike hoft;
Yet not, in vain fecurity, reclin'd,
The events of battle fill my anxious mind.
Perchance the Gods, too partial to the foe,
Our ftrength may wither, and our hopes o'erthrow;
For Odin long has prov'd their guardian care,
By Woden fhielded in the ftorms of war;
And ftill the favoring God his aid affords,
And bears him harmlefs mid defcending fwords.
How oft has Scandia mourn'd her heroes' doom,
Swept, by that arm, in thoufands, to the tomb!

Before his might her hofts have fhrunk away,
Like mountain fnows before the vernal ray.
Then let the all-conquering force of fpells be tried,
And range the Powers of magic on our fide;
Bid panic terror hover o'er their fight,
Chill the pale foe, and turn their fteps to flight;
So may thy friend a double triumph prove,
And, with a nation's wrongs, avenge his flighted love."

The monarch ceas'd,—the words the wizard took,
While farcafm fmil'd contemptuous in his look.
" Dread'ft thou that feeble race? Can Grymer's foul
Thus bend to phantom terror's vile controul?
Do thoughts like thofe which little minds debafe,
Become the leader of a warlike race?
Thy mighty Woden, and his Gods, at moft,
A narrow fway, and power precarious boaft.
In time's firft day-fpring, when as yet the earth
Knew not its place, nor ocean roll'd to birth;
Alone one torpid, vaft abyfs, was feen,
Uncloth'd with form, undeck'd with cheerful green;
Ere man the breath of firft exiftence drew;
Thofe fons of Bore the mighty Ymir flew,
By fraud his race confin'd, ufurp'd the fway
O'er the blue manfions of unclouded day.
Yet ftill in fear their ill-got rule they hold,
Still dread the day, when vengeance uncontroll'd
Shall burft its chains, and, in deftruction hurl'd,
A fiery deluge wrap the finking world.
Then go, and Valhall's feeble Gods defpife,
For Powers more mighty in thy aid fhall rife;—

Thofe Powers who o'er the gloom of night prefide,
Live in the ftorm, and on " the whirlwind ride ;"—
Shall whelm in duft the foes prefumptuous boaft,
And roll dark ruin o'er their proftrate hoft."

The Wizard ceas'd—with brightening hopes infpir'd,
The Scythian monarch to his tent retir'd.

Forth from his camp the dire Enchanter ftray'd,
Mid the weird horrors of the midnight fhade,
Till a lone dell his wandering footfteps found,
Fenc'd with rough cliffs, with mournful cyprefs crown'd,
There ftay'd his courfe : with ftern, terrific look,
Thrice wav'd on high, his magic wand he fhook ;
And thrice he rais'd the wild funereal yell
That calls the fpirits from the abyfs of hell.
When, fhrilly anfwering to the yell afar.
Borne on the winds, three female forms appear ;
Dire as the hag who, mid the dreams of night,
Purfues the fever'd hectic's trembling flight.
With geftures ftrange, approach the haggard band,
And nigh the wizard take their filent ftand.
Near, in a rock, adown whofe rugged fide
The lonely waters of the defart glide,
O'ergrown with brambles, op'd an ample cave,
Drear as the gloomy manfions of the grave.
Within, the fcreech-owl made her mournful home,
And birds obfcene that hover round the tomb ;
Dark, from the mofs-grown top, together clung,
Ill-omen'd bats, in torpid clufters, hung ;
And o'er the bottom, with dank leaves beftrow'd,
Crept the black adder, and the bloated toad.

Thither the magic throng repair'd, to form
Their fpells obfcure, and weave the unhallow'd charm.
Muttering dire words, thrice ftrode the wizard round;
Thrice, with his potent wand, he finote the ground;
Deep groans enfued; on wings of circling flame,
Slow-rifing from beneath, a Cauldron came ;
Blue gleam'd the fires amid the fhades of night,
And o'er the cavern fhot a livid light.

Now op'd a horrid fcene : all black with blood,
The infernal band, prepar'd for flaughter, ftood.
Two beauteous babes, by griffons borne away,
While lock'd in fleep the haplefs mothers lay,
Whofe fmiles the frozen breaft to love might warm,
And e'en the unfparing wolf to pity charm,
The hags unveil'd ; and fportive as they play'd,
Deep in their hearts embrued the murderous blade ;
Their dying pangs with fmile malignant view'd,
And life's laft ebbings in the fanguine flood.
Now, mix'd with various herbs of magic power,
In the dark cauldron glows the purple gore :
The Night-fhade dire, whofe baleful branches wave,
In glooms of horror, o'er the murderer's grave ;
The Manchineel, alluring to the eye,
Where, veil'd in beauty, deadlieft poifons lie ;
The far-fam'd Indian Herb, of power to move
The foes of nature to unite in love,
The ferpent race to infant mildnefs charm,
And the fierce tiger of his rage difarm,—
Known to the tribes that range the tracklefs wood
Where mad Antonio heaves the headlong flood;—

The * Monster plant that blasts Tartaria's heath ;
And Upas fatal as the stroke of death :
Boil'd the black mass, the associate fiends advance,
And round the Cauldron form the magic dance.
Three times around, in mystic maze they trod,
With hideous gesture, and terrific nod ;
While Runic rhymes, and words that freeze the soul,
From their blue lips, in tones of horror, roll.
The wizard rais'd his voice, the cavern round,
Wild-shuddering, trembled at the fearful sound ;
In mute attention stood the haggard throng,
As thus he woke the incantatory song.

From the dreary realms below,
    From the dark domains of fear,
From the ghastly seats of woe,
    Hear ! tremendous Hela, hear !

I.

Dreadful Power ! whose awful form
Blackens in the midnight storm ;
Glares athwart the lurid skies,
While the sheeted lightening flies ;
When the thunder awful roars ;
When the earthquake rocks the shores ;

---

* BAROMETZ, Tartarian Lamb :——A plant found in
Tartary and the northern parts of China : It is covered
with a very beautiful kind of furze or wool, of a bright yellow, and in its form has some resemblance to a LAMB, ap-
pearing to stand upon four legs, from so many roots to
which it is attached. It is said to be of a nature so destruc-
tive to every other species of vegetables, that none will live
within its vicinity.

Mounted on the wings of air,
Thou rul'ft the elemental war.
When Famine brings her fickly train ;
When Battle ftrews the carnag'd plain ;
When Peftilence her venom'd wand
Waves o'er the defolated land ;
Rufh the ocean's whelming tides
O'er the foundering veflel's fides ;
Then afcends thy voice on high ;
Then is heard thy funeral cry ;
Then, in horror, doft thou rife
On the expiring wretch's eyes.

From the dreary realms below,
  From the dark domains of fear,
From the ghaftly feats of woe,
  Hear ! tremendous Hela, hear !

II.

Goddefs ! whofe terrific fway
Naftrande's realms of guilt obey ;
Where, amid impervious gloom,
Sullen frowns the ferpent Dome ;
Roll'd beneath the envenom'd tide,
Where the fons of forrow 'bide ;
Thee, the mighty Demon hoft ;
Thee, the Giants of the Froft ;
Thee, the Genii tribes adore ;
Fenris owns thy fovereign power :
And the imperial Prince of Fire,
Surtur, trembles at thine ire.

Thine, the victor's pride to mar ;
Thine, to turn the scale of war ;
Chiefs and princes at thy call,
From their spheres of glory fall ;
Empires are in ruin hurl'd ;
Desolation blasts the world.

From the dreary realms below
　　From the dark domains of fear,
From the ghastly seats of woe,
　　Hear ! tremendous Hela, hear !

III.

Queen of terror, queen of death !
Thee, we summon from beneath.
From the deep infernal shade ;
From the mansion of the dead ;
Nieflehm's black, funereal dome ;
Hither rise, and hither come !
By the potent Runic rhyme,
Awful, mystic, and sublime ;
By the streams that roar below ;
By the sable fount of woe ;
By the burning gulph of pain,
Muspell's home, and Surtur's reign ;
By the Day when, o'er the world,
Wild confusion shall be hurl'd,
Rymer mount his fiery car,
Giants, Genii, rush to war,
To vengeance move the Prince of Fire,
And heaven, and earth, in flames expire !

From the dreary realms below,
   From the dark domains of fear,
From the ghaftly feats of woe,
   Hear! tremendous Hela! hear.

He ceas'd—the flames withdrew their magic light,
And, cloth'd in deeper horrors, frown'd the night.
At once, an awful ftillnefs paus'd around,
Hufh'd were the winds, and mute the tempeft's found,
One deep, portentous, calm o'er nature fpread,
Nor e'en the afpin's reftlefs foliage play'd ;—
Such the dire calm that glooms Carribean fhores
Ere, rous'd to rage, the fell Tornado roars :—
Not long, for lo! from central earth releas'd,
Shrill through the cavern figh'd an hollow blaft ;
Wild wails of woe, with fhrieks of terror join'd,
In deathful murmurs groan along the wind ;
Peal following peal, hoarfe burfts the thunder round ;
Redoubling echoes fwell the dreadful found ;
Flafh the blue lightnings in continual blaze ;
One fheet of fire the kindling gloom difplays ;
And o'er the vault, with pale, fulphureous ray,
Pour all the horrors of infernal day.
Now heav'd the vale around, the cavern'd rock,
The earth, deep trembling, to its center fhook,
Wide yawn'd the rending floor, and gave to fight
A chafm tremendous as the gates of night.
Slow from the gulph, mid lightnings faintly feen,
Rofe the dread form of Death's terrific Queen ;
Of wolfifh afpect, and with eyes of flame,
Black Jarnvid's Witch, her fell attendant, came;

O o

Than whom, no monster roams the dark abodes,
More fear'd by friends, more hated by the Gods.

More frightful, more deform'd, than Fancy's power
Pourtrays the demon of the midnight hour,
In hideous majesty, of various hue,
Part sallow pale, and part a livid blue,
A form gigantic, awful Hela frown'd;
Her towering head with sable serpents crown'd;
Around her waist, in many a volume roll'd,
A crimson adder wreath'd his poisonous fold;
And o'er her face, beyond description dread,
A sulphury mist its shrouding mantle spread.
Her voice, the groan of war, the shriek of woe
When sinks the city whelm'd in gulphs below,
In tones of thunder, o'er the cavern broke,
And nature shudder'd as the Demon spoke.

" Presumptuous mortal! that, with mystic strain,
Dost summon Hela from the realms of pain,
What cause thus prompts thee rashly to invade
The deep repose of death's eternal shade?
What, from the abodes of never-ending night,
Calls me, reluctant, to the climes of light?"

" Empress supreme! whose wide-extended sway
All nature owns, and earth and hell obey;
The solemn call no trivial wish inspires;
No common cause thy potent aid requires;
The dooms of empires on the issue wait,
And doubtful tremble in the scale of fate.
The glow of morn, on yon extended heath,
Will light the nations to the strife of death.

There Saracinia's fons their force unite
With Scandia's monarch, Woldomir, in fight;
By ftrength combin'd, proud Odin to o'erwhelm,
The fierce invader of the Scandian realm;
By Woden favor'd with peculiar grace;
Friend of the gods, and odious to thy race.
Then, in the impending fight, thy fuccour lend,
And o'er our hoft thy arm of ftrength extend;
The hoftile bands, protected by thy foes,
With dangers circle, and with ruin clofe;
With wild difmay their fhrinking ranks pervade;
Whelm their pale numbers in the eternal fhade;
And wing, with certain aim, the miffive dart,
Or point the faulchion, to the leader's heart."

Thus Ulfo fpoke—and Hela thus return'd.
" Know, while in primal night creation mourn'd,
The eternal caufe, the great, all-ruling mind,
The various term of human life affign'd;
Irrevocably firm, the fix'd intent
No power can vary, and no chance prevent.
Mark'd, by the fates, for years of bloody ftrife,
Rolls the long flood of Odin's varied life;
Nor is it ours the ftern decree to thwart
By open violence, or by covert art
Yet ftill the power is left us to annoy,
Whom rigid heaven denies us to deftroy;
And, tho of life fecure, the hoftile chief,
The wretched victim of fevereft grief,
Shall mourn his arms difgrac'd, on yonder plain,
His laurels blafted, and his heroes flain."

She ceafed ;—in thunder vanifhing from view,
The fiends, the cauldron, and the hags withdrew.
Back to the camp the Inchanter fped his way,
Ere, o'er the caft, arofe the firft faint glimpfe of day.

ODE TO CONSCIENCE.

BY THEODORE DWIGHT, ESQUIRE.

HAIL Confcience, faithful inmate of the breaft!
   Thy fmiles can charm to fweeteft reft,
Thy frovns can wake the keeneft woe,
Without thy aid even heaven would grow
A cheerlefs void of deep diftrefs,
And angels want the power to blefs.

When great Jehovah's voice creation form'd,
   When worlds unnumber'd fprang to inftant birth;
When morning ftars to ecftacy were warm'd,
   And man ftood ruler of the boundlefs earth,
Thou in the realms of light and love,
Did'ft dwell emboffom'd with the Etherial Dove.
" Where Guilt fhall dare extend her reign,
" And Satan ftretch his dark domain,
" There let the tides of horror roll,
" And torture rend the finking foul."
The GODHEAD fpoke,—Creation round,
Deep trembled to its utmoft bound.

Hail mighty Confcience ! hail !
 When the black deed of guilt is done,
Thou mak'ſt the quivering wretch turn pale,
 And ſtartle at the ſun.
When Murder fearleſs of thy power,
 Lifts up the fateful knife,
And in the dark and midnight hour,
 Deſtroys the guiltleſs life ;
High ſwells thy awful voice :
Awaking at the fearful ſound,
The fiends of vengeance gather round ;
 The villain ſtarts at every noiſe,
His ſoul, to judgment ſummon'd, ſhakes,
His frame convuls'd with horror, quakes ;
'Till urg'd to fate by all-refiſtleſs fear,
He owns his crime, and dies the victim of deſpair.

 When the quick tide of life ſwells high,
 And Pleaſure hourly wantons nigh,
 The Sceptic braves thy ſtern command,
 Nor dreads thy executing hand.
 But when the powers of life decay,
 And ſickening nature waſtes away,
 When Age brings on a lengthening train
 Of weakneſs, dire diſeaſe, and pain,
 When Death uplifts its horrid form,
 And Juſtice wakes the avenging ſtorm ;
 Torn with diſtracting doubts and fears,
 Thy terrors thunder in his ears :
 Pale ſpectres haunt the ſhades of night,
 Deep bluſhes meet the morning light,—

Above he fees the tempeſt lower,
And floods of wrath around him pour,—
Wide yawns beneath the world of woe,
Where waves of burning vengeance flow.

Impell'd by conſcious guilt he ſtrives to fly,
Far from the light of God's all-ſearching eye,
And plunging headlong in the midnight ſhade,
Calls rocks and hills to ſhield his guilty head;
'Till robb'd of Hope,—life's lateſt ſtay,—Deſpair
Breathes the faint wiſhes of unutter'd prayer:
In dread ſuſpence, his laſt ſad refuge fled,
His ſchemes all fruſtrate, his deluſions dead,
Heaven ſhut from view, annihilation vain,
He ſhrinks from life, and flies to endleſs pain.

Not ſuch thy lot, O. man* divine!
Peace on the bed of death was thine.
Calm with a retroſpective view,
Thy mind look'd paſt exiſtence thro;
In bright, and regular array,
And blazing on the face of day,
  The deeds of virtue ſtood;
Conſcience beheld them as they ſhone,
Approv'd and hail'd her darling ſon,
  And God pronounc'd them good.
And when the meſſenger of death,
Receiv'd thy faint expiring breath,
Soft ſlumbering on the bed of peace,
Thy voice bade every ſorrow ceaſe,

---

* Mr. ADDISON.

While to the world's aftonifh'd eye,
Thou fhew'd'ft with what repofe a virtuous man can die.

 Hail Confcience! hail the good man's friend!
  Thy fmiles thro' life his fteps attend;
 And on his dread departing day,
  Impart a fweet, and gladfome ray,
To cheer his foul, to footh his dying breath,
To light his path-way thro' the vale of death,
And ope his profpect to awaiting fkies,
Where Faith looks forward with prophetic eyes,
And fees unmov'd the moon in blood expire,
The fun in darknefs, and the earth on fire,
Stars, planets, fyftems, into ruin hurl'd,
And the laft trumpet rend a guilty world.

COLQLOO,——AN INDIAN TALE,

Thrown into Englifh Verfe.

BY WILLIAM DUNLAP.

COLWALL! the Women crie;
 Colwall! the dales refound,
Colwall, the hills reply,
 And hollow caves rebound.

Wild fhrieks thro thickets ring,
 Faft flies the dark-brown night:
" Come ye Warriors bring
 The Captive ta'en in fight.

Draw tight the cutting bands!
  Bring matches blazing blue!
Now! now! the victim ſtands
  To mighty Colwall due."

With ſcorn the Captive ſmil'd.
  With ſcorn he ey'd the throng,
Then thus his pain beguil'd,
  With high exulting ſong.

SONG.

And are theſe all the means ye know
  To give a warrior pain?
Oh give your fires a fiercer glow;
  Remember Colwall ſlain.

My father gloried in his ſon.
  My warriors came from fight,
None ſtaid behind; the ſcalps we won.
  Declar'd our matchleſs might.

Who has not heard Cololoo's fame?
  My nation well ye know,——
And dreadful is the Tiger's name,
  And fear'd by every foe.

Pain does not lie ſo near the ſkin,
  More burning pine-knots bring!
Cololoo's all at peace within,——
  And Logan's fame he'll ſing.

RECITAL.

Then whilſt from every limb the red ſtreams guſh,
  And round him glows the fire;
Whilſt thorns and nails transfix the quivering fleſh,
  The death ſong riſes higher.——

SONG.

Aged Logan led the fight,
  Logan's fame is ever new,——
Logan feiz'd a treacherous White,
  His murder'd Children rufh to view:

" Curfes blaft thee! pale-fac'd Savage,
  Ruin feize thy ruthlefs kind,
Train'd to rapine, fkill'd to ravage,
  Gain, the God that grafps thy mind.

Now ye red men take your fill,
  Give the fcalping knife its due,
The red right arm is bare to kill,——
  This my children, this to you."

Reeking from the white man's brain,
  Lo! he lifts the fcalp on high;
" Logan does not wifh thee pain,
  Fly to death's dark caverns, fly!

See they come! they come to meet us!
  Raife the yell that makes them quake,
Say,—fhall puny white men beat us?
  Men that every blaft can fhake?

Men that fear the rufhing rain,
  Men that fear the clouded fky,
Men that fhrink and howl at pain,
  Nor know to triumph when they die.

Now ye Tiger tribe be brave,
  Think that Logan fees the fight;
Scalps on fcalps adorn my cave,
  Glad'ning to my children's fight.

P p

Sulph'rous fmokes obfcure the view,
   War! the hills and dales reply.
Now ye red men, now be true!
   Ye know to fight! ye dare to die!''

Hand to hand the Warriors rufh,
   Shouts and yells in echos die;
Tom'hawks cleave, and bay'nets pufh,—
   They fly! they fly! the white men fly!

One brave band alone remains,
   One alone of all that band,
Every fhot and blow fuftains,
   Red like ours his heavy hand.

See they fink,—he's left alone,—
   Still our Warriors ftain the fields;
See! he falls, but fighting on
   Sits, and ftill his fword he wields.

Logan feiz'd the brave man's arm,
   Longing, look'd upon his face;
Logan will not do thee harm,
   Tho' thou art of faithlefs race.

Logan's fons had been like thee,—
   White men fhot them from the bufh;
The brave fhall not be harm'd by me,—
   He's dead,—he's flown,—and all is hufh.——

None thy beauteous corfe fhall wound;
   None thy hairy fcalp fhall tear;
Thou fhalt fleep with warriors round,
   Thou the dead-mens, feaft fhall fhare.

Seize the fcalps, and count the flain;
 White-men, weep your brothers' woes!
Eafe our dying chiefs from pain :—
 White-men learn to fear your foes !

So, Logan triumph'd o'er the foe ;
 Logan's fame was fairly won :
So, Logan laid the white-men low,—
 ——But fet is Logan's fun.———

Why bring ye not the heated ftone
 To fear and feam my manly breaft ?
Why fure the torture is not done !
 Such pain Cololoo bears in jeft.

RECITAL.

Round his head Idiego hurl'd
 His hatchet keen and good ;
Whizzing, fierce the weapon whirl'd,
 And quiver'd in the wood.

Reldor then with fullen ftride,
 His knife was in his hand,
Advanc'd, and thus aloud he cried,—
 And cut the twifted band.

Reldor takes thee for his fon,
 Colwall in battle flain,
In many a fight his fame he won,
 Nor fhrunk from death or pain.——

Silent now the warrior train
 Bear the blood-ftain'd chief,—
No more they weep for Colwall flain,—
 No more is known of grief.———

ODE TO TIME.*

FULL oft the Painter's pencil, oft the Bard,
    On canvas, or on Fancy's airy scene,
Hath shewn thee laughable, with grisly beard
Stiff-starting from a peaked chin ;
A few white hairs thin-scatter'd round thy head,
Thine eyes turn'd grey with age ;
Thy nose quite shrivell'd, like a pointed hook,
Thy visage bearing all a wrinkled wizard look :
Bent down and crooked was thy form,
And tottering on thy weak, lank legs,
Like some slim weed amid the shaking storm :
Thy blood, poor miserable dregs
Of life, crept thro' each wind-puff'd vein,
Which seem'd as tho' 'twould burst with ev'ry strain :
Thy long and dangling arms a scythe sustain,
To top off men as they cut down their grain :
Most laughable indeed! thus to deform
A God in power first, as first in form !

But look ye painters ! hear ye bards this truth !
His face shall ever bloom unfading youth.

---

* This Poem was originally published, in an imperfect
state, in No. 20 of the 3d volume of the Gazette of the
United States, for July 6th, 1791, with its present signa-
ture. The great alterations which it has since undergone,
and the many important additions now made to it, form a
sufficient excuse for the conduct of the Editors in placing
it among the Original Poems.

Bright golden locks adorn his head,
  Majeſtick beauty ſeems his form ;
Where'er he ſteps, his awful tread
  Sounds like the thunder of the ſtorm.

Imperial Rome ! once miſtreſs of the world !
Who rear'd her palaces, her towers on high,
Bade her tall obeliſks aſſail the ſky !
In ruin lies, by his ſtrong arm of power hurl'd.
Some broken arch, or nodding tower,
  Falls prone to earth each paſſing hour ;
And oft the wary traveller hears the ſound
Of ſome lofty column broke,
By TIME's rudely ſhattering ſtroke,
When down it comes loud-craſhing on the ground,
And hills and vales, the horrid roars rebound.

Behold yon figure ſtarting on the ſight !
His awful brow around,
With palm and laurel bound ;
His forceful eye with genius bright,
Seems now in Fancy's view to roll,
And ſpeak the bloody Cæſar's warlike ſoul !
But Cæſar ! thou art gone !
And TIME ſhall bid thy ſtatue follow ſoon.

The ſpacious Forum where great Tully's voice,
A clear and ſwelling torrent pour'd along,
'Till the tumultuous faction check'd their murmuring noiſe,
And mute—with dumb attention hark—as to the ſong
Of Orpheus, did fierce Cerberus of old,
When he with muſic's tongue his tender ſtory told ;
Touch'd by TIME's deſtructive, potent wand,
Lies in ruins mouldering on the land.

From Rome the Mufe now turns her eagle-eye,
To where the fun burns in the weftern fky,
Where Niagara loud and ftrong,
His deep majeftic torrent rolls along :
From many a noble ftream and lake fupplied
The rufhing tide,
With rapid force moft awful roars;
While echo fwells the folemn found upon his folitary fhores.
But lo! the boiling flood check'd by a rocky mound,
It madly foams, and whirling round,
In one ftupendous fheet,
From the dizzy awful height,
Fierce rufhing, headlong thunders to the ground.
The trembling groves, and caves around,
For many a league the dreadful fhout refound—
And while the bellowing flood midft craggy rocks below
Boils into foam, above the heaven-depicted bow
In rapture holds the wondering traveller's eye,
And all his fenfes thrill with heavenly extacy.
But hold my Mufe! reprefs thy airy flight,
Nor give thy quick'ned foul to fweet delight;
For e'en thofe haughty rocks, that rear on high
Their fhaggy heads, and rend the vaulted fky
With their loud-roaring founds fublime,
Shall bow beneath the fhattering hand of TIME.

Yet waft away! oh! diffipate thy fears,
For now thro' the deep gloom of future years,
A beauteous fcene beneath the weftern fkies,
Refplendent burfts upon my ravifh'd eyes.
Where thro' uncultur'd wilds Ohio rolls,
And hears the rav'nous wolf's terrific howls;

Or fees upon his fhores at midnight hour,
The cruel favage exercife his power ;
Sees him with a demoniack's joy elate,
Commit the haplefs victim to his fate,
And while with grinning rage, the blazing wood
He quenches in the Prifoner's hiffing blood,
Hears the fhrill fhrieks that pierce the diftant air,
And freeze the heart of pity with defpair :
There TIME's command fhall bid thofe horrors ceafe,
And wild Ohio fmile with fcenes of peace.
Where beafts of prey prowl o'er the defert ground,
Some future youths fhall liften to the found
Of wifdom, flowing from the fage's tongue,
In tones attractive as the voice of fong.
Then fhall fair temples, villas, cities rife,
To beam new fplendor on the natives' eyes ;
The heaven-taught Painter, Sculptor, and the Bard
Shall there in future ages feek reward ;
The voice of mufic warble thro' the air,
And all the glorious arts of peace appear.

But now again, the Mufe prophetic, fighs,
While fcenes of future defolation rife.
She fees her City, fair Columbia's pride,
A heap of ruins fpreading far and wide : ·
She fees her ftreets once beauteous to behold,
Partition'd off, the fhepherd flock to fold ;
The crumbling bricks, and feparated ftone,
By pale-green mofs, and fcattering fern o'ergrown.
The wiley fox from broken arches peeps.
Thro' the deferted dome the weafle creeps,
The owl fits whooping on the temple door,
While hops the fqualid toad along the floor ;

The hiſſings of the deadly ſnake ſhe hears,
The warning rattle, trembles in her ears.
Begone deluſive fancy! may thy wand
No more deform the beauty of our land!
Be unprophetic all thy gloomy views,
The airy offspring of the weeping Muſe—
But all too true alas! thy words may prove,
When TIME's deſtructive power ſhall o'er their beauties
[move!

Ere thrice ten times the God of day,
Has drove his flaming, annual Car,
Adown the roſy weſt;
My ſlender frame of clay,
With TIME and fierce diſeaſe at war
May moulder into duſt:
Theſe grief-ſtrung nerves of mine may ceaſe to move
In ſad vibrations to the voice of Love;
With many a hapleſs Bard whoſe tender breaſt
Now knows no more the goading thruſt
Of pride, or penury his nerves of feeling tear.
But hold! ah hold thy lifted hand!
Nor lowly bow,
Beneath thy awful blow
The Father of Columbia's favor'd land:
Oh ſpare! the glorious Patriot ſpare!
Nor give the ſtroke of fate,
Until his equal ſhall appear
To fill with equal dignity the lofty chair of ſtate.

BIRTHA.

Philadelphia, July 1791.

AN ODE,
ADDRESSED TO MISS ****.

BY THE LATE REV. JOSEPH HOWE, OF BOSTON.

NEVER did parting Youth feel more
    Than I, fair Maid, when from the fhore
Thy veffel fail'd away;
And can not then my prayers prevail,
Nor love, nor vows, nor tears, avail,
    Nor aught procure thy ftay?

Was it for this that I fo long
Liften'd, to Fortune's fyren fong
    Liften'd with rapturous joy?
Did fhe, for this, infpire my heart,
With hopes that we fhould never part,
    And thus thefe hopes deftroy?

Amid the much-admiring crowd,
While thus I figh'd my griefs aloud,
    I fcarce refrain'd to fpeak;
Shame held my tongue, while from my eye
The pearly drops, full plenteoufly,
    Stole trickling down my cheek.

Thus, near fair Tibur's filver flood,
The Roman Bard, gay Horace, ftood,
    And faw Galatea fail;
And thrice he warn'd her, o'er, and o'er,
And told the fates Europa bore,
    In hopes he might avail.

In hopes he might avail to move
The fixed purpofe of his love,
   From fuch a dangerous choice.
But all in vain, like me, he tried,
Galatea ftill did firm abide,
   Deaf to his moving voice.

  " Then go, if naught," the Bard rejoin'd,—
  " Can move the purpofe of thy mind,
    " Go, and may bleffings follow thee ;
  " Let every gentle gale attend,
  " Let every wave thy voyage befriend,
    " But think, ah think! of me."

Nor lefs to heaven did I prefer,
For thy dear fake, my pious prayer.
   O winds, O waves, agree!
Winds gently blow, waves foftly flow,
Ship move with care, for thou doft bear
   The better part of me.

And think, and think, I alfo faid—
On all the vows which we have made,
   On all thofe charming fcenes,
Which once, with glee, we pafs'd away,
Pleafed in each other, night and day,
   Nor envied kings and queens.

MESSAGE of MORDECAI to ESTHER.
FROM A MANUSCRIPT POEM.
BOOK II,——THE CONCLUSION.

BY TIMOTHY DWIGHT, D. D.

THOU know'ft, O Efther! from thy infant years,
    To rear thy form, to nurfe thy opening mind,
To teach thee every virtue, every truth,
To form thee finifh'd, lovely, great, and wife,
Was all my care fupreme.   Friendlefs, alone,
An orphan fcarcely budded, well thou know'ft
I found thee; as a darling flower (the rofe,
That blooms in Sharon, or at Hermon's foot
The lilly of the vale) from midft the wild,
With every care remov'd thee to my field,
And faw thee rife, and bloom, and fend abroad
A fragrance, richer than the Arabian gale.
Why all adorn'd with beauty's living bloom,
In form as fome young Virtue of the fkies,
Of tincture died in health's immortal ftream,
Of eye refplendent, as the morning fun
Looks thro' the cloud's fair opening, and of grace,
Where heaven was pleas'd to move in mortal guife;
Why form'd with foul, fuperior to thy kind,
With thoughts expanding thro' the world's wide round,
And pinion'd to the fkies; with hardy mind,
Patient and daring, as the hero ftands
Upon the deadly and fierce flaming breach,
Serene while Death walks onward; yet more foft

Than the pleas'd infant fmiles the favage dumb;
Why all accomplifh'd, and why angel all,
I ponder'd long, and now from Heaven I learn.
This mighty hour the Eye Omnifcient mark'd,
While fair, beneath his forming hand, uprofe
Thy varied excellence. For this Heaven gave
Thy virtue, gift fupreme, that virtue crown'd
With wifdom's power; that wifdoms cloth'd divine
With beauty's angel form; that form around
Diffus'd the light of Heaven; and all adorn'd
With grace and fweetnefs, dignity and love.
On that proud day, when, from an hundred realms
Summon'd, came many a lord, and chief, and king,
Magnificent, to grace the monarch's feaft,
And all the pomp of Perfia round him fpread;
When Vafhti's infolence, beyond all thought,
Her prefence to the illuftrious train refus'd;
When, taught by Memucan he wifely bade
The haughty fair one wear the crown no more;
Even then a field I faw, by Heaven outfpread,
To give thy virtue fcope, and rich reward.
Pondering, I brought thee to the eunuchs' Prince;
Amaz'd, amid all Perfia's beauteous maids,
Thee, thee alone he gaz'd. Convinc'd, I knew
The crown referv'd for thee. With no furprife,
I faw thee lifted to the world's great throne:
'Twas thus the Skies decreed. But, O blefs'd fair!
Not for thyfelf the Heavens thy beauty gave,
Thy grace, thy wifdom; nor, for thee alone,
Did Mordecai uprear thy precious bloom.
Heaven's gifts are virtue's aids; for virtue us'd,
Are us'd aright; or elfe are given in vain.

On thy great power to blefs, all Ifrael builds
A folemn claim. A voice, as thunder loud,
Awful, majeftic, from thy nation founds,
And bids thee rife to fave. Their caufe thou know'ft
The caufe of heaven. In them religion lives ;
From them Mefliah fprings, by whofe blefs'd hand
All nations good, and life, and glory gain.
The world's great happinefs on them fufpends.
Creation's end, and Providence' great fcope.
Go then, thy nation fave. Should every ill,
Even death, betide ; yet what is life, or death,
When Ifrael calls, when God demands our life.
And know, O fair ! if thou thy voice withhold,
Yet to the ruling Heavens, whofe piercing eye
All mortal things furveys, ten thoufand paths,
From danger's deepeft caves, lead up to day :
Paths, tho' by man unfeen, yet ftrait, and plain,
To God's all-piercing view. Thro Death's dark vale,
Such paths fhall Ifrael guide to life and peace.
Then from the fkies indignant, while thy race
To peace and joy afcend, thy faireft day
Of duty, glory, loft, thy foul fhall feel
The piercing anguifh of a wounded heart,
And wafte with keen remorfe, and fad defpair.

Thus wrote the feeling Prince. Awhile, in deep
And folemn contemplation fat the fair,
Pondering the forceful meffage. Rouz'd at length
From off the fofa, all that foftly fweet,
Angelic fmile her face forfook ; her eye,
Kindl'ng with facred fire, fhot forth a ray
Of funbright glory ; high her bofom rofe ;

Her pulse beat high, and loftily she walk'd
The fpacious room. Surpriz'd, her virgins ftood,
While thus her faithful Hatach she addrefs'd.
Go tell illuftrious Mordecai, my foul
Is warm'd to this great deed. His daughter's heart
Shuns not for Ifrael, or for Heaven, to die.
Undone by me, no duty fhall demand
Another's bofom ; loft by me, no hour
Of real glory fhall another crown
With fame, and life divine. Let Ifrael's race,
Thro' Shufhan's walls, with prayers, and tears, and fafts,
Implore the Skies; and tho no bright'ning hope
Prefents the king complacent; yet, to morrow,
My feet fhall tempt the court of gloomy danger,
And if my life's exacted, let me die.

ESTHER AND MORDECAI.

BOOK III.——(*The Beginning.*)

FROM midft a fhining cloud, whofe borders fair
    A golden light upturn'd, look'd forth the fun.
As clear, as bright, uprofe the Perfian Queen,
In all the pride of beauty. Rob'd in pomp
Of Afian fplendor, forth fhe flowly mov'd,
Attended by a royal train, that gave
New glory to the Fair. Strait to the throne

* L. 3. Up rofe the fun and up rofe Emily. CHAUCER.

Of fovereign majefty fhe bent her way.
Before her open'd wide the ivory gates,
On golden hinges turning; where, in purple
And gems, and gold, attir'd, with pomp fupreme,
With port auguft, and afpect fternly dread,
She faw the Monarch thron'd. Full on his eye
She dawn'd in all· her beauty, rob'd in white
With filver intertwin'd, and flowers of gold.
Around her diadem, mid rows of pearls,
Twinkled unnumber'd ftars. Two cupids fair
Befide her walk'd in blooming innocence;
And two her train fupported. From their hands,
Flowers fell, and fragrance, that the palace wide
Breath'd living odours. Soft and fweet the air,
The lovely Queen affum'd; her large, black eyes,   •
Mildly refulgent, fhone, two morning ftars;
While o'er her cheek, with lambent beauty, play'd
Colours, which neither flowers, nor gems, nor clouds,
Nor rainbows ever fhed. Full on the King
She-caft a fweet, and foul-explaining fmile
Of foft complacence; fuch as angels fhow,
To greet their fellows, when, from errand high
Return'd, they meet the fovereign euge blefs'd
The Monarch gaz'd; and, tho' his heart was fix'd
In all the fternnefs of Afiatic ftate;
Yet in the beams of beauty, foul infpir'd,
His foftening bofom melted. Fairer far
He view'd her, than when brought to blefs his arms
With virgin innocence. As in calm fkies,
Twixt two fair planets, walks in pride divine
The afcending Moon, o'er all the the immenfe of heaven

Reigning fole queen, and with enchantment fweet
Softening the world to filence.   With mild eye,
She looks her empire round, and fees the ftars
With joy before her hide their little lamps,
And plains, and groves, and mountains in the beam,
Shadowy, afcend and brighten.   Fair fhe fmiles,
And triumphs in her beauty ; while the bard
Eyes the bright queen, and wakes a thoufand dreams,
And thinks her emprefs of the realms above.
So rofe in all her bloom the wondrous Fair,
And fo the Monarch gaz'd.   Spontaneous mov'd
His arm unbidden, and to greet the Queen,
Reach'd forth the golden fceptre.   As the Fair,
Advancing, touch'd its ftarry point, he cried,
O Queen, what wifhes in thy bofom rife?
What prayer begins thy voice? Even to the half
Of Perfia's vaft domain, that prayer is giv'n.———

END OF VOL. I.

LIST OF SUBSCRIBERS.

THIS Lift is incomplete ; feveral of the Subfcription Papers not being feafonably returned to the Editors. This they regret the more, as they are well affured of there being one Paper, in Philadelphia, which contains the names of more than Thirty Encouragers of this Undertaking.

N. B. Where the Editors have been unable to learn the addrefs of a Subfcriber, the Name is printed without any addition.

MR. Jofeph Adams, Litchfield.
Thomas Allen, Bookfeller, New-York, 6.
Richard Alfop, Middletown.
Mr. Gilbert Afpinwall, New-York.
Jonas Addoms, M. D. New-York.
John Allen, Efquire, Litchfield.
Thomas Amory, Bofton.
Jonathan Amory, jun. do.
Aaron Auftin, Efquire, New-Hartford.
B
Rev. Azel Backus, Bethlem.
Gideon Ball, Catfkill.
Jofeph Barrel, Efquire, Bofton.
Auguftus Bates, Delaware.
Major Ezekiel P. Belden, Wethersfield, 2.
Samuel Bettle, jun. Philadelphia.
Uriel Blaau, Catfkill.
Jacobus Bogardus, do.
Jeremiah Boone, Philadelphia.
Walter Bowne, New-York.
Col. Aner Bradley, Watertown.
Mr. James Brace, Litchfield.
Elifha Bridgeman, Weft-Hampton.
R r

Mrs. Mary Bringhurst, Philadelphia.
Edward Bringhurst,   do.
Joseph Bringhurst, jun.   do. 6.
Charles B. Brown, Esquire, do.
Mrs. Broone, New-York.
William Brown, Esquire, Guilford.
Doctor William Buel, Sheffield.
James Burges, Washington.

C.

Aaron Case, Kent.
Doctor Jesse Carrington, Goshen.
Mrs. Betsey Chester, Wethersfield.
Thomas Chester, Esquire, do.
John Church, Hudson.
John Clark, New-York.
Doctor James Cogswell, do.
Doctor Mason F. Cogswell, Hartford.
Mr. James Cole, Catskill.
Mr. Norman Collins, Harwinton.
Arnold Colt, Esquire, Wilkes-barre, 6.
Miss H. Copperthwaite, Philadelphia.
Vicompte de Cornillon, Hartford.
Mr. Daniel Cotton, jun. New-York, 2.
Mr. Elias Cowles, Litchfield.
Doctor Thomas O'H. Croswell, Catskill.
Mr. Younglove Cutler, Watertown.

D.

David Daggett, Esquire, New-Haven.
Samuel W. Dana, Esquire, Middletown.
Hon. James Davenport, Stamford.
John Davenport, Esquire, do.
James Davidson, Kenebec, 2.
Jonathan Davis,   do.
Hon. Thomas Dawes, jun. Boston.
Doctor William De Wese, Philadelphia.
John Doan, Catskill.
Elijah Doty, do.
Mr. William Dunlap, New-York.
Theodore Dwight, Esquire, Hartford.
Miss Sally Dwight, Northampton.
Mr. Nathaniel Dwight, Hartford.

E.

William Edmond, Efquire, Newtown.
Mr. William Edwards, Northampton.
William Ely, Efquire, Springfield.
Noah Evereft, Catfkill.

F.

Michael C. Fifher, New-Jerfey.
Rev. Ebenezer Fitch, Williamftown.
Rev. Abel Flint, Hartford.
J. A. Fonda, Manor of Livingfton.
Abraham Franklin, New-York.

G.

Rev. John S. Gardiner, Bofton, 3.
Hon. Ezekial Gilbert, Hudfon.
Angelica Gilbert,   do.
Afhley Gilbert, Catfkill.
Mr. Afa Gillet, Litchfield.
Mr. Judfon Gitteau,   do.
Mr. Chauncey Gleafon, Simfbury.
Chauncey Goodrich, Efquire, Hartford, 3.
Elihu C. Goodrich, Efquire, Claverack.
Mr. Thomas C. Green, Bookfeller, New-London, 6.

H.

Hon. Nathan Hale, Efquire, Canaan.
Samuel Haight, Catfkill.
Jared Harrifon, Watertown.
Reuben Hart, Stockbridge.
Rev. Reuben Hitchcock, Sunbury, (Georgia.)
Mr. Roger Hitchcock, Litchfield.
Mr. Elnathan Holly, do.
Ph. L. Hoffman, Manor Livingfton, 2.
Thomas H. Hooker,
Samuel M. Hopkins,   hen.
Benjamin Horner, jun. Ph
Hez. L. Hofmer, Efquire, Hudfo
Titus Hotchkifs, Watertown

J.

Ifaac Jackfon, Philadelphia, 2.
William Jackfon, Wethersfield.
Ammiel Jenkins, Hudfon.
William Johnfon, Efquire, New-York.

K.

Ephraim Kirby, Esquire, Litchfield.
William Kellogg, Cornwall.

L.

Benjamin Lane, Manor of Livingston.
Mr. Lyman Law, New-London.
David Lawrence, Hudson.
Mr. Samuel Lawrence, Hartford.
George R. Lawton, Philadelphia.
S. Lawton,   do.
Oliver Lazier, Catskill.
Doctor Michael Leib, Philadelphia, 12.
Mr. Elisha Lewis, Hartford.
John Livingston, Manor.
Abner Lord, Lyme.
John H. Lothrop, Esquire, Hartford.

M.

David Manwarring, jun. New-London.
Mr. Elisha Mason, Litchfield.
Nicholas S. Masters, Esquire, New-Milford.
Mr. Samuel McNeil, Litchfield.
Mr. Donald G. Mitchell, do.
Simeon Mitchell, Wathington.
John Montgomery, Harpersfie'd.
Benjamin Moore D. D. New-York.
William Moore,   do.
Benjamin J. Moore, do.
Anthony S. Morris, Philadelphia, 2.
James Morris, do.
Perez Morton, Esquire, Boston, 2.
Jon. Ogden Mosely, Esquire, East Haddam, 6.
M. Muller, Bolton, 2.
Thomas Mumford, Esquire, New-York.

O.

Andrew Onderdonk, New-York.

P.

David Parmele, Esquire, Haddam.
Christopher Paterson, New-London.
Miss Lucy W. Payne, Philadelphia.
Miss Sarah Pemberton, do.

Mr. David Pierpont, Litchfield.
John Pinkerton, Jun. Philadelphia.
Timothy Pitkin, Jun. Efq. Farmington.
M. Samuel W. Pomeroy, Bofton.
Cath. Powell,   do.

R.

Sampfon Rea, Philadelphia.
Tapping Reeve, Efquire, Litchfield, 3.
James Rivington, New-York.
Mr. Mofes Rogers, do.
Stephen P. Tols, Kent.
Mr. John Royfe, Hartford.

S.

Major Mofes Seymour, Litchfield.
Capt. Samuel Seymour, do.
Mr. Dudley Saltonftall, do.
Doctor Daniel Sheldon, do.
Mr. Samuel Sheldon,   do.
Reuben Smith, Efquire, do.
Mifs Mary S. Smith,   do.
Mr. James Stone,   do.
Mr. Samuel Shethar,   do.
Mr. Ledyard Seymour, Hartford.
Mr. Jonathan Scott, Watertown.
Aaron Smith, Efquire, Watertown.
John C. Smith, Efquire, Sharon.
Mr. Thomas B. Saltonftall, New-london.
Capt Levi Stone, Kenderhook.
James S. Smith, Red-Hook.
Elnathan Smith, Jun. Efquire, Berlin.
William Pitt Smith, M. D. New-York.
Elijah Steele, Jun. Cornwall.
Elifha Stevens, Waterbury.
Mr. Afhbel Stoddard, Printer, Hudfon, 6.
Doctor Jofeph Strong, Middletown.
Zephaniah Swift, Efquire, Windham.

T.

Mifs Sally Talman, Philadelphia.
Peter Bodine Ten Broeck, Claverack.
John C. Ten Broeck, Hudfon.

Nathaniel Terry, Efquire, Enfield.
Peter Thompfon, jun. Philadelphia.
John Titus, New-York.
Mrs. Dolly P. Todd, Philadelphia.
Doctor Eli Todd, Farmington.
John Townfend, New-York.
Hon. Uriah Tracy, Litchfield.
John Trumbull, Efquire, Hartford.
Mr. Tudor, Bofton.

U.

Townfend Underhill, New-York.
Union Library Society, Wethersfield.

V.

Hezekiah Van Ordon, Catfkill.

W.

George Warren, Windflow.
Mr. Elijah Waterman, New-Haven.
General Samuel B. Webb, Claverack.
Mr. Jofeph Webb, Wethersfield.
Doctor James Wells, Berlin.
William W. Wetmore, Catfkill.
Levi Wheaton, Hudfon.
Roger Whittlefey, Efquire, Southington.
William W. Wilkins, Efquire, Philadelphia,
Rev. Jofhua Williams, Harwinton.
John Williams, Efquire, Wethersfield,
Ezekiel Williams, Efquire, do.
Mr. Ezekiel Williams, Jun. Hartford.
Mr. Solomon Williams, Lebanon.
Frederick Wolcott, Efquire, Litchfield.
Mr. William W. Woolfey, New-York, 2.
Lieut. Samuel Woodruff, Litchfield.
Meffrs. Charles R. and George Webfter, Albany, 12.

Litchfield, June 1793.

www.ingramcontent.com/pod-product-compliance
Lightning Source LLC
Chambersburg PA
CBHW021213270326
41929CB00010B/1108